the night at times square

Also By

C.M. FRANCIS

The Day I Died

One Term Left

the night at times square

C.M. FRANCIS

This is a work of fiction, and the views expressed herein are the sole responsibility of the author. Likewise, certain characters, places, and incidents are the product of the author's imagination, any resemblance to actual persons, living or dead, or actual events or locales, is coincidental.

The Night at Times Square

Copyright © 2023 CM Francis

ISBN: 9798324754082

All rights reserved. This book or any portion thereof may not be reproduced or used in any manner whatsoever without the express written permission of the publisher except for the use of brief quotation in a book review.

Cover design copyright © 2023 by Liana Moisescu
First printing, 2024

*To Denise Buckley & Hank Skladanowski,
who showed me all the wonders of Cleveland.*

Chapter 1
Rhiannon

Change.

The only thing I need is change, or at least that's what Mom says. What she really means is that my parents are doing the next, *last* option: moving me in with my aunt at the outskirts of Cleveland, Ohio.

Yep...*Ohio*.

We drive our SUV from Brooklyn to the middle of nowhere on I-90 West. In New York, we were in bumper-to-bumper traffic, whereas here, seventy is listed as the speed limit. I haven't seen an exit for twenty miles, let alone a rest stop. Our car travels on the Berkshires, winding uphill until my ears pop. The window paints a picturesque landscape full of forest greens, caramels, and ambers.

Dad rolls down his window, his hand sticks out, and he waves his arm, like it's swimming. Because I'm sitting behind him, the breeze blows into my eyes. I shut them. "Dad, could you—"

"I know, I know." He rolls up the window. "It's just the smell of nature. I love it!"

For a while, my parents hold hands, his thumb circling around Mom's pointer finger as she sighs for the tenth time within two minutes. She glances into his eyes while he continues to zoom past the car on our right. They think I can't hear them because I was listening to a burned Linkin Park CD, but my player died two hours ago.

"Jenn, this'll be a good thing," Dad says and kisses her hand. She smiles weakly, *very* weakly, yet the crease on her brow gives her away. Mom's complexion is made-up with a flowery dress and jean jacket; it took her a half hour to decide which outfit she'd wear.

"Maybe she should be homeschooled again." She stares out the side window. "You said it yourself: she only has one year left of high school, and then she can do whatever she pleases."

Dad rubs one eye while keeping the other on the road. We wear the same attire: sweatpants, sweatshirts, and a small ponytail. However, unlike me, it works for him. "If we continue with homeschooling, she'll end up living with us for a majority of her life." Once we're on an abandoned section of the highway, he stares at Mom. "Is that what you want?"

Say yes, Mom...Say yes.

"I guess not." She leans on Dad's shoulder with another sigh, and internally, I sink. "I just can't leave my baby for an entire year."

"It's only until Christmas. Aunt Vicky and Rhiannon will drive to New York." Mom's eyebrows raise, and I can't help but scoff at that comment. *Aunt Vicky will drive us?* She hates driving in Cleveland, let alone New York. While visiting Mom at NYU way back when, Vicky got in three fender-benders and had a near-death experience. She swears off driving anywhere near New York state.

"Okay...they'll fly," he says. "Rhie can show your sister the ropes of New York City! Didn't you tell me Vicky hadn't been there in twenty years?"

"She went to Manhattan for an art conference, but she didn't sightsee. Plus, she only comes to Brooklyn once a year at Christmas. You would think that with all the world traveling she does, she'd be an expert at the United States."

"Maybe she'll explore good ol' U-S-and-A, since this is her last year of teaching." He nudges Mom and wiggles his eyebrows. "Only eight more years until you become retired."

"Just because my sister and I have an eight-year age gap doesn't mean I'll retire in that many years." She laughs and squeezes his hand. "But maybe if we took Vicky to see the sights of Manhattan, it would inspire her to move back home. We have an extra bedroom, anyway."

"See?" Dad knocks elbows with Mom's shoulder again. "This'll be a great opportunity for her, for all of us. All we need is—"

Change. Rhiannon will thrive at Hawken School. She'll make many friends, just like her old school. Hopefully, she'll break out of her introverted shell and be happy...always happy. Perhaps she'll get a boyfriend, or at least a date for all the school dances. After what happened last year, a new school, new scenery, new life might be a pleasant surprise. Change is good.

It's the same lines I've heard since May when Aunt Vicky volunteered to have me stay with her in Richmond Heights.

The. Exact. Same. Thing.

And I can't take this anymore.

Taking off my headset, I lean forward with a wide grin, a grin that says, *I need you to stop talking, or I'll start crying again.*

"What are you guys talking about?"

Dad reaches behind his seat and squeezes my knee. "Just talking about how much we're going to miss you." He glances at me in the rearview mirror, and I lean back on the window. The wooden landscape zooms by, tree after tree after tree. The sun is clear without a cloud in the azure. Once October hits, I won't see the sun until April because of Ohio's gray skies.

Mom and Dad silence themselves for the rest of the car ride. He turns on the XM Radio, listening to Christmas carols year-round. Even though I used to hate this type of music before Thanksgiving, I enjoy it now because it means winter's coming, and half the school year is gone.

The final three hours are serene with a twenty-minute power nap. When I wake up, Dad flicks the right blinker and turns on the exit ramp. A two-lane street appears for miles and —

"There!" Mom yells and points.

Dad slams on the brakes: *SCREECH!* I hold on to my punching bag so it doesn't fly through the front windshield. Multiple cars swerve out of our car's way, yet as my ears perk up, expecting noises, I hear nothing.

That's weird.

He turns on the hazard lights and backs up twenty yards, continuing into Aunt Vicky's driveway. Her house is two stories tall with a basement, a farmer's porch, and a path ending at the foot of an outdoor stairwell. On either side of the cobblestones, giant bronze heads blend in amongst the garden.

Once the ignition is turned off, my parents jump out of the car and walk to be greeted by Vicky waving her arms above her head as she steps off the rocking chair. I freeze and can't move.

This is a good thing, Rhiannon, really good. Fresh start, fresh environment, fresh change.

With a deep breath, I slide out of the car and stare at the two-lane street practically empty of cars passing by. After I turn around, Aunt Vicky embraces Mom and then shakes hands with Dad. It's been three years since we saw each other for more than a day, yet she looks the same. Her hair is dyed auburn, her eyes are the same brown hue as mine, and her tight curls bounce with each step. I used to be tanner, but now we're alike, and the one thing I've known about Vicky is her wardrobe: different shades of black and blue with fluorescent-colored earrings and necklaces.

When she spots me, her eyes grow wide. "That's Rhiannon?" She looks at Mom and back at me. "I...I wouldn't even recognize her. How much weight has she lost since I last saw her?"

Thirty pounds, give or take.

"Let's go inside," Mom says and guides Vicky off the farmer's porch. They step into the house with Dad following, leaving me alone outside. My aunt has two buildings; one is a regular house and the other a studio for her art. The two times I visited her were amazing. She taught me how to weld and blow glass. But the last time I visited her was freshman year, and when I started hanging out with friends over summer, I declined her invitations. For junior year, she didn't even attempt to ask.

When she stared at my weight loss as a huge shock, I should have known our relationship had completely disappeared.

Once I enter the house, I see the decorations are similar and completely different. I remembered the furniture being placed in identical spots, yet the actual pieces are altered; the walls were always filled to the brim with paintings, photographs, and mono prints, but the artwork has changed. Above the entertainment system, lights lay across the counter. The display shelf carries some more bronze heads, and in between two shelves is a framed tapestry with the embroidering, "Fore Play." Her small television has an antenna, and on the back wall, hundreds of DVDs stack behind glass cases.

As I walk through the small hallway, more artwork hangs in the quaint kitchen. I open her refrigerator to notice the abundance of greens, filtered water, and a dozen eggs. On top of the refrigerator, many wine bottles are propped up, and as I open the cabinets, zero paper plates are here, only ceramic ones. Aunt Vicky reaches for a bottle and grabs the cork opener.

"Did you guys make it here okay?" She twists the screw until it doesn't move: *POP!* After she pours a glass for herself and Mom, she pours a tiny glass and hands it to me.

"No, thank you," I say and stare at the tile. "I don't drink."

"I know you don't." She laughs. "But tonight, I'm letting you. Tomorrow is your first day at Hawken School, and we have to celebrate!" She holds the glass closer to me. The burgundy liquid bubbles swishing around.

Before I can protest, Dad walks up to me and lays his hand on my shoulder. "She can't. She needs to help me with her stuff from the car, and you know me, I'm weak and fragile."

He could have said, "*She's* weak, *she's* fragile," but he doesn't.

Aunt Vicky is persistent. "Kirk, it's just a little—"

"We'll do it right now. Catch up with your sister," he says and practically dashes us out of the house. For the next hour, we unload the car in silence, Dad bringing my belongings to the bottom of the stairs and me carrying them up into my new bedroom. The spare room is next to Aunt Vicky's, but it's closed. There's a sign reading, "Do not enter until Halloween begins!"

I didn't bring too many items, just the necessities, and the last bag I brought is my small stuffed giraffe named Maybelline. I toss her against the headboard, bouncing off the bed and onto the floor. Next to the door is the upstairs phone with a cord between the phone and receiver (I didn't think those existed anymore!). As I am about to leave, a hanging calendar catches my eyes with Monet's lily pads. On top, it reads, "September 2022."

The only thing left is my precious punching bag, Joy.

"Aunt Vicky?" I peek into the dining room. "Where should I put this?" I point to Joy, and her brow frowns.

"Um..." She stands and looks around. "I think downstairs? And please, I prefer Tori now." It is everything in my power not to roll my eyes.

I call Dad from outside, and he scurries by my side. With him holding the front and me holding the back, we carry the bag carefully down the rickety steps. Aunt Vicky's—I mean, Aunt Tori's—washroom is cramped, so we shuffle past the half bathroom and into the unfinished basement with a printed seashell couch. Four blank canvases sit in the corner with a wooden closed case near it.

When I glance at the overhanging boxes, I see labels in Mom's handwriting. She probably shipped items she knew I wouldn't want. They weren't important to me anymore, like fashionable dresses, tops, and jeans, and three photo albums stuffed to the max. Those pictures should make me smile, the black-and-white pictures of snow in Manhattan, Sadie and I at the color powder 5K, and the guy whom I loved gazing out the window at Vinegar Hill House restaurant.

Sometimes, memories should be treasured, while others, like these, should be destroyed.

Then, I do a double take: Fujifilm X-T4. Why would Dad even bother packing that? He knew, *knows*, how I can't photograph anymore. I jump as high as I can and push the unopened camera farther against the wall. Mom and Tori still chat and echo through the basement, but as soon as he runs up the stairs to shut the door, he cups his hand to his ear: silence.

Joy and I will enjoy the basement.

Dad adjusts the punching bag to the opposite side of

the room. Placing the punching gloves on the dryer, he lifts an invisible microphone and mimics the echo. "Ladies...ladies, ladies, ladies and gentlemen...men, men, men...I give you...you, you, you, the incredible...ble, ble, ble...Rhiannon 'The Beast' Broderick...rick, rick, rick!"

He points at me as I put on my gloves. I change my voice so it's whiny. "Uh, thank you very much. Don't worry, I promise the match will be very quick and *very* painful, for my opponent, not for me, of course."

For the next five minutes, I release my frustration and anxiety, pouring my soul with each punch. Although I usually have the music of Linkin Park to pump me up, an encouraging Dad is even better.

"Children?" Mom opens the door. "Time for dinner!"

Dad speaks into the invisible microphone. "Coming...ing, ing, ing." Before we rush up the stairs, his arms hovers around my waist and shoulders. I close my eyes and nod. With one arm on my shoulder and his other arm on my back, he embraces me for the first time since January. "I'm so proud of you, Rhiannon. Really, I am."

My eyes fly open, and his water. I thought he was disappointed in me, the same way it seems everyone viewed me nowadays. But as I stand wrapped in his arms, I know that's not the case.

Maybe change is a good thing after all.

"I'm gonna call you every night, whether it's Tori's cell phone or the house," he says and breaks away to look at me. "You're positive about no cell phone? Maybe an iPhone or a Galaxy? Or how about a Tracfone?"

I tilt my head. "What's a Tracfone?"

"Never mind," and he chuckles. Once we release, he brings me a CD folder and opens it. As he flips the pages, around ten crisp white discs fill the multiple pages of the binder, each one labeled, "Dad's Mixtape," with a number.

"Just in case you get sick of your music."

"I doubt it." I shut the thick binder. "But thank you."

"Plus, each one has a Dad Joke written by your old man. I should label everything, especially the chocolate records. Those are pretty sweet." A smile grows on his face as he wiggles his eyebrows. Sighing, I shake my head while smacking my forehead.

"Daddddd..."

He chuckles as I hop up the stairs. Mom and Aunt Tori are already eating while Dad and I fill our plates. After we sit down, Aunt Tori stops mid-chew and looks at my dish. "You don't like my chicken?"

I look at Mom and then at my aunt. "I'm a vegetarian."

"Last time I saw you, you could take your father to a chicken wing eating contest." She glances at Dad. "That was, what, last Christmas?" I stare at my plate and all the vegetables it carries.

Christmas was before New Year's Eve.

New Year's Eve was before New Year's Day.

New Year's Day was before—

Mom holds my hand. "A lot has changed for little Rhiannon." If I glance up, I will break down, so I stare at my food and wonder how hungry I truly am.

My aunt's gaze burns a hole in my scalp. She clicks her tongue, but she doesn't say anything. Dad changes the subject to how enthusiastic I must be feeling going to the private academy of Hawken School. Because Aunt Tori is an art teacher there, I attend for free.

Mom, Dad, and Tori engage with one another, laughing and reminiscing about previous family gatherings. Tori's phone lays front-side up, and it vibrates. A picture of a man pops up. She flips her phone over.

"Who's that?" I point to it.

She smiles. "Don't worry about it."

I'm silent for the rest of dinner, but my mind whirls nonstop questions. Will I get homesick being away from my parents? Will I miss Dad's corny jokes? And, most importantly, How much does Tori know about the reason for coming to Ohio?

When everyone finishes, Aunt Tori slides out her chair and stands with her plate. I sit and wait, staring at the lack of food before me. Mom whispers to Dad, the frown on his face growing. I wonder what—

And then, Aunt Tori wraps her arms around my neck. It's meant to be for a hug, yet it feels like a boa constructor squeezing its prey. I'm frozen and stiff, goosebumps form along my body, my esophagus tightens, and the hair at the back of my neck sticks up. I pant, my heart pounding against my chest, my breathing unsteady.

"Say something!" he shrieked. I hit his chest, his fist, and at one point, his face, but my punches were weak against his muscular arm.

I push out my chair and knock my aunt backward in the stomach. "S-s-sorry." I stumble out of my seat and steady myself. But my rapid heartbeat doesn't stop, and my left leg quivers. The breaths in and out of my lungs are quick, like a rabbit when someone steps too close. My vision blurs no matter how wide my eyes expand.

Black spots sporadically hit my eyes. I gaze at the reclining chair, the television, different pieces of artwork, but those dots keep popping up. I shut my eyes and attempt to steady my breath.

Is another blackout coming on?

"Rhie?" Aunt Tori whispers. As I open my eyes, she glances at me, confused about what is happening, and then stares at Mom.

Before Tori opens her mouth, I say, "I-I'm just tired, that's all. I-I-I'm gonna head in early." Her eyes drift to the back porch; it's still light out, not even sunset.

Once she nods, I climb the stairs, sit on my bed, and lean forward, trying to catch the air by hanging my head below my knees. I try to clear my mind, to meditate, to make my head blank, but nothing's working. I shoot my head up and look at objects around: a nightstand with a water bottle and a digital clock, a tiny closet that has been painted speckled colors, and a plastic grocery bag tucked in the corner.

It'll have to do.

I grab the bag, tie it tight, and breathe into the plastic. Come on, Rhiannon, go to your happy place. High grasses, open fields, rustic barn, three horses. No one's here for miles upon miles upon miles...

Gradually, I open my eyes with my breath even, and I lie down on the old mattress, stretching to grab Maybelline off the floor and holding her tight. Although I've only seen places like my happy place in Western films, being so isolated from everyone would be a wonder. The mental visual of that location is heaven because no one can find me. Cleveland and even Richmond Heights are too crowded for me now.

I roll on my side and shake my head; this is not how I wanted my first day in Ohio to be like.

At least I didn't black out.

After a few moments, everything returns to normal, and I grab the suitcase in my new room. The mattress takes up most of the floor space. The tiny dresser with a television is at the end of the bed. There's a giant, creepy doll with huge eyes staring at me, and I turn it around. I unpack my clothes, toiletries, and necessary school supplies and toss them in the room's corner.

Finally, I finish unpacking as much as possible and throw into the DVD player a classic black-and-white film. Then I hear someone whining through the air vent. Scooting to the shaft, I listen by putting the film on mute and leaning closer to the floor.

"I don't understand why you won't tell me." Aunt Tori's louder than normal. "You were crying when you begged for me to take her."

Mom sighs a loud, long sigh, and another chair slides across the floor. "Kirk," Mom says. "We really need to tell her."

"I know," he says. "I just don't want to relive it."

As he runs up the stairs, I dash into bed, shut the lights, and close the door. Although I don't turn off the television, I flip away from the door, shutting my eyes. When Dad opens, he whispers, "Rhiannon?" My lungs fill with as much oxygen as possible and release it with a tiny snore. He walks closer and hovers around me, but I won't open my eyes. After he kisses my forehead, he backs up and closes the door.

At ten o'clock, Mom and Tori scamper up the stairs and fall asleep. I'm stuck listening to the sound of crickets, the occasional car zooming, and the air conditioner in Tori's room. There's nothing like the "silence" of New York: Chinese takeout at 3 a.m., singing at all hours of the day, and celebrations with friends and strangers.

Tossing and turning, my mind won't shut off, so I creep down the stairs and boil some milk to help me fall asleep. Once the milk bubbles, I sit on the rocking chair in the enclosed patio and sip the scalding liquid.

There's no AC in this corner of the house, but it's nice. In Aunt Tori's backyard, the terrain sharply swoops down to a stream. On the other side of the creek, multimillion-dollar homes fill the streets an acre apart, identical with different colors, their lights turned off. However, one house remains alive, and if I perk my ears, I can hear the booming of a base.

I bet they're seniors. I bet they're having a blast, focusing on "the end of an era" and living it up. I bet girls are losing their virginity, and tomorrow, they will secretly tell one friend while the guys scream the news to the world.

For one second, I wish I had the guts to enter the stranger's home, put on a happy-go-lucky smile, and eventually, be one of the popular crowd again. For one second, I think, *Must be nice.*

But after last year, I doubt I'll ever be friends with anyone again.

Chapter 2
Austin

"Chug! Chug! Chug!"

I'm upside down, gulping away at the keg. The beer dribbles along my nose. This is the last hurrah of the senior year's summer, and with school tomorrow and my parents away on different business trips, I figured, *Why not?*

My family's housekeeper, Allison, comes tomorrow, anyway.

"Chug! Chug! Chug!" a few jocks continue to chant. Part of me wants to throw up the grotesque taste of cheap beer, but the other part of me wants to live it up.

They bring me right-side up and cheer me on. I throw multiple high fives, fist bumps, and for those *true* friends, a chest bump. I have a giant backyard with an in-ground swimming pool. No one uses it currently, but during the summer, all my friends swam here. Well, the guys swam, the women laid on lounge chairs wearing skimpy bikinis.

I jog to the patio's chair and grab the elixir of life: H$_2$0. After I twist it open with my mouth, I gulp that water faster than any beer today, or ever. It tastes so good, my taste buds are washed out, and my lips regain their form. When I'm finished, I crumble the bottle and shoot it into the recycling basket, but it falls from being overly stuffed.

"Hey, Austin." Right when I turn around, a tall, blond girl kisses me. She lays her arms against my shoulder, although my hands don't touch her. "That was fun last week."

Last week? Last week? What was last week?

She giggles. "You know! When we fooled around?" With three beats of silence, she frowns and takes her hands away from me. "Do you even remember my name?"

Was it Monica? Rachel? Phoebe? Shit, those are the girls in *Friends*.

Once I chuckle to myself due to my *Friends* reference, she slaps me across the face, but her hit is weak. "You're *such* a dick!" She stomps to the opposite side of the room and glares my way.

I think her name is Kate...like eighty percent sure.

"Dude!" Greg slams his hand on my back. I wince a little and step away. Sure, I might have a couple of inches on him being six foot three, but I have a swimmer's body: lean with a six-pack. He's bulky, his letterman jacket stretching at the arm seams. "I challenge you to see who can drink more shots."

I grin and glare down at the boy. *Challenge, eh?* I rub my hands together and am about to say, "Challenge accepted," when my stomach growls; if I don't eat anything right now, I'll vomit.

My body is telling me yes, but my liver is telling me no.

"Nah," I say, "I'm gonna grab something to eat." My keg stand was the first taste of alcohol for tonight, yet I'm already tipsy. I slap Greg as hard as I can, yet he doesn't move a muscle. In fact, his boasted build hurts my hand.

Please say it isn't broken.

"You're such a pussy, Jackie Chan!" He cackles. "Get it? Jackie Chan!" He laughs so hard he falls to the floor. I grit my teeth and force a laugh. *Good one...Haven't heard that joke in an hour.*

I open the sliding door and enter the house: an L-shaped couch, a massive plasma TV hung on the wall, two lamps one at each side, and twenty professional photographs of me, from an infant to my senior picture that I received days ago.

I plop on the couch, and the room sways. While I search for another water, a strange girl hands me one. She's petite, white hair with blue highlights, and a neck tattoo that might as well ask, "Do you want fries with that?"

"Thanks," I say as I slide closer to the girl. As I sip my water, her hand graces my basketball shorts closer and closer to my waist.

Damn, this girl knows what she wants. My reputation is intact.

I toss the water bottle and wrap my arm around her. "What's your name?" But as soon as I ask her that, someone's stare bores into my skin. I glance behind the neck tattoo girl and behind "Kate." My heartbeat quickens. Jessyka. She leans against the banister with a sheepish grin, her long nails tapping the railing maniacally.

"Um...excuse me?" The neck tattoo girl waves her hand in front of my face, and I force myself to glance at her. "And yours?"

Why is Jessyka here? We agreed we needed to end this. My thoughts and worries are spiraling out of control, and although I already realize I've had one chug too many, I want Jessyka to disappear.

"I'm Austin." I grab two tiny glasses from the coffee table. "Shots?" I never drink a shot *after* beer—*liquor before beer, you're in the clear, beer before liquor, you've never been sicker*—but I need to get a certain someone out of my mind.

The stranger stretches her hand and brushes against my arm. "Cheers." We click our whiskey and chug them in one swoop. I wince from the burn sliding down my throat, and once I look at the girl, she sips the drink like it's water. She finishes it and wipes her mouth with her hand. Her lipstick rubs off on her fingers. "How about another?"

This girl *really* knows what she wants.

I push the thought of Jessyka to the back of my head, wrap my arm around the girl's neck, and kiss her. As we release, her eyes dash from my left eye to my right, her eyebrows raised. "Is that it?"

Immediately, I pounce on her and try kissing again. She plays with my hair and yanks it a little too hard. Her tongue slobbers into my mouth, and at one point, I've stopped kissing her altogether and let her tongue play with my tonsils. She's having fun, for sure, but I can't stop thinking about Jessyka: blond hair, hazel eyes, tall frame.

When I peek to glance her way, she's gone. My heart sinks, and the thought of her makes my stomach flip in a knot.

Wait. It's not the thought of her making my stomach move.

The alcohol swishes in my stomach, and suddenly, I'm nauseous. After I bring my hand in front of my face, I shut my eyes. "Austin?" As I open my eyes, the neck tattoo girl strokes my arm. "Are you okay?"

She's kind, being worried about me. *There are other girls out there, Chang. Stop thinking about the one you can't have.* With one last kiss, I say, "Don't move." I run toward the closest bathroom, shut the door, and slide on my knees to the toilet, but as I dangle above the open seat, nothing happens.

"Austin?" a deep voice asks.

"Yeah?"

"I'm coming in," and he does. "Jesus." Troy stands in front of me. He's built like all the swimmers, tall and lanky, yet muscular, his cornrows tight to his African American skin. He rummages through the medicine cabinet and the multiple drawers until he finds a facecloth. After running it under water, he kneels down and holds the cloth over my forehead: warm, but not hot. I close my eyes, breathing as slowly as possible. I place my two fingers against my pulse. It's rapid but slowing down. *Keep breathing, Austin, keep breathing.*

"Better?" he asks.

"Yes, thank you, Nurse Troy."

He laughs and punches me in the abs. "I thought Asians were lightweights."

We are.

The Night at Times Square

While I lie down on the rug's center, Troy switches the face cloths and rubs my back in a circle. "This isn't the best time to tell you this," he says, "but I'll say it; your back is so sweaty."

I laugh. "Oh, you know you love my *moist* shirt." We chuckle and turn to silence. It's amazing how one drink can switch from something fun to something not, the mixture of emotions running through my veins.

Neck tattoo girl and her eagerness to hit the bedroom.

Greg and his peer pressure to drink more beer.

And Jessyka...oh, Jessyka...

I shake my head and push my thoughts of her away. "Shit." Troy stops moving his hand, shuffles his body, and lifts me like a rag doll. "It's time for you to go to bed. You're crying."

I am?

Troy kicks the door open and yells, "Okay! Everybody out!" I shut my eyes and continue to sob. I dig my head in his chest and want this night to be over. As soon as he says those words, everyone leaves, including the neck tattoo girl, "Kate," and Jessyka.

While Troy climbs the stairs and walks to my bedroom, I weep more than I'll admit. Maybe I cried due to Greg's "hilarious" Asian jokes, maybe it's 'cause the neck tattoo girl was a poor kisser, or maybe it's because I can't have Jessyka.

As Troy tucks me into my bed, I sniffle and finally calm myself down. "Troy?" He glances up, a worried crease on his face forming. Although I've stopped hysterically crying, my eyes still water. "I love you, man."

If anyone else peeked into the bathroom moments ago, they would just pull out their iPhone, snap a picture, and post it on Instagram. I can see it now: *#BigAsianBaby*.

"Love you, too, even if you only say it whenever you're drunk." Troy smirks, walks to the door, and says, "Now, we got practice tomorrow. Drink plenty of electrolytes."

I try to thank him, but if I speak, I'll start crying again. After I nod, he leaves, and I stare at the water and Gatorade on the nightstand. I reach to grab either of the two, but I can't stretch far enough.

Screw it, and I fall asleep in an instant.

My eyes fly open. I'm lying on my back with a splitting headache. The air conditioner is so loud I contemplate turning it off. My ceiling fan is set for slow, except it sways. Right below the ceiling, my glass-case comic books of The Flash are propped up. I rub my temple and glance at the full Gatorade and water.

I shoulda listened to Troy.

I try to focus on my alarm clock, yet it's still blurry. Once I grab my glasses, I give a sigh: 5:30 a.m. Practice doesn't start for another hour, so I can either:

A) sleep a little longer,

B) take some Tylenol and grab some plain bread, or

C) take a shower to sober myself up.

Option A seems the most promising.

As I snuggle under the sheets and comforter, I hear a long *FLUSH*. Did Troy spend the night, after all? When a girl opens the door, my mouth falls onto my sheets.

"You wear glasses? What are you? Four-eyes?" Jessyka chuckles and walks to the giant beanbag chair with an extra pillow and knitted blanket. She folds the sheet and places it on the edge of the bed. *Did she sleep here last night?* My throat tightens, and my eyes grow wide. She rolls her eyes and exhales. "Don't worry; I snuck in after *everyone* left. If you really want to get rid of me, stop hiding your spare key in the same spot," and she bats her extended long lashes.

Her voluptuous body wears a skin-tight crop top and miniskirt, a signature look for her during the summer.

"You weren't supposed to come here anymore," I mumble and rub my forehead. She opens the sliding drawer beneath my nightstand and hands me two Tylenol.

She sits next to me cross-legged and holds my hand. "I was worried about you, that's all." Her fingers trace my palm, and without thinking, I close my eyes. Jessyka's skin is smooth, and her lotion smells like lilacs. After she touches my hand, she leans into my face and kisses my mouth. It's been six months since we have kissed each other, and I automatically wrap my arms around her, her lips soft nibbling on mine. As she releases, she whispers, "Want some more?"

What the hell?

Scrambling, I try to get out of bed, but my sheets tangle like a spiderweb. I fall to the carpet. She jumps off the bed and lands, straddling my body, and I instantly feel my boxers getting tighter.

"Jessyka." Somehow, I unwrap myself and stand. "I'll say it again, we—"

"Can't," we say.

"Yeah, I get it." She rolls her eyes, her head lowered. But she spins around and gives a hopeful smile. "What if we *could,* though? I mean, Strong and I haven't been happy lately, and I think it's time. You and I talk often—"

"Yeah, texting—"

"But still." Jessyka holds her warm hand against my icy one. "Don't you remember when we..." She lowers her gaze, releases our hold, and clasps her hands. "I don't know about you, but I *crave* it."

Maybe I do, Jess, maybe I do. But I just can't.

I open my mouth to give her my rehearsed speech; I practiced it every morning with the hope I won't have to repeat it. "Listen, Jessyka, it's over. Strong is my friend, and you and I have to end it. If you break up with him, I'll..." Her eyes glimmer with plea, and I stare at the mattress. "I still won't date you." I prepare myself for the inevitable, a weep session or a slap on my face. She could say the worst thing imaginable.

However, what she *does* say is far, *far* worse. "I think I'm in love with you."

The whole thing started with an argument between Strong and Jessyka. They began bickering constantly, so often he told me he was ending it. He became drunk, and I called for an Uber. She was the last person at one of my parties, and I told her the truth: *You can be an asshole at times.* Her outer shell disappeared, and we were up all night talking until we slept together. The next day, Strong told her that he wanted to make it work, and although I hadn't had sex with her since, my mouth remained shut, too scared to let him know. I should have told him right away, but I just couldn't. Jessyka and I agreed to end it back in February, although we texted, called, and visited each other's homes without Strong's knowledge.

I shake my head, throw the "I'm in love with you" comment away, and say, "Jessyka, I seriously can't," and before she says anything else, I hop out of my bed and slam the bathroom door behind me. Immediately, I shower to sober up and to erase her from my body and my mind. It's no use though; the more I try to forget about her, the more clear it becomes. Although we didn't cheat physically over the past six months, the texting, calling, and sneaking made us cheat emotionally. Which is worse...*so* much worse.

It's now almost 6:10 a.m. I grab my favorite humorous T-shirt from the clean clothes hamper and speed down the freeway in my car, Jeffy.

"Come on, baby," I say, tapping the dashboard with one hand and rubbing a Mickey Mouse bobblehead on the passenger side. As I speed up, Jeffy purrs. This Honda Civic '07 may be rusty, but I love him because I purchased my car with my money. For three summers, I worked at a movie theater with tons of overtime. My parents offered to pay, but I needed some responsibility in my life.

Jeffy has a weird smell, though. Maybe it's weed. I'll add a new air freshener later.

Once I land in the parking lot, I dash through the double doors and follow the courtyard path as a shortcut. I'm glancing at my Fitbit when I collide with another person.

I stand and moan, rubbing my head and wanting to adjust my pants. I'm about to say something to lighten the mood as I glance down. A girl who looks to be about my age crosses her arms with a frown. I study her face and clothing: short brunette hair with a tiny ponytail, dark-brown eyes, and loose clothing of sweatpants and sweatshirt, even though it's already seventy-five degrees out here.

She's kinda hot.

I offer my outstretched hand to help her up, but the stranger ignores it, lifts herself up, and brushes the dirt off her pants. Once she notices my stare, she sighs. "Well?" she asks and gazes into my eyes. *Who is this girl? Why is she here so early? And why don't I recognize her?*

When I'm about to shuffle forward, she steps back with her eyes widening. I recoil. "Sorry" is all I say and run toward the Olympic swimming pool.

I sprint so fast I could be recruited for the track team. Passing the STEM classroom, passing the science labs, and passing the wood shop, I'm finally in the locker room. I strip down to my swimming trunks, grab my goggles and nose piece, and leave with the rest of my belongings on the floor, including my glasses.

As I barge through the locker room door, the swim team turns around, and every person silences. My teammates wear bathing caps, eager to swim the warm-up laps.

I tiptoe to the bleachers and take the first available seat. There are two people looking at me: Coach Desjardins, who is pissed, and Troy, who is trying *so* hard not to laugh.

Then I can feel the burn of a stare. *Is it Jessyka? I told her not to be here.* However, when I glance outside the giant windowpane, the only thing I spot are rustling bushes, probably from a rabbit or a squirrel.

"Mr. Chang." Coach taps his foot, and I shake my head and face forward. "What's your excuse this time?"

Rather than saying something snarky as always, I shrug. "No excuse; just overslept." *And I have a hangover that won't quit.* "Oh, by the way," I say and face Troy, "I love you."

Now, everyone laughs, including Coach, until his eyes narrow.

For a minute, he stares at me, and if I wasn't the number one swimmer on the team, I bet he would suspend me for being late on the first day. However, I *am* the best, so a little slap on the wrist will suffice.

"As I was saying," Coach resumes and looks at the rest of the team. "This year will differ from before. Your captain"—he points to Troy—"is one of the best. He'll guide you throughout the year."

Then, the team and I dive into the pool for the warmup. Although everyone else stays behind Troy, I swim as fast as I can, passing him easily. When I spin at the edge of the pool, he shakes his head and keeps his easy pace.

Once I complete two laps, I leap out of the water and watch everyone else finish. Clapping my hands, I yell, "Come on, boys! Hurry up!" and a few teammates chuckle while Coach groans.

By the time they finish, I shiver and jump repeatedly. The swimmers line up behind Troy, and with a cough by him, I reluctantly step back. I'm a firm believer that a captain should be the best swimmer, but Coach chose second best, for some reason.

He reads off a handful of names, Troy's and mine included. "As of now, these are Hawken's eight best swimmers. Wouldn't it be fun if we have a little competition to start off the season?"

He divides us into two teams: two freestyle, two breaststroke, two backstroke, and two butterfly. Troy and I dominate the butterfly, so we choose to be the anchor. The first is the freestyle stroke, so two juniors will swim at the front. They seem nervous, but I know as soon as they climb on the diving board, it'll disappear with their minds clear.

With a blow of Coach's whistle, the two freestylers dive. I remember these kids last year, and their number one thing they wanted to improve during the summer was their diving. They definitely accomplished that.

The monarchs in my stomach already form, but it's not because of the rush of adrenaline; it's because I didn't practice nearly enough as I should've in between last season and today.

The breaststroke goes next and then the backstrokers. Neither team will give up on this race, and I don't know if it's the hangover, my nerves, or the fact it's hot as balls in this arena, but I sweat profusely.

Neck and neck, the two backstrokers swim as my teammates' noise grows. Troy steps onto the platform, and I follow. He puts his goggles on, and I'm cursing myself because I forgot to put in my contacts. He leans down and looks at me with a smirk.

This Troy is determined. This Troy probably practiced every day in the summer. This Troy wants to win.

But I won't let him.

"Ready?" Coach asks, but neither of us speak. My light flashes before his. After I leap into the air and dive, a rush of icy water hits me like a punch in the gut. Coach must have our training pool ten degrees cooler than usual because he wants us to prepare for meets.

When I come up for air, I pull my arms toward my body with my palms outward facing, elbows higher than my hands. They're pushed down and back through the water while my legs move at an equal pace in upward and downward motions. My knees bend to allow a continuous, fluid stroke. Swinging my arms, I push my hands down, sweep them under my body, and break the surface. I hear Coach whistle and cheer Troy on: "Thatta boy!"

Troy's winning.

My neck and face and body align, perpendicular to the edge of the pool. I catch up to him, and this is when I don't see him. His palms must flop facing inward, his legs spread apart, and his breath uneven. With the last millisecond, my hand slams against the tile.

"Holy shit," Coach says and grins, staring right at me. I squint at the scoreboard to find out who won, and after adjusting my eyesight, my mouth flops to the bottom of the pool. Every teammate talks to me, about me, and my disappointing career:

"He lost! I can't believe he lost!"

"Wow! Troy's the new golden boy."

"If Austin doesn't shape, he'll get kicked off the

team."

I float, my chest inhales like a balloon, and I steady my breath. During the summer, I swam at an easy pace, lifted light weights, and pretty much took those three months off. However, Troy pushed himself, proving he can win. If I don't motivate myself, my captain is running my ship.

I climb the underwater stairs, remove my bathing cap, and shake until my hair sticks up straight. My messy hair must make me look like Wang Ling from *The Daily Life of the Immortal King*.

"Looks like you got some competition!" Troy reaches out a hand for a congratulatory handshake, but I hug him.

This is what I need. I'll buckle down and take practice more seriously. Maybe I'll practice on the weekends, Saturday *and* Sunday. And I'll definitely stop drinking—or just not drink as much. Like, three times a week instead of five.

This man, this marvelous man, shall be my muse.

Actually, the word *muse* refers to the nine muses in Greek mythology, who were known for beauty and music. So, Troy isn't my muse, per se, but the equivalent.

I'm about to tell him this when his eyes follow someone behind me, his face brightening. "Hold on," and he jogs as fast as he can on the slippery tile. I don't have to turn around.

"Did you win, babe?" his girlfriend asks, and they must be kissing from the lack of conversation.

"I did! It was close, though," Troy says. "Austin!"

Should I run? Should I return to the water for an extra hundred laps? Should I—

Troy claps my shoulder, and I flinch, if only for a second. Turning around, I only look at him.

"Aren't you going to give me a hug?" His girlfriend grins.

I don't look at her. "I'm good," followed by a nervous chuckle.

"Come on." She bats her eyes again. "It's not every day you'll get lucky enough to be beaten by Troy Strong."

With a deep sigh, I half hug Jessyka, and she blows gently against my ear. When we pull away, she stares at my trunks. Something tells me the two of us aren't over, despite what I told her hours ago.

What type of shit did I get myself into?

Chapter 3
Rhiannon

In my aunt's bedroom, an alarm rings, and I immediately shut my eyes and turn away from the door. I've been awake since three o'clock, watching the ceiling and clutching Maybelline. She still has coffee stains on her front two paws, no matter how many times I wash her.

"Rhiannon?" Tori opens the door and knocks, in that order. "Do you want to take a shower?"

"Sure."

I wait until I hear her feet scurry down the stairs. In the shower, scalding water hits my back at a higher-than-normal pressure. I stand there for five whole minutes, leaning on the tile wall and collecting my thoughts. Every year, butterflies formed in my stomach, anticipating the first day of school. I would spend the night before changing my clothes so I picked out the perfect outfit. When I woke, those butterflies swarmed, but in a good way.

Now, I feel nothing.

After I turn off the water, I change into my sweats and trudge down the stairs. Mom drinks an espresso and Dad has tea, both reading the newspaper. I give them kisses on their cheeks and scoot my chair to the table. Without missing a beat, he slides his mug to me. Aunt Tori has twenty mugs stuffed in a cabinet, and no two are alike. Today, I drink from a glazed mug, reading, "What are you afraid of?" I turn it around and listen to the college radio station.

"I made sure there's no meat in your omelet." Tori puts it in front of my plate next to the cloth napkin. When I glance up, she smiles, wearing a white nightgown. On it is a bright sun with a pair of sunglasses, and in tiny print, it reads, "I'm just one big fucking ray of sunshine."

She taps her slipper and bounces. "Well? Aren't you gonna try it?" I stare at the perfect omelet: tomato, onions, asparagus, mushrooms, and garlic. Yet, I don't get hungry anymore and slide my plate over to Dad. Tori sighs and stomps away.

"You could have appeased her," he whispers and bites the omelet. He moans, savors the flavor in his mouth, and touches his chest. Once he swallows, he scarfs the entire omelet, bite after bite. "Never mind. This is *terrible*." He takes another bite. "Absolutely *terrible*." And another. "You'd *hate* it," and he finishes the rest of my omelet in thirty seconds with a loud *BURP*. "Hey, why don't eggs tell jokes?" He leans toward me. "They'd crack each other up."

He nudges my arms with his elbow, and before he tells another joke, Mom sighs and says, "Let Rhie finish her tea, okay?" I smirk and sip Dad's mug.

After I grab my beige backpack lying on the living room couch, I notice three Polaroid cameras lined up against a briefcase in the corner. Aunt Tori picks up one of the three. "I'll have you take a picture of me and Hank, since it's the beginning of our last year."

"Who's Hank?"

She gasps. "You will *love* him!"

While I roll my eyes, Tori hops down the outdoor stairs. Before I follow, Mom coughs. I turn around. "Go easy on her, okay?" Mom smiles and taps my arm. "Who knows? You might enjoy her company."

As the four of us walk to our cars, Mom wraps her arm around my shoulder all the way through the path. Once we reach the driveway, she embraces me and so does Dad. Even though they haven't left yet, I miss them already.

"Hey, Rhie?" Dad whispers, and I glance up. "Try to be happy."

After we break apart, Tori and I wave at them as my parents back out into the street. A few cars swerve out of their way, but no beeping occurs. I jog to the end of the driveway and watch their car become smaller and smaller, blending into the other vehicles until it can't be identified.

I stare into the abyss, and it hits me how I'm alone without them. They brought me to therapy, allowed me to choose my homeschooling studies, and even took me to Coney Island for sunsets, including during a freezing February.

"Rhiannon?" I turn around, and Tori's head sticks out of her truck's window. "We're going to be late." I nod, walk back to the truck, and hop in.

The drive is pleasant with many cute houses beneath the tall trees. On this sunny day, rays catch my eyes whenever we reach a spot free of leaves. Tori whistles to whatever indie songs plays, currently a tune by Of Monsters and Men "From Finner."

We park near three murals, and when we enter the art room, hundreds of art pieces align. In the back, a Mozart record plays. Above the entrance, there's a sign reading, "Fair Play" that looks identical to the one at her house. There's a ladder leading to a secret passageway, covered by a black trash bag.

Tori yells to the trash, "How many days 'til graduation?"

"Oh, honey, too many!" A man pops out of the garbage's passageway and stuffs the bags into a ball. He struts his way down the wooden stairs with his piercing blue eyes, bald head, white beard and mustache, thinner frame, and a dark blue polo. Once he finishes his descent, he rambles. "I attempted to change the film of my eight-millimeter camera. I got it on Etsy!" He squeals, places the camera on the counter, and tosses the trash bag into a large bin.

"I tried to call you last night but there was no ans—" He stops when he sees me, eyes widening and mouth dropping. He scans me, squints, and nervously laughs. "Tori, I don't know who this girl is, but, my gosh, the resemblance is uncanny."

Tori beams. "Hank, this is Rhiannon. My niece."

"Pleasure," and he shakes my hand with a firm grip. While I drop my gaze to the floor, I notice Hank and Tori both have two different colored socks on. As I glance up, they stare at each other, and he mouths, "What the hell?"

"Rhie, why don't you go exploring?" Her hand motions as she looks at her watch. "You have plenty of time before school starts. Try to be here at eight o'clock, okay?" She's eager for me to leave, and I bet Hank will ask her a thousand questions about who I am, why I am here, and what happened.

"Sure," and I put on my Walkman and backpack, exit the art room, and enter the hallway. In the arts section of the building, many vibrant paintings fill the walls, and one mannequin wears a rainbow skirt composed of tissue paper. The next section is a huge room with large round tables and small raised ones. There's even a study hall with a fireplace near the entrance.

This layout is strange.

As I circle around the room, someone taps on my shoulder. I jump and rip my headset off my ears. "Can I help you?" the woman asks. When I turned around, I must have wandered into her desk. This secretary blinks her long eyelashes behind her tiny glasses, sporting a fluorescent yellow skirt and dull gray tee.

"I'm just browsing. My Aunt, Tori—"

She snaps her fingers. "You must be Rhiannon! Welcome to Hawken! Do you want some coffee? Tea, perhaps?" She continues to speak on and on, asking questions about Brooklyn and Manhattan and my past life. My palms sweat as my heart pounds.

I need to get out of here.

"Where's the bathroom?" I ask, interrupting her. She stops talking and points behind her. I walk in that direction, then stop, and as soon as the secretary is occupied, I sprint outside.

I wander around the buildings with my music player around my neck: freshly mowed lawns, beautiful gardens, and thirteen bronze statues of hawks. When I read the stone tablet in front of the birds, the thirteen hawks represent thirteen alumni fallen soldiers, and each bird is unique. Did Tori make those?

Cutting across the path, I trudge through different courtyards, but I recognize I passed this area twice already. Am I lost? *Shit.* Stopping, I glance at my analog watch and sigh again.

SLAM!

Someone knocked into me. We fall on the mulch, and I curse at the minor pain coming from my tailbone. My sweatpants have mud smeared on my shin.

The person sticks out their hand with the sound of a mouth breather. I ignore it, not-so-gracefully hobble back on my feet, and wipe my pant leg. As I'm staring at eye level, I notice his chest: lanky, muscular arms, and T-shirt reading, "I'm into Fitness, Fit'ness Taco into My Mouth."

I shade my eyes from the sun and peer at his face. Asian descent, thickly framed glasses, full lips, and dark hair, reminding me of an anime character I can't quite place. His chest fills with a rapid breath, and I'm guessing he ran. When I focus back to his eyes, he appears vacant and blank, staring at me for far too long.

"Well?" I ask colder than I mean to and fold my arms.

He's about to touch my arm when I back up. All he says is "Sorry" and dashes off again. The guy hops over the outdoor furniture like a gazelle, his drawstring bag stretching longer with each step. I stare at him until he pushes through the double doors and enters the building.

I follow his path with my eyes fixed on the entrance. Maybe he knows a shortcut to Tori's, or a different adult can steer me in the right direction. When I reach it, I stop, whiff the smell of chlorine, and peek through the window. It's an Olympic-sized swimming pool, just like my old school.

On the right, a group of boys sit on the bleachers, and on the left, a man and a boy stand on the tile. The guy who slammed into me jogs on his toes and sits in the first row. When he looks my way, I hide behind the bushes.

What are you doing, Rhiannon?

I shake my head and continue on the path until I reach the three murals. With my back against the oak tree, I slide down, land on the lawn, and close my eyes. The gentle breeze brushes my face as I attempt to practice meditation. *In through the nose, out through the mouth.* Almost no one crosses my path, and those that do, ignore me.

This is perfect.

Maybe I'll begin a new book, like *They Both Die in the End* or *Before I Fall.* As I rummage through my backpack for some reading materials, I stop, rest my hands on my lap, and continue to meditate. The sides of my lips twitch, like a smile wants to break through the permafrown I now own. Perhaps I'll let it.

BEEEEEEP!

My eyes fly open as the bell rings. *Was I asleep?* Drool falls onto my lap. Yep, definitely asleep. I stumble from the lawn to an upper branch and glance at the art room.

It's impossible to sneak through Tori's class without interrupting, but I don't want to be late, especially on the first day. After I crack through the doorway, her entire class turns around, including my aunt.

"Rhiannon?" Tori's eyes widen. My throat closes up, and my heart quickens so loud it must be audible. She steps forward, yet I remain frozen. "I knew I should've come out and found you when you didn't come back. I'm so sor—" Her hand hovers close to my arm, and suddenly, I snap and pull my hand behind my back.

"I don't wanna be late." I force a smirk. She winces like I just slapped her across her face, lowers her arm, and returns to the front of the studio. I swallow, feeling guilty for being miserable for the past two hours. I should say something, like how it's not her fault I might be tardy and how I am truly trying to make the best of this school.

But am I?

As I hold my breath, I stare at the clock, bolt out of there, and jog through the hall. Once I pick up the pace, another *BEEP* plays over the loudspeaker.

"Welcome staff and scholars," the announcer says. "This is Principal Gemetta wishing a warm welcome. First of all, we're going to have a great year. Have you seen this weather?" I roll my eyes and sniff the armpits of my sweatshirt. Deodorant holds its place, but I can't say the same for the sweat stains.

As I read the signs above the classroom's door, I exhale: Mr. Lane's English Room. Finally, I enter. There are about fourteen kids sitting in rows and columns, fifteen including me. Unlike my old school, the students wear clothing that could belong to a fashion magazine. Even the girls who sport leggings with loose tank-tops purchased their attire from Lululemon, Under Armor, and

Zella. Currently, everyone is reciting the pledge of allegiance. There are two seats left, and both are in the front.

Great.

After the pledge, I scurry to my seat with my head hanging low and plop at a desk. I take my Walkman off my neck, wrap my headset around itself, and slide it under my chair. A girl goes *PSST* as I turn in her direction.

This girl reminds me of a supermodel with long legs, extremely thin figure, and straight hair that is so blond it's practically white. She wears a crop top, ripped jeans, and four-inch sparkly heels.

"That's so cool?" She points to my Walkman. "I think my parents had one of those when they were our age? It's, like, retro? I wonder where you got it?" She ends every sentence as a question.

I'm about to reluctantly answer when Mr. Lane says, "A new student! How exciting!" My cheeks redden as he stares at me. He looks at me, like he wants me to say something, but I don't. He leans forward and signals for me to rise. "Well?"

How many days until graduation?

With a deep breath, I stand, and the girl who was fascinated by my Walkman squeals. "She's *so* little? I feel like I can carry her in my purse?" A few guys laugh as I grow redder. I'm aware of my height, being five foot nothing, but still; can't everyone just leave me alone?

"Miss Clement," the teacher says with authority, and all that the girl does is blow a gum bubble and pop it. He turns my way and eggs me on.

Sighing, I mumble, "I'm originally from New York,

and I now live with my aunt, Ms. Benner." I stare at the desk, wanting the humiliation to be over, but his glance hovers above me. I face him.

"And your name?"

"Rhiannon...Rhiannon Broderick."

"Oh my gosh?" the same girl asks, or says. "Like the singer? Of 'Umbrella'?" Then she sings, and soon, half the class chants the same catchy yet obnoxious tune.

"No," I say, and the girl sighs. "Like the song by Fleetwood Mac."

She nods, but everyone silences, except for Mr. Lane.

"Well, welcome to Hawken School, Miss Broderick!" He practically squeals, and after a beep, he clears his throat. "My apologies. It's just we never have new students this late in their high school career."

"Who's the new student?"

All of us, including Mr. Lane, turn to the door: a man wearing sweatpants, sweatshirt, sneakers, clip board, and a whistle hanging around his neck. This guy has to be the physical education teacher. He grins and stares at me. I sink even further into my seat.

"Say, we have a great women's swimming program here," the man says. "Not as good as the boys, but still." The guys chuckle, and the girls roll their eyes. *Sexist much?* I'd join them in their actions, but the man continues to look my way. "Have you ever swam competitively?"

I swallow. "No." Lie number one. "I don't like to swim." Lie number two. "Besides, I don't know *how* to swim," and that's three lies in under a minute. Must be a record.

The man opens his mouth, yet Mr. Lane steps in. "It

was great seeing you, Mr. Desjardins," and he practically pushes Mr. Desjardins out the door.

With five seconds of excruciating muteness, Mr. Lane hands out the syllabus for Honors English. I write my name at the top and keep my eyes glued to the paper. When we're halfway through the syllabus, I feel someone's eyes on my right side. I shoot up, and a different guy—dirty-blonde hair, bulky muscles, and carries two gallons of water—scans me.

He peeks to ensure Mr. Lane doesn't see him. "You know," the guy says. "You'd be pretty hot if you'd smile more." I grit my teeth and try as hard as I can not to drop my mouth.

Who does this guy think he is? The only guy who has the audacity to say that is Tom Holland, and for Tom Holland, you bet your ass I'd smile for him.

The students within earshot giggle and go, "Oo." But I don't break a sweat and lean to my right.

"This is my smile." A stoic face pours out of my body as the guy drops his smirk. "And *you* might look halfway decent if you'd quit taking steroids. That way, your face won't resemble Deadpool's." No chuckles nor snickers come from the classroom. I'm guessing this guy has popularity written all over him because everyone stops laughing.

Except one.

I turn around and redden: the guy from the courtyard. He laughs so hard he hiccups. "Excuse me," says Mr. Lane. "Something funny?"

"Actually, yes. Fleetwood's got jokes."

He glances my way. The edge of my lips curls up for

one second, but then I continue with my notes and jot down the *extremely* important information: *always bring something to write with*. When the courtyard runner raises his hand, Mr. Lane points at the back of the classroom. "Yes, A—"

"It's Austin," the boy interrupts the teacher, turning bright red. "Um, I was gonna ask you if I can borrow a pencil?" Mr. Lane glances at Austin and back at the attendance list. After he grabs a pencil from his desk, he tosses the boy an unsharpened one.

"Whatever, *Austin*," and he resumes with his syllable. I remain staring at Austin, who has a huge sigh of relief.

What's that about?

The girl who asked me about my Walkman taps at my back, and when Mr. Lane tells us to gather into groups of four, she asks, "Do you want to join us?"

I blink. *Some stranger wants me to join her group?* I can't help but nod without time to think. The guy who reminds me of Deadpool is in our group, too, and Austin is the fourth. He leans back in his chair, rocking back and forth, back and forth, and I secretly hope he falls so he realizes the danger he puts himself in. The amount of pain he can get from falling off a chair is the equivalent to pain from falling off a bridge.

"Can you be our scribe?" the girl asks me and points to the guy and Austin. "Their handwriting is messy? And I'm afraid I'll break a nail?" She shows off her lovely manicure with a unique design.

I nod, grab a pen, and write my name first. When I glance at Austin, he opens his mouth to give me his name, but I already jot it down.

"Gregory, Greg for short." Greg smiles wider, encouraging me to do the same. After I write his name down, I glance up. I start with a stern face and creepily force my cheeks to upturn. Austin laughs, and I immediately drop my face.

My cheeks are hot. I shake my head and force myself to stare at the girl. "I'm sorry, what's your name?"

"No need to apologize? Jessica?" She giggles. When I write her name down, she frowns. "You spelled it wrong?" Does she spell it with one S? "It's J-E-S-S-Y-K-A?"

I snort, loud. Is she serious? Did she change her name to some weird spelling? Or did her parents hate her as an infant? As soon as I see how pissed JessYKa is, I wipe my smirk off my face.

"Sorry," I whisper again and erase half of her name. My cheeks flush, yet both Greg and Austin snicker, like they're trying hard not to laugh, and every second, their laughter grows until they can't hide it anymore. When I glance at Jessyka, she's red, but it's not out of embarrassment.

For the rest of the class, Jessyka barks orders, tells me to write faster and neater, and maniacally taps her fingers. My wrist becomes sore from all the scribbling.

Once the bell rings for biology and calculus, it's time for lunch, and I hover around my desk. I pretended to be gathering my things, taking notebooks in and out of my bag, and finally, I put my headset on to Linkin Park. After I peek to see if the hallway is empty, other than the couple making out, it's clear.

I step out, put my hood up, and trudge through the

immense cafeteria, spreading out thirty tables with wide open spaces. To my surprise, there're more tables with a solo student. One guy sprawls his book across the high counter, another one eats just raisins, and the last one scrolls through her phone with a puss on her face.

With my protein drink in one hand and my granola bar in the other, I stare at one abandoned table against the far wall. My music blares in my ears so I can't hear anything as I hop onto an elevated small table. Before I repeat my CD again, I open my CD binder and pull out another burnt disc labeled, "Dad's Mixtape #1." On the bottom, it reads, "Why couldn't the bicycle stand up on its own? It was two tired."

Once I slide the CD into the player, I hit the Play button: the instrumental version of "Running Up the Hill." My foot taps along with the beat, and I shut my eyes. While listening to the music, Austin plops in the chair across from me. I press the Pause button on the CD player, but I don't take off my headset. "Fleetwood, right?"

"Rhiannon, actually."

He leans back in his chair. "You don't mind if I call you 'Fleetwood,' do you?"

No one has called me "Fleetwood" in nine months, I wanted to say. But I don't feel like explaining this to a guy I barely know and shrug, sitting back against my chair. His brown eyes narrow, like he's trying to figure out who I am. I lose this staring contest and lower my eyes.

He's dressed impeccably, unlike before. He wears three layers, a white tee that I barely see, a gray sweatshirt, and a rustic jean jacket. For bottoms, he sports ripped black jeans and a navy-blue sneaker, and he no longer wears his glasses.

"Listen, Fleetwood," he begins, and I look up. "Jessyka means well. She's just self-conscious sometimes, that's all. She's not like Narcissus." He chuckles, but I have no idea what he is referring to. "You know, Narcissus, the son of a Greek nymph who fell in love with himself? Hence the term *narcissist*?"

My mouth opens slightly, not because of him defending Jessyka, but because he knows mythology better than I do.

"Anyway..." His face turns pink. "I'm sure someone made fun of you, once upon a time, right? Everyone's going through the same thing."

I crinkle my nose. Jessyka and I are *not* the same, and we definitely haven't gone through the same shit. The fact Austin said such a thing pisses me off, and I wish I could punch him in the face. However, I'd get expelled, regardless of my relation to Tori.

I stare at him, the perfect nose, the swoop of his gelled hair, the usual charming smile that most popular people carry. His eyes draw to my lips, and I press Play, and read my novel, *They Both Die in the End*. Unwrapping the granola bar, I ignore him, despite his mouth's movement. Finally, he jumps down from his seat and walks away.

"Oh my gosh," a girl says within earshot, "he's so dreamy."

"I know, right?" says another. "I heard he's a take-charge type of guy."

"I heard he can make you feel weak and fragile."

"I heard he enjoys being the one in control."

Why would anyone search for a guy like that? Before I read, I search to find Tori waving at me. My cheeks flush while I wave, and she gives me a thumbs-up.

This I don't reciprocate.

Once I return to my book, my eyes can't concentrate and instead watch Austin. His table is full with a few people standing around it. They're laughing at something, but I'm fixed on the apple he tosses repetitively. He smiles wide, a charming grin he must use to get away with pretty much anything.

Was I like that? Effortlessly having the popular crowd into me? My eyes focus on his apple, up and down, until he stops. When I peer into his eyes, he notices, and rather than giving me a sheepish grin or even a tiny wave, he turns away.

This is the last year of my high school career, and every time I turn off my alarm is one step closer to graduation. As for college, I won't be attending, not anymore. In a perfect world, I'd live on a farm in the middle of nowhere, alone. Maybe I'd be staying in Montana, climbing the mountains or woods, or I'd live in Alaska and scope Aurora Borealis.

I stare at my food and drink and toss both items into the nearby barrel. Shaking my head, I read my book, the words coming off the page as I enter a new world and leave the old one behind, and no matter what, I won't think of that night in Manhattan.

New Year's Eve
Times Square
11:30 p.m.

"Rhiannon, where are they?" Sadie asked with her eyes watering. A guy bumped her right hip, and she stumbled into the crowd. I grabbed her wrist and yanked her closer to me between 41st and 47th Street.

I squeezed her hand to comfort her. "We're almost there." But I didn't know if that's true. She smiled at an equal height, her being in flats. I remember her saying how guys like short girls the other day, and due to that, she purchased ten pairs of shoes with no extra height. When I glanced at her, her eyes fluttered. She gazed into my eyes, frowned, and whined *again*.

"Why do your fake eyelashes look so good? I hate these! I shouldn't have bought the cheap ones!"

Although I wanted to say, *Told ya so,* I said, "I'll take yours off as soon as we find our group."

Our eyes darted from the performing stage to random spots in front of us, but mostly we watched down on the crowded pavement. My camera bag strap hopped to the beat of my high heels with Maybelline sticking her head out of the pouch. As Times Square drew closer to midnight, there were thousands of people morphing into one mob. Because it's about thirty degrees warmer than normal, many spectators tossed their coats onto the ground. Piles of trash were thrown on the streets and sidewalks, and people were packed like sardines, so we shuffled in order to move.

"Oh, I almost forgot," Sadie said while we maneuvered around. "Wanna have *The Hunger Games* marathon again? I know you only like the first two movies, but it'll be fun!"

I laughed. "Only if we watch *Up* first."

"Fine." She rolled her eyes. "We can watch that movie *again*," and nudged me.

"What day?"

"Friday night?"

I stepped near the sidewalk and stopped shuffling. "I can't. It's Xavier's and my anniversary."

Sadie narrowed her eyes. "What do you mean? You just had your two-and-a-half-year celebration. What is it *this* time? First time you laid eyes on him?" and she batted her eyes.

"We're celebrating the first time we slept over." I tried to smile, but she scoffed and began walking.

"Really? I mean, it's not that big of a deal. You haven't even had"—she glanced around us and whispered, "sex yet." I couldn't help it and laughed, but that wasn't the best reaction to her. She rolled her eyes. "Wow...it's like you don't care about our friendship."

On the word *friendship,* I mouthed the word at the same time that she said it.

To be honest, maybe Sadie and I won't have as strong a connection in the future as me and Xavier. She planned on attending Florida State, staying there indefinitely since she hated the cold.

Still, we should spend as much time together as we can.

I stopped moving and forced Sadie to turn around to look at me, reluctantly. "I'll see what I can do. Who knows? Maybe we'll cut out every quarter-anniversary." She hugged me, pulled out her phone, and opened Snapchat. After she chose the cat filter, we stuck out our tongues and pressed the button.

Sadie added the beautiful picture of us to her story, labeling the caption, "Times Square with my bestie!" and tagging me. Instantaneously, my phone started to blow up with all the comments:

"You look so GORGEOUS! #highheeledqueen."

"Her makeup is flawless! #fiveminutebeauty."

"OMG, your hair! #sojealousofyourhighlights."

Although I don't speak, Sadie frowned because we spent the same time getting ready for tonight, the same amount of money spent on our hair, and the same height thanks to new footwear. Yet, everyone complimented me and not her.

We continued to shuffle toward the stage. I clenched my necklace as every moment passed by. In my coat pocket, my iPhone vibrated, and I released my pendant to check it.

Xavier. The text read, "Where are you? I'm on the

pole."

Grinning, I stopped moving and squinted above the crowd. Across the street, a guy stood on top of the streetlamp, searching the massive crowd. He wore his usual attire of bright yellow-and-black sneakers, sleek jeans, and a leather jacket. But it didn't matter; his heavy footing was *so* loud that I could hear it, even with the crowd's noise.

I jumped repetitively until he spotted us. He waved us over and smoothed his gel so there wasn't a hair out of place. I giggled and dragged Sadie behind me. Before we reached our crowd, I asked her to close her eyes so I could pluck the fake eyelashes away.

"I'm going to throw up," she said, and I sighed. "Seriously! I'm so nervous! What if Duff doesn't remember me? Or worse: remembers the *wrong* name."

"Don't be silly, *Stephanie*." She lightly slapped my face.

As I continued barging through the millions of people, Sadie tightened her grip on my palm.

"I Googled him," she said.

"You don't say," and I gave her a side-eye.

"Did you know he's gone to a different school every three years? He moves because of his dad. He's an Army guy, or something." Before I could breathe into the conversation, she continued. "He's traveled around the world! That's why he has an amazing British accent. Xavier told me Duff might end up moving next year, but if he begs his Dad, Duff will stay with Xavier! It's like fate is bringing us together."

"You might want to refer to him as 'Finley' instead

of 'Duff.' It makes him sound less of a douchebag."

Sadie laughed and nudged me. "He could never be a douchebag."

We maneuvered our way to the sidewalk as my grip on Sadie's hand loosened. She's liked Finley Duffy for the past two and a half years. And ever since she first saw him, she told me she was going to marry him, although she wasn't in any of his classes.

With ten feet between us and Xavier, my hand got yanked by some stranger, and Sadie and I separated. I yelped and almost fell because the new heels were higher than usual.

But hey, Manhattan was warm tonight, and I took advantage.

I stumbled with my arms outstretched to find my balance. A gentle hand scooped my stomach effortlessly, and I immediately found my equilibrium.

"My hero," I said, turned on my camera, and photographed the perfect smile that Xavier always held. After I put my camera away, we kissed, wrapped our fingers together, and walked toward Sadie. She moped and sat down by the sewer.

"I can't do this." Her fingertips shook. "I'm not like you, Rhie. I don't know how to even talk to guys, never mind flirt with them."

Ever since Xavier and I began dating, she put me on a pedestal that I didn't deserve. Whenever my boyfriend and I kissed, Sadie whined and said, "Why can't I have that?" But she didn't know anything other than our surface-level depth. Like other couples, our relationship was much deeper, but I swore to him I wouldn't tell anyone about our conversations, even her.

I released Xavier's hand, lifted her head, and wiped the running mascara from her cheek. "Take a leap, Sadie. That's the only way you'll know if you have a chance. And"—I gripped her shoulder—"you're braver than you think."

She stared into the distance at Finley Duff: Finley with his long-sleeve polo and Hogwarts sweatshirt, Finley with his piercing blue eyes to match hers, Finley with his bleach-blond tips and his large Adam's apple.

I linked my arm with hers and marched toward our friends. Well, not our "friends" per se, more like acquaintances. The ladies huddled among themselves while the guys kicked a hacky sack around. Xavier and I separated to hang with our groups.

Half of these juniors I didn't recognize and half were on the swim team. Lizzy, captain of the team, flicked a lighter and held her cigarette under the flame. With a deep breath of the tar, she glanced in my direction.

"Will you *please* come back on the swim team?" she asked and took another puff. "No one beats you at the butterfly stroke. You can hold your breath for so long!"

I peeked at Sadie, who rolled her eyes. When she was about to protest, I slightly stepped forward so I stood between the two. "Sorry, but it stopped being fun for me." Actually, I still loved it, even missed it sometimes.

"Come on, Rhie!" Lizzy finished her cigarette, threw it onto the sidewalk, and snuffed it with her high heels. "Not everything *has* to be fun. Besides, winning is the greatest high you'll ever experience." It's true; with each win, I got a rush that I couldn't explain. But, I'd rather focus on my future career of photography than play a silly game.

Marching back to Sadie, I squeezed her hand and shook my head.

"You don't know what you're missing." Lizzy sighed and pulled out yet another cancer stick. "It's a great way to stay in shape, too." My hand dropped to my side, and she reddened. "Not-not-not that you are *out* of shape. I was saying..." Her voice trailed while her eyes landed on my midriff.

I was embarrassed about my weight. At the end of sophomore year, I stopped taking PE since it was no longer required, and I quit the swimming team 'cause I didn't have enough time to spend with my boyfriend. Slowly, I gained a pound here and there, but I didn't try to lose it and gained thirty pounds.

When Lizzy opened her mouth to say something, I whispered, "Excuse me," and walked to the edge of the sidewalk. As I watched Sadie, Lizzy, and everyone else, they didn't notice me, and rather giggled, that stupid laughter all the girls used when they wanted to be heard by a guy.

Then, Lizzy sidestepped to her right and caressed Xavier's arm. He squirmed, cleared his throat, and moved away from her, but with the last puff of her cigarette, she nudged his arm and whispered something inaudible. Yet, I could read her lips perfectly fine: "You can do better than her."

When she mouthed, she looked at me.

My blood boiled. *Who does she think she is?* Xavier frowned and stepped backwards. Apparently, she still didn't get the picture and slid next to him with her eyes landing on me again. She egged me on, like she was saying, "Come at me, brah." However, I had a better plan.

I jogged-ish to the lamp post, jumped higher than he did earlier, and whistled using two fingers. His grinning face turned my way.

"Romeo, Romeo, wherefore art thou Romeo?" I said in a poorly made British accent and glanced at Finley. He didn't seem amused, shaking his head and gazing at the stars. Xavier laughed, sprinted to the post, and started climbing.

"I'm coming, Juliet!"

I leaped into his arms and embraced him. His cologne smells so good tonight, like a musky cigar. He might be short for a guy, being five foot six, but being five foot nothing made him the perfect height for me.

Whenever Xavier and I saw each other, it's like the world stopped. The noise faded, and we were the only people left on Earth. If an apocalypse happened full of zombies, we'd save each other, or we'd *both* be zombies and communicate using grunts.

Once we released our hug, we smooched, giving each other Eskimo kisses. Sadie pointed to her mouth and pretended to gag. This night would be perfect, except there's ten people in between Finley and Sadie.

"Everybody, put your hands up!" said DJ Kevin.

We bounced to the rhythm, hopping and giggling nonstop, even Xavier. I sang my lungs out, and he joined in. Then I nudged him and pointed to our group of friends. He gave me one head nod and bounced until he reached Finley. Sadie spun around and said, or screamed,

"What are you doing!"

"Sometimes, fate needs a little help!"

Xavier and Finley continued to hop around and stopped once they reached us. She opened her mouth and stared at his lips. Although I literally needed to close her mouth, Finley couldn't stop gazing at *her* lips while he opened another can: Duff Beer, from *The Simpsons*.

Hastily, I pulled out my camera and took a great shot of them. As soon as the flash went off, Sadie turned a shade of purple. "Why'd you bring your camera here? Someone might steal it!"

"I have insurance," I said and tried not to roll my eyes. "Besides, I absolutely love it. It's like tiny pieces of my soul are in each picture."

"That's deep, Broderick," Finley said, but I didn't look in his direction.

"Thanks for the sarcastic comment."

"It wasn't."

Now, I spun and peered at him with his smile widening. *Was he being genuine?* He grinned and stood next to my boyfriend, leaning on Xavier's head. *Nope, he was* definitely *being sarcastic.*

"Oh, shut up, Duff." I pretended to be upset and punched him in the arm. He laughed, but continued leaning. He knew Xavier felt self-conscious about his height, so why would Finley make fun of him now? "Come on, don't be a dick."

It's times like these when I'm so glad my crush on Finley was just a phase.

He petted Xavier's hair, and although it was only some teasing, Xavier's fist tightened, his eyes narrowing.

He grabbed Finley's hand, dragged it behind his back, and squeezed. Finley laughed at first, but as Xavier's hold became tighter, Finley struggled and winced.

"Mate," Finley said and attempted to turn around. "Come on—" Xavier twisted the younger boy's arm. Finley tried to push away and wiggle free, yet it was no use. With every sudden movement, Xavier rigidly brought the limb closer.

When Finley inhaled, like he was about to scream, I rushed over to my boyfriend and placed my hand on his shoulder. Xavier froze and loosened the grip. I whispered, "It was only a joke. He's your friend, remember?"

His eyes fluttered as he released Finley's hand. Before anyone could do anything, I held Xavier's hand and dragged him ten feet away. He sighed and sulked beneath his shoulders.

"It's not working...the medication..." I continued to rub his back and waited for him to continue. Two months ago, his mother switched health insurance, and they wouldn't cover all their expenses. Xavier was bipolar, so having the proper medication was crucial. He told me the day he found out he had the disorder and ways to make me feel safe. If he was angry, I would tell him, "It's not me you're mad at," or "Let's go for a walk and calm down." It was working, but no one was aware besides me.

"Did you try working on your car? It usually calms you."

He held up his grimy hands, a classic sign of time spent in the auto shop. "But it's not helping." Sighing, he kissed my hand. "I'll go to the doctor's tomorrow, or as soon as possible. I don't...I don't like feeling this way."

I laid my head on his shoulder, and he put his head on mine. "Do you want to see a therapist?"

He scoffed. "Therapists are overpaid listeners who use the phrase, 'and how does that make you feel,' too often." He chuckled, but there was sadness between his eyes as he glanced down to the cement.

I held him as if all the people disappeared. I hated seeing him like this; he confided to me how scared he was because he didn't know how everyone would react to his condition. I wanted him to realize how much I supported him.

Xavier looked down, held my chin, and gently kissed me. I stared into his eyes, and he grinned, tickling my ribs. "Come here, Juliet." While he picked me up, I wrapped my legs around his waist.

We kissed not really caring about PDA or the disgusted glances nearby adults gave us. When we stopped, I unwrapped my entire body and leaned against his forehead. Then, he peeked behind me, tapped my shoulder, and pointed.

I turned around, and the Matchmaker 3.0 was underway. Finley and Sadie shook hands and kept on talking, or yelling, but whatever. Xavier and I high-fived each other, and he added his arm to my waist.

"They grow up so fast," he said and pretended to wipe his invisible tears.

When DJ Kevin played a slow song, Xavier bowed to me, and I curtsied. Rather than holding me and swaying like normal high school couples, we waltzed, apart and together, apart and together, apart and together. As we did this, my dress rode up. I blushed, pulling it down with my hands.

Xavier stopped dancing and leaned into me. I smelled his after-dinner mint. "You are so hot, Rhie." Still holding hands, he made me twirl. "Seriously."

My biggest fear was losing Xavier, and at this moment, my weight was my biggest flaw. "What if I gain *more* weight? Like fifty or even a hundred pounds?" I whispered. He raised my head.

"I would be happy, because then, I wouldn't *need* to go to the gym anymore. In fact, I *encourage* it! Hell, the two of us will gain three hundred pounds, live in our mansion—"

"Because your app is gonna take off."

"—yes, because it *will* take off."

Xavier was one year older than me, and he said he was prepared to be a computer science major with a prototype for his newest app. He wouldn't let me *glance* at the plans because he wanted it to be perfect.

"We won't need to grocery shop!" He lifted his shirt, revealing gorgeous abs, and let his stomach drop. I laughed. "We'll order it!"

"And live happily ever after?"

Squeezing me tight, he kissed me. We waltzed back and forth. "Besides," he said and wiggled his eyebrows. "I love a girl with a little meat on her bones."

I scoffed and glanced up. "Really?"

"Yeah! As far as I'm concerned, you've gotten hotter since you've gained weight." I laughed and dug my face into his shoulder. "Oh, guess what? I got into Ohio State."

"That's amazing," I said, but my heart skipped a beat. If he chose Ohio, we'd be separated for a majority of the school year.

He clasped my hands and smiled that perfect smile. "I already did research on photography schools closer to Ohio State. There's Columbus College of Art and Design, and I know it's a little further north, but Cleveland Institute of Art is there, too. If you went there, you could room with your aunt and visit me every Friday, Saturday, and Sunday."

I couldn't help but scoff. "I haven't spent quality time with Vicky in three years."

Xavier wrapped his arm around me. "No time like the present!"

"For Christmas this year, she bought me earrings, and I don't have my ears pierced." Not to mention how we barely speak, how we act like we're on two different planets, and how I avoided all her texts, calls, and invitations to visit her house.

I didn't want him to go anywhere but New York.

Before I could let him know this, a loud *DING* bellowed above the crowd. The entire audience stared at the giant clock. "One minute to go!" DJ Kevin said over the loudspeaker. On the Times Square building, there were giant numbers dwindling down until the ball dropped: 59...58...57...

The group chanted, and they paired off. Finley and Sadie awkwardly stepped closer together, their cheeks blushing more each second. Once everyone yelled, "Happy New Year!" Xavier dipped me. He kissed perfectly with just the right amount of tongue. As he brought me up, I glanced at the underdogs. Finley and Sadie made out. Sure, they don't seem to know what they're doing, but it's sweet.

Xavier wrapped his body over mine. "Well, would you look at that?" He rested his head on my shoulder, and we closed our eyes.

"When they get married, I better be the maid of honor."

"Oo! And I can be the best man! Can you imagine? Power couple. Or *married* power couple. Do you think they'd get hitched after us? Or before? Eh, it doesn't matter. Would Duff be my best man? I mean, I guess he *could,* although—"

Sometimes, he rambled out of control. I pressed my fingers against his lips, and he immediately stopped talking and smiled.

"I was doing it again, huh?"

I nodded and said, "But it's oh so cute."

He spun me around and kissed me. "I can't wait for our anniversary. I already got reservations at the Vinegar Hill House." I opened my mouth to tell him about how frustrated Sadie was with me, but then I closed my lips and kissed him one more time.

She'll get over it.

With his finger, he twirled my necklace: pink leather, toggled chain, and at the clasps, a heart engraved with the word "Love." He kissed the heart pendant and laid his head against mine. I loved this boy, this guy, this *man,* and I didn't want this night to end.

Like a mind reader, he whispered, "Rhie, what do you say you and a few of our closest friends hang out at my place? Continue the festivities?"

I opened my mouth, but then closed it. I didn't need

a watch to know how late this party was going to end. Besides, I was an early bird, not a night owl.

Before I said anything, he dragged me closer and placed his hands on my waist.. "My parents aren't home," he whispered in my ear with a soft kiss, "and there's plenty of Pinot Grigio to go around."

I should have said, "Let's go to my house, just you and I."

I should have said, "We should stay in Times Square."

I should have said, "No."

Stupid, stupid me.

Instead, I kissed him for a long time. I held him tight, as if he was saving me or I was saving him. He touched my necklace at the same time I held on to it. As we released our breath, our heads leaned into the others. I said, "Absolutely," and then he smiled.

That fucking smile.

Chapter 4
Rhiannon

"Okay, everybody, stand up and spread out," Tori tells the class.

At the same time, they raise and spread out so they're arms-length apart. She leans to her side and glares at me. I remain sitting, continue reading *Before I Fall,* and ignore her. Sighing, she resumes with the rest of the class.

"What part of the body is from here"—she points to her hips—"to here?" She points just below the neck.

Greg leans toward the guy next to him. "I didn't know this was an anatomy class."

"That's *precisely* what this is, Gregory." On her SmartBoard, Tori clicks to the next slide on her armature slideshow. Everyone giggles; this armature was poorly made with arms sticking out from her ribs, her eyes looking like something Picasso would've made, and her feet three sizes too big. Behind the artwork in the picture is a young girl with a gap-toothed smile.

I turn a shade of red as Tori smiles at me. "My little

niece with her first sculpture."

"She looks like a hillbilly," Greg says at a volume for the whole class to hear.

Before everyone laughs, she turns and faces him. "What part of the body am I referring to, Mr. Lowell?"

I mouth, "Torso."

The smirk on Greg's face vanishes, and he remains silent. "How about the upper half of your leg?"

Thigh.

Still, nothing. "Or how about here?" She turns around and gently taps her butt. I snort quietly and hide behind my book.

"Your um..." His face becomes redder and redder. "Your ass?"

Tori snaps her fingers. "Yes! Your glutes!" With a smirk, I roll my eyes and resume reading the rest of my book. When I finish, I search my backpack for another book, yet there's nothing here I haven't already read. I need to check out the library.

Once the bell rings, the class scatters, and I just sit, dreading my next class. My feet shuffle to the door while Tori cleans up for her next class. Before I leave, she asks, "Why don't you switch into Hank's class?"

I stop walking, spin around, and stare blankly.

"If all you'll do is read and doodle, at least doodle in a drawing class." I shrug with my eyes falling to the floor. "Rhiannon, talk to me. What exactly happened?" My throat tightens, my heart pounds against my chest, and my eyes dim in a fog.

I stared at Xavier, yet he ignored me. He didn't turn around, didn't say sorry, didn't give a shit. My precious camera, the one thing that I adored, was utterly destroyed.

"Rhiannon?"

Shaking my head, I glance up and force a chuckle. "I want the extra time with you, that's all." However, even Tori knows how much of a lie my statement is, so she casts me away by saying one cold sentence.

"I have another class."

I step out of her classroom, and she shuts the door with a loud *BANG!* Wincing, I immediately regret not telling her the true reason I don't love photography.

Never mind love. I don't even like it anymore.

For the first twenty minutes of PE, we warm up, and I choose to jog around the gym with my sweatshirt's arms rolled up. It's an easy pace with my heart rate barely changing. When I first started to run eight months ago, my lungs fell out of my body, and my heart rate soared through the roof. But now it's different.

It's amazing how you can motivate yourself when you're alone.

On lap number four, I pick up the pace, and as I increase my speed, I glance at Austin. He's Mr. Desjardins's intern. Since there's close to nothing to do, he lifts weights daily, doing legs on Tuesdays and Thursdays and arms on Mondays and Wednesdays. Fridays are spent working out on the rowing machine.

The girls in my class drool more than he sweats.

Austin stops rowing and wipes sweat from his brow.

His pits and neck are a dark gray while the rest of his shirt is practically white. He dabs his forehead to reveal his six-pack. When I glance up, he stares at me, smiling.

Although I redden, *damn it*, I ignore him and continue to sprint until Mr. Desjardins blows his whistle.

"Gather round!" Everyone sits on the bleachers divided by their groups of friends, and Jessyka and crew are the largest. A pink-haired girl and I sit far apart from everybody else. We glance at each other but say nothing. She pulls an iPhone out of her pocket and reads something. Then, I notice everyone is on their iPhones. Some scroll through mindless social media while others text away.

Was I like that? Being so oblivious because of my phone?

Austin jogs over to Mr. Desjardins with a Santa Claus bag and shakes the brown cloth upside down. Out pops two foam headgear and four gloves.

I light up.

"Yesterday, we completed your training in CPR. Now that's out of the way, our first unit is boxing. I'll be training you starting Monday, but for today, we need a benchmark. What's a better way than having a boxing match?"

One would think Mr. Desjardins is a softie with a higher voice than expected, fifty years old, round in the belly, clean shaven with two dimples, and completely bald. He reminds me of Mr. Clean.

"Any volunteers?"

Jessyka raises her hand and looks around with pursed lips. Any motivation I had disappears as I lean back on the bleachers. Ever since I spelled her name wrong, she enjoyed any sport involving my humiliation.

"I need one more girl to volunteer," Mr. Desjardins says and crosses his arms. But no one moves a muscle. While Jessyka's friends giggle, he sighs and gazes at the ceiling. "All right then. I'll just pick someone." He scans the bleachers, his eyes moving from group to group until his eyes land on the pink-haired girl.

"Brielle," he says and waves the two girls to come to the center court. Jessyka dashes to Mr. Desjardins first, and Brielle takes tiny steps until she reaches him. He adds punching gloves and safety equipment on her head while Jessyka gets the same things from Austin. I stare at his perspiration building in his hair and forehead, and when they catch each other's glance, he looks away.

"All set?" Austin asks with a squeak. She's about to touch his arm as he pulls away.

Not only does Jessyka intimidate the girls, she intimidates most guys, too.

The two men step back, and the ladies tread to the gymnasium's center. With his whistle resting on his lips, Mr. Desjardins says, "I want a clean match, okay?" I, as well as everyone else, know Jessyka won't let *that* happen. He steps back and blows.

Brielle hunches behind her shoulders, her hands covering her head before the first punch is thrown. Jessyka hops repeatedly and dashes to the left and to the right. As she steps forward, Brielle steps back. From this angle, it looks more like a tango lesson than a boxing match.

Jessyka leaps forward and nails Brielle's right arm. Her hand immediately lands on her side, and with that,

Jessyka takes advantage. Using the same hand, she punches Brielle in the face, and with the opposite hand, Jessyka nails her stomach. She falls to the ground, wheezes, and doesn't move.

Austin sprints to her aid, and soon after, Mr. Desjardins walks to her and hovers. The girl remains conscious, but stares at the space in front of her. I turn around and see Jessyka's friends laughing. One whispers, "She didn't stand a chance."

My fists tighten. Why wouldn't Jessyka go easier on her? This was the first match before we had any training. Did she take boxing lessons before today? Maybe she does gymnastics or cheerleading to help increase her upper body strength. Does her motivation involve anger issues?

Austin squats down, rubs Brielle's shoulder, and says, "Breathe, just breathe...Pretend no one else is here...Pretend you're in the Bahamas, sipping mai tais." Mr. Desjardins coughs, and Austin turns red. "I-I-I mean *virgin* mai tais, 'cause there's *no* way you've had the real stuff. There isn't any alcohol for anyone our age, really." Brielle gently scoffs and rolls her eyes along with Mr. Desjardins.

Jessyka jogs back to her friends. Rather than jumping on the bleachers, her friends climb down the stairs and hover near her. I lean forward and try to listen.

"Can you believe her?" asks one of her friends. "I heard a girl in my math class lost her virginity to Austin, and she described it as an out-of-this-world-experience. It's so unfair that Brielle's getting all of his attention. I wish he would give *me* some." This girl whimpers like an injured dog. Jessyka wraps her arm around the girl's shoulder.

"You'll get him soon, hon," she whispers into the girl's ear, but not so much that me or Brielle can't hear it. "I mean, if I *accidentally* break her arm, so be it." I gasp, and she turns red, jumps up, and fights back tears.

Mr. Desjardins sighs and rubs his temple. "Jess..."

She fakes a shocking expression and says, "Why, I was only kidding."

"You better be." But once he turns around, the wannabes giggle and return to the bleachers. When Jessyka and Brielle return to their places, Jessyka puts up her gloves, smirking and snarling. I glance from one girl to the other and then at the teacher. He yawns with his whistle hanging near his mouth, waiting to begin. Doesn't he realize how vicious Jessyka can be? She continues to dance, pumping her gloves against one another, and Brielle sighs and looks at me.

Raising my hand, I say, "I want to go." I can feel everyone's stare from behind me. Austin and Mr. Desjardins blink. In the past, Jessyka might have been an awful competitor, and they're surprised I volunteer. If she's been a bully in the past, today, it ends.

"Well, I don't think—" Mr. Desjardins starts, but I've made up my mind and march to Brielle. Austin removes her gloves and headgear and adds them to me. She watches him strap my boxing glove as tight as possible and gently puts on the helmet.

Before Brielle returns to her seat, she says, "Kick some ass."

Oh, I so will.

Mr. Desjardins stares at Brielle and back at me,

saying, "On the sound of my whistle," and steps back. I forget about the crowd, the teacher, or Austin, and focus on Jessyka. She jumps repeatedly and glances at her friends. Me, though? I only watch her. I study how often she bounces, how high she can fly, and how long before she tires.

The whistle blows, and I step to the left and to the right. I see Jessyka's eyes spring like a ping-pong ball. I leap two quick steps, hit her in the left abdomen, and return. Then I'm in control, hopping light on my toes, and waiting for her next move.

Jessyka huffs and lowers her eyebrows. When she swings at my face, I block it and punch from the other side. My punch hits her cheek, and she stumbles backward. Some girls go "Oo" in the crowd.

She screams and charges in my direction. However, I just slide to the right, and she continues her plow into Mr. Desjardins. She reddens as Austin chuckles. Without meaning to, I grin, hold out my outstretched arm, and motion with my glove.

Come at me, brah.

Her anger boils over the pot, trying to hit me anywhere possible—abs, shoulders, face, even knees—but I block every single shot. I notice her swings are slower, her punches sloppier, and her tongue sticking out sideways. With one hit, I nail her in the headgear.

Immediately, she collapses, and my first instinct is to ask, "Are you okay?" However, with a jog over by Austin, she winks at me and continues to speak about the *excruciating* pain she's in. Mr. Desjardins blows his whistle twice and unwraps my gloves and my headgear.

Austin lifts Jessyka and carries her to the opposite side of the bleachers. After setting her down, she removes her shoes and raises one foot. "I think it's broken," she says.

I snort loudly and sit next to Brielle. Staring at my hands, the palm is full of calluses, and the pinky fingers are black and blue. Jessyka laughs while Austin massages her foot. Doesn't she have a boyfriend who *isn't* Austin? Was his name Tom? Or Tim? It doesn't matter; he doesn't seem interested in her. And why am I even thinking about—

"Austin!" Mr. Desjardins points to his watch and taps his sneaker. "You are my intern, yeah? Get the next two girls ready!"

Hastily, he puts on her shoe and ties it using bunny ears. But when he stands, he stares at me and steps forward. My heart thumps more than it has all day, running laps or boxing. His lips curl up with a slow clap. I stand to take a bow, and he whistles.

Is he flirting with me?

As I sit down, two different girls take center stage with awful formation. I don't know this, but I can tell, *feel*, Austin watching me. I concentrate on watching girls at my sport. They hold their punches still while waiting for the sound of the whistle.

"Jessyka!" Austin yells. When I turn to see what's going on, she's inches away and punches me in the face. I instantaneously feel a bruise beneath my eye and a possible tiny cut on my cheek.

But that's not what I'm worried about.

I stand and am about to sprint into the bathroom,

wishing and hoping this endeavor will end. However, I stop moving. Red appears in sporadic spots until the gymnasium bleacher morphs into a fireplace.

No...no, no, no—

Xavier turned around, picked me up, and held me by my throat. He lifted me off the rug and slammed my back against the fireplace. "X...Xavi—" But it's like he didn't want to listen to me.

"Fleetwood?" I can hear Austin trying to make light in this situation, but something won't let me leave this memory. Or this nightmare.

"Say something!" he shrieked, mucus falling all over my neck and body. I hit his arm, his fist, and at one point, his face, but my punches were weak. As my arm fell to my side, I struggled to stay conscious.

"Rhiannon?" Austin's hand touches my shoulder, and it's like someone shot me out of a cannon. I stumble out of the bleachers and clench my chest. My heart throbs, and my stomach drops. I heave, and as I look up, everyone silences, even Mr. Desjardins. On the other end of the gym, Jessyka trudges with an adult escorting her.

How long was I out for?

When I glance through my stinging eyes, Austin touches my shoulder again. "Are you—" I sprint through the gymnasium, through the locker room, and through a stall, vomiting. My heart beats at a rapid pace, my inhales uneven. I close my eyes and try to keep steady with my head lowered. For the rest of the period, I lay on the floor, hug my knees, and attempt to breathe.

Chapter 5
Austin

"Aren't you leaving?" Mr. Desjardins asks and points to the exit of the gymnasium. "You don't want to be late for your next class. I know your punctuality isn't so keen, so..."

I remain staring at the ladies' locker room door, currently shut. As I glance at my watch, my right leg fidgets. Where is she? Rhiannon hasn't come out yet, and after she stared at me, all she did was bolt into the girls' room. But when Coach and I sprinted to comfort her, she had locked it. Was it food poisoning? Did she have a concussion? Or something else?

Jessyka slapped Rhiannon in the face as if she were a punching bag. She stood and walked three steps, but then stopped and stared into my eyes with a look of fear. Her eyes glazed, her lips parted, and her body swayed. I held her arm so that she wouldn't fall, but her touch froze my arm. As Jessyka narrowed her eyes, Rhiannon just stared at a specific spot. Jessyka smirked at first, but after about ten seconds, she drew pale.

I snapped in front of Rhiannon's eyes while holding her arm. She didn't blink, and her breathing was unsteady. When I glanced at Coach Desjardins, he whispered into a walkie-talkie, "I don't know," and looked at me. "Do you think she's having a seizure?"

Shit, was she?

Within ten seconds of the question being asked, the daily police officer and guidance counselor bolted through the doors. Jessyka raised both hands. "I didn't mean to," she said, and they surrounded her. She held her arms up farther and stormed off. "I swear! It was only a nudge!"

I faced the frightened girl and called her name: "Fleetwood?" Her eyes fluttered, like a force field was between us, and I was trying to get her to break through. Ten seconds later, she remained glaring into the abyss, and Coach paced, biting his nails.

My hand slid from her forearm to her shoulder. "Rhiannon?"

She gasped and stumbled back, and I released her. She blinked multiple times until she looked at me. Although I tried to stay collected, my hand held my chest. She turned around to watch Jessyka being escorted out of the gym. Holding her breath, Rhiannon sprinted through the crowd and into the women's locker room.

Everyone, including me, stared at Coach. With his clueless reaction, I ran to the locker room, but it was locked. I sprinted to him and spoke to the walkie-talkie. "Can I have the nurse in the gymnasium, please? We may have an injury."

As I waited for her arrival, he smacked his lips and weakly replied, "Who wants to box next?" A few ladies raised their hands, and as soon as they lined up to get their equipment, I jogged in front of the door and waited.

It's been twenty minutes since then. Still no movement.

The nurse came as fast as she could, and when she asked Rhiannon if she was okay, the only thing uttered was, "I'm fine." None of the girls seem to care, though, other than Brielle. Every once in a while, she glanced toward the door, and once the bell rang, she hovered until everyone left.

The second bell rings. I still wait and watch the clock's hand: *Tick! Tick! Tick!* It appears she's not coming out, and when I turn around, a creak is heard from the door. I spin around, and Rhiannon steps out onto the gym's floor. However, once she notices me, she halts and crosses her arms. I whiff her breath. It smells like a combination of vomit and mint gum.

She immediately draws pale, yet she doesn't stop her glare. "Well? Why are you still here?" Her words are cold, but her voice trembles.

I shrug and bring my hands to my sweatpants pockets. "I just...I just wanted to know if you're all right."

"Oh." Her eyes fill with water as she glances at the floor. "Yeah...I'm fine." A beat later, she whispers, "Thank you."

Although she can't see my face, I turn red and nod. We walk from one end of the gym to the other in silence, and as we enter the main hallway, we part, she slugging to the left, and me sprinting to the right.

One class later, it's time for an upper body strength workout. The weight room is spacious, with a blue mat in the middle. Different machines align three sides of the mat, and the last fourth has free weights, five benches, and a massive wall mirror.

After I put in my AirPods, I grab my weights, sit on

the bench, and do a set of fifteen shoulder presses. Metallica booms in my ears. I try to tune out the rest of the swim team, or at least attempt to focus on my weights. But I can't concentrate. No matter how hard I try, my mind wanders back to—

Troy taps my shoulder, and I turn off my heavy-metal music. "Are you going on Ms. Benner's field trip next week?"

I blink a few dozen times to concentrate on what he's saying. *Who has a field trip, again?* He slaps me on the arm, and although I laugh, I wince and wonder again how much training he had over the summer.

"The art field trip?"

I snap. "Oh! Yeah! That!" I laugh and place the light weights on the bar. As I glance at Troy, his weights are at least three times heavier than mine. "Both classes are going, Ms. Benner and Mr. S, right?" I look at Coach for a second and then at Troy. "Do you want me to bring some liquor?"

"Shh!" He holds his hand against my mouth. "Do you *want* to get suspended?"

I grin. "Wow," I whisper. "Has this man changed his mind about underage drinking? Are you going to be a priest? Holy Christ our lord?" He punches me, a *real* punch. I rub my arm while screaming internally because, damn, that hurt.

He holds dumbbells weighing sixty-five pounds with ease. "Weekends are okay." He leans into me. "But that's it. I want to get a scholarship, you know?" I nod and pick up the fifty pounders, but I can only lift two reps before I struggle. I lay it down and grab the thirty-five.

The Night at Times Square

"Save me a seat on the bus?" I ask, huffing between reps. He smiles while making the reps seem so easy.

"You bet your ass I will."

When I arrive at home, I remove my sneakers and place my keys in the key bowl. I drop my bag in the living room and walk toward the kitchen. Dad paces every three seconds while on the phone with an important client, although that's how he treats every phone call. As I grab a plate and fill it with vegetables, chicken, and mashed potatoes, I glance at him and give a head nod. He does the same, and then we move our separate ways.

For the past ten years, this has been our routine, barely talking other than the usual, "How was your day?" On days like this, when I have too much in my mind, we don't speak at all.

Footsteps scurry down the stairs and pound toward the living room. Mom tries a little harder to keep our family together, but that's not saying much.

"Hey, Mom." I stuff a piece of chicken in my mouth. She mumbles to herself, her hair is half in a ponytail and half out, and she sports two different socks. In one hand, a thick folder with different files sticking out, and in the other, a picture of a woman, not too much older than me. I place my food on the extra cushion. "Mom?"

She ruffles her hair, lets all her locks fall, and puts the elastic band around her wrist. After she sighs, she storms through the living room and into the kitchen. "Are you kidding me, Tao?" I hear her slamming something onto the kitchen's island. "What's her name!"

"I'll call you back," Dad says and disconnects the call. He groans, and I would guess he's rubbing his forehead.

"I already told you; she's my secretary!"

Back and forth, their noise level grows, and eventually, they shout, like they're contestants who need to win the million-dollar prize. Their Chinese accents become apparent, so much so they switch from English to Mandarin. I can't understand them anymore. This has been a routine, too, the constant fighting between Mom and Dad. They don't even share a room together.

Are they waiting for me to leave so they can get a divorce?

I shake my head and turn the television's volume up. As soon as I finish eating, our housekeeper Allison walks through the living room, picks up my plate, and nods. The argument stops once they see her, and Mom and Dad resume their businesses, him back on his phone and Mom leaving the kitchen.

"Al—" She stops. "I mean, Austin." My cheeks fluster as I stare at the mindless television show on Netflix called *The Floor Is Lava*. I hear Mom sigh. "Turn it down," she says, her voice sounding more annoyed, angry, and upset than usual.

However, I don't know what I'm supposed to do.

Before she leaves, I try asking, "How was work today?" Mom freezes and faces me with a crease in her forehead. I give her a wide smile, a genuine one, too. "Didn't you have a big operation today? I think you were separating conjoined twins. How long did it take?"

She sighs again. "How much money do you want?"

My mouth flies open. Apparently, my family and I are further apart than I thought. "I...I really wanna know, that's all."

The Night at Times Square

She stares at me before she answers, but all she says is, "Fine," and runs up the stairs and slams her door.

I guess I'll learn about how the conjoined twins went another night.

Mimicking Mom, I sigh, turn down the volume, and scribble random answers on the homework.

At ten o'clock, I close my door and hop into the bed. My death-metal music calms me, and I normally fall asleep listening to it with my AirPods in my ears. Not tonight though with my brain restless. No matter how hard I try, my mind turns back to Rhiannon.

I turn off my music and scan social media to find her like Twitter, Instagram, TikTok, and Snapchat, but she's nowhere. With one last bit of hope, I try Facebook, and only one person shows up. My eyes brighten, staring at Rhiannon in a black-and-white photograph, but it's different. This girl smiles widely, her hair long, highlighted, and curly. She wears a low-cut dress, a leather jacket, and high boots. Although she's a little heavier in this picture, it's definitely her.

Under the bio, there's a quote. "When you photograph people in color, you photograph their clothes. But when you photograph people in black and white, you photograph their souls," by Ted Grant.

I don't know who that is.

Then I lie down on my bed, turn on the side, and stare at the stranger I've known for just one week. This girl must have had tons of friends, was popular, and lived her best life. However, this Rhiannon is not like the old one.

When I click to learn more about this stranger, it's set

to private. I request her, and every three seconds, I hit refresh. After about ten minutes of tapping the same button, Jessyka messages me: "I'm lonely" with a picture of herself wearing nothing except lingerie. I toss my phone on the nightstand, shut the lights off, and think about how I need an actual bedtime playlist.

Chapter 6
Rhiannon

This is hell.

I stand in line for the bus. It's about one quarter filled as I glance at my fellow students through the windows. No one sits, a jock grabs a smaller boy and plays keep-away with another guy, and a girl applies makeup while side-eying any female *without* cosmetics.

When I board the bus, I fill in the first available seat, hastily pulling my Walkman out of my drawstring bag and putting on my headset. I hit Play to listen to the instrumental version of the song "Lonely" by Billie Eilish. Sinking in my seat, I finally breathe and close my eyes. But I feel someone's stare, and I can't help but peek.

Austin.

The bus becomes more filled, and the students move slower and slower because they're searching for a safe place to sit. He taps his fingers on the back of my seat with one hand and scrolls his iPhone with the other, wearing AirPods. When he stops, he glances at his Fitbit and at me. I immediately focus on the outside world.

"Aus!" a boy, who I don't remember, yells. "Right here!"

"Don't get your tampons in a bunch, Troy."

Troy holds one particular finger up and laughs.

Austin pushes my seat, and I turn around. Climbing up the sides of the seat so he's off the floor, he moves like a monkey, swinging with his backpack toward the rear of the bus. Once he reaches Troy, Austin leaps over him and lands at a window seat.

"Boys!" the bus driver yells. "Sit down!"

Austin holds both arms up and says, "My bad."

All the guys near him laugh.

"Oh my gosh," a female voice says, in a non-hush volume. "Austin doesn't care about what anyone says."

Out of the corner of my eye, I spot this blond girl biting her lips. She plays with her necklace. "Have you had sex with him yet?" another voice asks.

She shakes her head. "But I mean, come on; it's only a matter of time. Half of the senior class has hooked up with him," and she waves seductively in his direction. He winks, and Greg nudges him and humps the air.

My gaze focuses outside as I turn the music louder. The bus parks near the art studio. From years past, many murals fill in the concrete walls. There's one mural I cannot stop staring at: a painting of a woman, dark hair and olive skin, her eyes closed as her hair flies in the wind. The Japanese maple loses its pink leaves falling to the grass. On the other side, a huge flower lies with deep scarlets at the pistil that flows through multicolored petals.

PLOP!

The Night at Times Square

I rip my headset off my ears, turn, and sigh. "Are you excited for the field trip?" Aunt Tori's wild curls bounce as she eagerly waits for my answer.

No, actually, I'm not. The only reason kids are thrilled to visit the Cleveland Museum of Art is because they got a free day from school.

"Well?"

I smack my lips. "Sure."

"What are you excited to see?"

Tori, please give me a break. "I don't know. I've never heard of this museum before."

She gasps, and it's everything in my power not to stand up and find a different seat. "I can't believe that!"

I grew up in Brooklyn. Every weekend, Sadie and I checked out unique and wonderful gallery displays. For some galleries, the owners wanted to know what *I* thought of the artwork, and I told them the truth; some were amazing, some not so much. Before everything happened, I was promised my own exhibition as a senior gift at the Aperture Gallery.

"Didn't you love photography?"

Not anymore. "I'm switching passions."

Aunt Tori takes a deep breath to ask a billion more questions. *What's your new passion? How come it's no longer photography? Are you going to study in the art field or something different?* Mom and Dad asked me those questions, and I already gave them answers. That's probably why they shipped me off to Tori's; they couldn't take the lack of me liking anything, never mind having a passion for it.

Tori glances behind our seat and then faces forward. "You sure you don't want to sit with the other kids?"

When she says *kids*, I roll my eyes. To be a kid means being carefree, being naïve, being downright happy.

But rather than saying that, I say, "I'm not friends with any of them."

"Don't you want at least *one* friend?"

When I don't say anything, a crease in her brow deepens, and she opens her mouth to speak, then closes it, scoots to the edge of the seat, and talks to Hank. Today, he wears a wrinkle-free white shirt and plaid pants that are way too bright for my liking, but he pulls them off.

They discuss where everyone will meet, what time lunch is, and when the bus leaves. I press Play on my Walkman and stare out the window.

About a half hour on side streets, the bus driver flicks the left turn signal to drive on the highway. Aunt Tori taps him on the shoulder.

"Can we go the long way? I wanna show these kids something."

After a loud groan, he turns off the signal and follows the windy path. As we keep driving, my eyes grow. These houses are huge, bigger than any I've seen before, besides celebrities'. Half of these mansions even have a gate.

When we reach a stop sign, the bus driver pulls over and turns on the hazards.

"Excuse me, ladies and gentlemen!" Tori walks to the center aisle. Those who are sitting directly behind her stop talking. However, the farther back on the bus you go, the louder it remains. With a deep inhale, Tori sucks in as much oxygen as possible to help her project.

"For the next ten miles on Martin Luther King Drive, you'll see different countries represented by a flag. Some citizens and ancestors are proud of their heritage and keep their spot clean. I give you The Cultural Garden," and she points at the windows. The first one represents Italy, which Tori is one hundred percent Italian. Gardens along the streets, different bushes, flowers, and a nicely mowed lawn appear immaculate. Once she sits back down, the students' voices become deafening, like they had to make up for lost time.

Different countries around the globe are here, from Mexico to Japan, Canada to France, and Brazil to Egypt. When the bus slows down due to a traffic jam, I squint. China has overgrown grasses, weeds without dandelions, dying trees, and muddy terrain.

Isn't Austin Chinese?

Although I try to not look at him, I turn around. Across the bus, he leans forward. His eyes fix on China's garden. One of his buddies asks him a question, but he seems entranced and cannot stop gazing. It's like his stoic face, the water within his eyes, read—*scream*—sorrow. He peeks my way, just for a second. I turn around, blush, and resume watching the zooming cars go by.

The bus pulls into the underground garage. Most of the boys act like zoo animals, yearning to burst through the exit and run around at the exhibits. Before they are released into the wild, or in this case, the museum, Aunt Tori claps her hands and lowers her hands.

"Now, we'll meet for lunch at the cafeteria around noon." She glances at Hank. "Mr. S and I will circle the museum, so don't try anything disruptive, all right?"

Austin leaps up and says, "Scout's honor!" and he crosses his heart. Everyone laughs, including Tori.

"Mr. Chang, since you're so eager, why don't you give me a tour? That way, we can both keep an eagle eye on everyone." Her hand crosses an X on her chest. "Scout's honor."

He points to her, his way of saying, *Touché*.

Even though I'm in the front seat, I wait and watch each person stroll by. About halfway through the line, Austin trudges and scrolls through his phone, still wearing his AirPods. I still have my Walkman on, except I can only do so much besides press the Play and Stop buttons. It's times like this when I miss smartphones.

I linger until everyone leaves the bus. I'm contemplating if I should stay here or join everyone when the bus driver clears his throat. "I got somewhere else to go."

Reluctantly, I hop down.

Tori and Hank speak about the dos and don'ts of the behavior in the museum. *Ten bucks someone is gonna laugh when they see a naked painting.* I stand behind them. There are seven feet between me and the person in front of me. Once the students dash in different directions, I walk to Aunt Tori.

"Why don't we try the Alberto Giacometti exhibition together?" she asks. I know this artist. His signature was the human figure, creating long, stretched bodies in clay and plaster and later bronze. Personally, I find his artwork to be creepy, but what else am I going to do?

"Sure," I say.

Tori and I trudge in silence as we pass the enormous exhibition banners like Modern Art, Historical Pieces, Renaissance Era, and Ancient Asian Artwork. We're about to descend the stairs to the special exhibit when a loud whistle is heard.

"Tori!" Hank jogs with a plastered smile that screams, *Shit*. Once he reaches us, he huffs over his knees. "We got a problem."

He points to the second floor where Austin, Troy, and a bunch of other guys stand. They're yelling something, but I can't understand it. I lean forward and glance at Hank.

He asks, "Have you ever played the penis game?"

Tori snorts a little too loud. The penis game is when you say the word *penis* softly at first, and as the next person goes, they repeat it, only louder. The first person who refuses to say the word loses.

Hank chuckles along with my aunt, and they turn to face me. The old Rhiannon would laugh, and in fact, I'd probably play a role in these shenanigans. However, my face is stoic and stern. Goosebumps form on my arms, and even though I'm wearing a heavy sweatshirt indoors, I shiver.

Xavier and I walked along the streets of Manhattan on our one-year anniversary. We snuck in a little wine with dinner. We brought our own hydro flask filled to the brim and told our server we felt like "saving the dolphins," although I doubt he believed us. I was tipsy, and once we stopped at a cross light, I glanced at the billboard: a model with nothing on except tight underwear. The white, crisp Jockeys bulged out. I immediately giggled.

"What?" After he glanced at the billboard, Xavier's smile spread. "You can't keep a straight face!"

I loosely pulled away, yet he wrapped his arms around me. My grin stretched, and I pretended to be mad. "What do you mean? I can so keep one!"

The crosswalk signal turned green. We unwrapped ourselves and held hands, swinging our arms like a couple of goofs. "Okay, my Juliet. Say the word while keeping a straight face."

Once we jogged to the sidewalk, I glanced left and right. "Here? Now?" Many people looked our way, considering it was just eight o'clock at Times Square. There must have been hundreds of them! He nodded as I crossed my arms.

With a deep breath and a straight face, I said, "Penis." No smile, no laughter, nothing. I was very proud of myself.

Xavier blinked twice, held his breath, and screamed, "PENIS!" Probably half of Manhattan heard him. I burst out laughing.

"That's not fair!" I punched him in the muscular arm.

"Told ya you couldn't do it."

"Rhiannon?" Aunt Tori lays her arm on my shoulder, and I jump twenty feet into the air. I'm surprised I didn't fly through the roof. "You're okay by yourself, right?"

I want to plead with her to stay and tell her that Hank can handle them on his own, but I nod. The two of them power-walk to the escalator toward the boys.

After I glide down the stairs, I enter the Alberto Giacometti exhibition. The first art piece I see is the iconic bronze sculpture, an elongated body with minimum muscle and no fat. He stands with one leg forward and one leg back. There's an invisible barrier beeping whenever anyone draws too close.

The next few rooms are the same: different men, different sketches, and a skinny figure of a woman. The only fat you can see is her breast, sagging to her waist. But the rest is thin, *too* thin. My hands lower to my waist and press against the bones. I touch my ribs, trying to dig into the spine, but it's impossible to have the same proportions as Giacometti.

While I analyze the naked woman, my ears perk up when someone asks, "What is she doing?"

"Leave her alone, man," a voice, Austin's voice, whispers. I hear the footsteps dwindle and disappear into the next room. As soon as I'm sure they're gone, I exhale and step back.

For the next three rooms, I saunter among the sculptures. But as soon as I enter a new room, Austin and crew stand next to a different yet similar sculpture of a lanky, skinny woman with abnormally large breasts. He whips out his iPhone to take a picture and waves his hands, signaling the boys to squish together. The four boys hover their hands around the woman's chest.

"Say 'artwork,'" says Austin.

"Artwork!" and they laugh. I rub my temple and dash into the next room.

As I reach the last room, I stop short. This room was Giacometti's, just not the same as all the others. This one is an experimental room full of brightly colored paintings. These people he painted actually smile. I stop and walk toward two paintings, one of a canyon and the other of a tree hiding a house. Giacometti's strokes are pointillism, but rather than having simple dots, he used dashes. If you look close enough, you'd think it's an abstract piece.

I've been to countless art galleries, most of them being modern art. They were doing the same thing of trying to be different. Giacometti had his signature pieces, but by repeating identical figures over and over again, he grew bored. It wasn't until his death anyone bought his bright, fluorescent artwork.

For once, for a brief moment, I can see myself being happy here. Maybe I will start a routine where every Saturday morning is spent at this museum. Maybe I'll eat at different cafés or hole-in-the-wall restaurants. Or maybe I'll take out my camera, photograph below the river or high above in a skyscraper, like the Terminal Tower.

My mind whirls with possibilities as I step back, my eyes glued to the paintings, until the alarm goes off. Jumping, I spin and notice how close I am to touching an iconic sculpture. The security guard strolls up to me, and I can't move with my eyes closed.

"Ma'am," the security guard says and waits. When I open my eyes, the woman has a soft face, a dark complexion, and a genuine smile. "Just be careful next time, okay?"

I nod and exit the exhibition.

Once I climb two sets of stairs, my eyes wander between the modern art and the ancient artwork. The modern gallery has bold-colored walls, mono prints of Andy Warhol's *Marilyn Monroe*, and a baby stroller composed of trash. On my left, all I can see are dark walls with immense glass cases.

I wander around the Modern Art gallery until I stop at the unique painting. Unlike the bright paintings all over the walls, this one is gray, brown, and black. This picture is of a railroad track. The acrylic peels off in strategic places, almost like an apocalyptic way. Next to it is the backstory of the artwork: a World War II piece of Auschwitz. As my gaze follows the oil painting, I feel guilty.

Guilty for treating my aunt like shit and not appreciating everything she's done for me.

Guilty for all my parents did and not even uttering a thank-you.

Guilty for everything.

Tears fall from my face, but I don't wipe them. I let them fall. I probably would let a puddle form beneath my sneaker.

Then I feel someone's eyes glued to my back, and I don't turn red or blush. Rather, I turn around and stare at Austin. His dark eyes stay on mine, and for once he breaks the trance. I watch the painting for another minute before I leave the painting and the boy behind. Maybe he'll tell his friends about how much of a freak I am for crying over a piece of artwork, or he'll act like nothing happened.

At least my aunt won't mind. If anything, she'll be proud.

Chapter 7
Austin

"Austin!" Troy wraps his arm around my shoulder. "Don't tell Jessyka, but me and the guys are having a competition. Whoever finds the biggest"—he holds both arms around his chest—"wins."

"What do you win?"

He scoffs. "Bragging rights, my man."

I chuckle and continue to look at the railroad painting. Rhiannon stared at the painting for a full five minutes and let tears fall off her face, not caring who saw her. However, no matter how hard I try, I'm not moved by it. I figured everyone was inspired by the same picture, but apparently not. Other than her, no one our age cried because of a painting. Actually, no one of *any* age cries, 'cause it's not that good.

Troy stands next to me with his mouth open. His eyes move all over the painting, and like Rhiannon, he stares without blinking.

The Night at Times Square

"I can't imagine what they went through," he says. I turn to face him and tilt my head. "Auschwitz. That's what this painting is of. Remember that documentary we watched in World History class last year? When they first surrendered to end the war, Germany tried to cover up everything. Now, they're embracing it, not wanting history to repeat itself."

Although I faked an understanding, I slept through the entire video.

"Come on." He points toward the Renaissance Era with a grin. "They've gotta have some women in there."

I smile and force a laugh, but my eyes move toward the exhibit next to it. "You go ahead. I gotta take a leak." We walk our separate paths, and I head toward the bathroom. Once I see him disappear into the Renaissance room, I jog the opposite way and push into the Asian Art gallery.

There are dark amber walls with spotlights on specific sculptures, the high ceilings aligning the onyx above. I trudge through the gallery as the door closes behind me. Everything is in a separate case, from the carved clay to sewn cloth. I read every title and notice which nationalities created which pieces: Japanese tapestries, Nepal's Gods and Goddesses, and Chinese pottery. One vase is white with accents of green, blue, and orange with different fish swimming along the middle of the pot. A separate vase is made of jade, and on each side, dragons make up the handles.

My parents were born in China and lived there for ten years before they moved to America. They don't have accents; it's only apparent when they get heated in an argument because they took extra voice lessons so their accents disappear. When I was born, I was treated as an American. Sometimes, people make fun of the fact I'm Asian, but I just give them a sarcastic comment right back. Before now, before today, I really didn't care.

But as I sit, surrounded by my heritage and culture, I feel nothing, and that scares me. The fact—

My thoughts are rudely interrupted by a stranger swinging the doors to the gallery. I jump because no one was in this gallery moments ago. When I peer to the right, my heart quickens.

I scramble to my feet and am cautious not to set off any alarms. "I just want to talk," Jessyka says and steps forward with every word. She stares at my lips and licks hers. Similar to Medusa, her hazel eyes bare through my soul. I glance away and step back in fear I'll turn to stone. "Austin, please."

I stop moving, and although she said that in a whisper, within these walls, it bounced around like she announced it on a loudspeaker.

When I look up, Jessyka is a smoke show as ever. Her mascara eyes, the low-cut shirt, and the mini skirt that leaves little to the imagination. She wears high heels, higher than she normally does, so she is only three inches shorter than me.

She stands six feet away when she stops. *Good...good...Six feet apart, perfectly good distance.* Her lips curl as my pants suddenly get tighter.

"Well," I say, crossing my arms. "Let's talk." My voice is steady, but my knees quake.

"I just wanted to say that I think..." She fades and

lowers her gaze. Breathing in, she slowly sucks in all the surrounding oxygen, like she's suffocating me, but I attempt to mimic her mannerisms.

It's not working.

"I think you're right."

I'm right? About what? I've been avoiding her as much as possible for two weeks, and other than English and Art classes, I haven't said two words to the girl.

She smacks her tongue. "You said we have to stop. Remember?"

"Ye-yeah," I say. "You...you want to?"

"We really should end this." She smiles, but there is a hidden barrier making me think she doesn't mean it. "Troy is a great guy, you understand that, don't you?"

That question was like a punch in the face. Troy. My best friend. Ever since eighth grade, we've been inseparable, and I had to be the moron who slept with his girl one time...and kissed twice.

I back up three more steps. "Yes." I swallow. "I-I-I agree."

"Well," she says, with her arm sticking out. "Friends, then?" I stare at her shiny nails and wait for her to walk closer, but she isn't moving. So, I break the stillness of my body, shuffle to her with my eyes focused on her hand, and clasp it. We shake hands for ten seconds, and when I glance up to her breasts, her neck, and her eyes, I lower the gaze to her lips.

Once I move to her eyes again, the barrier she carried disappears, batting her lashes with a little giggle. "Do friends kiss on the cheek?" She raises her eyebrows and smirks. She's testing me. *Does she even like Troy?* Taking a step forward, she leans toward my ear and blows. I moan, my eyelids fluttering.

Friends give friends kisses on the cheek, right? Hell, if we were in Italy, we'd kiss on the cheek all the time. I can't help but nod and close my eyes.

Her breath smells like cigarettes, the stench I recall loving. However, this time, I lean back and hold my breath. She rolls her eyes as she pulls out a stick of mint gum from her purse.

After she kisses my cheek, she brings her head back. But when I open my eyes, she's closer than ever, licking her lips and refusing to stop staring at my own. "How about the other cheek?" Her hand strokes my arm. "We don't want your left side to be neglected, do we?"

I mean, that makes total, complete sense, right? In France, they give two kisses, not just one. I step forward, noticing how her deep red lip gloss glimmers. As she prolongedly kisses my cheek, I can feel the mark she leaves, like she's claiming me. Once she sticks another piece of gum in her mouth, I wipe my face with my palm in hopes no one will notice.

Troy is your friend, Austin. Don't mess this up...you've messed up too many times. Not only did I sleep with her, I constantly texted, had late-night phone calls, and ate the occasional dinners at her house. As I lean out of her reach, she smirks and unbuttons the top of her shirt, my eyes drawn to her imaginary nipple covered by her blouse.

Before she does anything more seductive, someone opens the double doors to the gallery. Immediately, I wander toward the glass case: a white stone carved of a dragon holding a dog in its mouth. Is the dog dead or alive?

"I'll..." Jessyka shakes her head. "I'll see you around?" she says like she's asking a question.

Does she always do that?

I nod and speed to the opposite side of the gallery. After she leaves, I sit on the extensive bench and lay my head in my hands. Why does Jessyka keep coming after me? Does she ever say, "This is a mistake?" She used a different wording, but she didn't *mean* it. Instead, she used high heels, a low-cut shirt, and voluptuous lips to make me want her more than ever.

Breathe, Chang...Breathe.

When I finally gained my stomach back, I look up. Rhiannon stares at the sculptures and tapestries, her hands clasping together behind her back. "Hey, Fleetwood." I attempt to smile, but it's forced. She glances in my direction with her cheeks reddening.

"I'm so sorry," she says, "I didn't mean to interrupt your conversation."

To be honest, I should thank her.

"Don't worry about it, really." I pat the empty seat next to me. "And don't apologize." Her eyes narrow, as if I was trying to trick her. During her path, I really stare at her: the short ponytail, dark brown that must be natural, baggy sweatshirt and sweatpants appearing to be three sizes too big.

When she reaches me, she sits on the opposite side of the bench. *Is she afraid of me? Or is she afraid of everyone else, too?* The two of us rest and stare at the glass cases in front of us. She holds her breath and turns to face me.

"I've never been in a place like this," she whispers,

and although most voices echo in this room, hers doesn't.

"I thought you were from Manhattan."

"I've been to many modern galleries, but not ancient artwork." She points to the Japanese tapestry, gently lays her hand back to her lap, and picks at her nails.

We wait for the other one to speak, and I cave. "What's your nationality?"

"I'm a mutt," she says. "My mom is fully Italian, but my dad is from different countries." She turns to face me with a stoic expression. "How about you?"

She's polite. She didn't say anything about how she knows I'm Asian. For all she knows, I could be Vietnamese, Japanese, Korean, or Cambodian. I glance down at her hands, and her fingernail draws blood.

Yep, definitely afraid of me.

"I'm a hundred percent Chinese. But I don't know anything about my heritage, so..."

Earlier when the bus stopped, I noticed China's gardens. Poorly kept, overgrown weeds, and dead everything else. Mom and Dad used to keep China's spot thriving, visiting it once a week, but now they're far too busy.

"I used to understand the language. Like, my mom asked me something in Chinese, and I answered in English. But now..."

A lump forms in my throat. I never realized how much the fact I don't know anything about my culture meant to me. My head lowers, and I try *desperately* not to cry. I mean, this girl barely knows me.

I hear the sliding across the bench before I see Rhiannon's hand quivering above mine. But then, she takes it away. My heart sinks. Why didn't she hold my hand? Or, more importantly, why did I *want* her to?

"Sorry," I say awkwardly and slide farther to the right side.

"Don't apologize."

I spin to face her, and she forces a smirk.

We sit in silence, and as I stare at her face, sorrow is written all over it. At our age, wrinkles form along the crease of our mouth, but not hers. She must not have any reason to smile.

But I want to give her a reason to.

I stand up and hold my hand in front of her. "Come on," I say with a nod, motioning her to follow me. "I've got something to show you." Cautiously, she grabs my hand. Once she is raised, she lets go.

Rhiannon follows me down the escalator and down the long, dim hallway. There are abstract, pop-out pictures, each one having a hue of color. In one illustration, the cobalt and navy and cerulean appear to be pixels. I jog some more and halt in front of her.

"I know these aren't New York, but—" I stop talking and move aside. She stares at me, blinking. With a deep breath, she steps forward.

I watch her the entire time. Her mouth parts as she walks to the first picture. Inside the tiny room are black-and-white photographs, no bigger than a ten-by-twelve canvas. She stops at each individual photograph; a little boy dressed in 1600s clothing, two children playing knights near a tiny waterfall, a nun dipping her hand in a foundation, a man ice-skating while holding a calm swan, and last, Hope Memorial Bridge. The photograph was taken at night during a firework display. This may be cliché, but this one is my favorite.

Rhiannon stares at this photograph for forever.

I sit on a comfortable chair, but I don't move my gaze. Her arms move from crossed to relaxed by her side. She tiptoes to the edge and bends down, like she's searching for hidden treasure behind the frame. When she finally looks at me, butterflies form, and my heart throbs.

What the hell is wrong with me?

She turns around and walks toward me. I scramble, jump, and wipe my sweaty hands on my jeans. Even though many people wander, it's like we are the only ones in the room. Rhiannon whispers, "Thank you."

And she smiles.

She hadn't genuinely smiled once at me, and although my goal had been to make her offer a tiny quiver of a grin, I hadn't imagined what it would feel like. Her smile reveals one dimple I didn't know she had, and her teeth are spot on, straightened, and bright white.

Was I staring at her lips?

I clear my throat, shake my head, and gaze toward the black tile. "You're welcome." Beads of sweat form along the back of my neck, and when I look up, she stares at her hands. Slowly, I bring my arm inches away.

"Aus!" Troy barges through the entryway, and even though I don't move, arm still outstretched, Rhiannon bolts around him. "There you are! Did you find any?"

I nervously laugh. "Any what?"

He brings both hands to his chest and shakes his arms.

"Not as big as yours, man." I stare at his tiny pecks.

"Here *or* there." He punches my arm. We walk to the cafeteria where Mrs. Benner and Mr. S stand, and everyone gathers around.

"You'll have thirty minutes to eat and visit the gift shop. Everyone should be on the bus in half an hour. We *will* leave without you." Mrs. Benner smirks, and most of the guys chuckle, although I doubt they'd actually leave.

My stomach growls as soon as everyone scatters. Once I pay for pizza and pasta, I glance for where to sit, but I can't find Rhiannon anywhere. So, I sit next to Troy. We're the only people resting at our table.

Even after I scarf down some food, my stomach hurts, but it's not from hunger. As I look for Jessyka, I see she's in the long salad line. "Hey, dude." I nudge and grab Troy's attention. "Can I ask you something?"

He leans toward me and smirks. "Are you having erectile dysfunction problems again?" Normally, I would laugh and say, "No, your mom is keeping me satisfied," but I only have a matter of time before Jessyka sits next to him.

"I'm serious." As I glance at the line, she receives a Greek salad from the cafeteria worker. But when she turns around, she notices me and blushes.

I should tell him about that one night months ago.

I should tell him about how it was a mistake.

I should tell him.

"Why..." I swallow, and my knee bounces. "Why do you like Jess?"

The grin on his face is wiped, and a crease on his brow forms. "I don't know, man. Jessyka's pretty great."

No, she's not.

"I mean, do you see yourself with her long term?"

Troy takes a deep breath and is about to answer when she sits in between us. She must have left her salad in the check out line because she doesn't have any food. "You guys talking about me?" She laughs, but I can tell she is worried I told him the truth.

He doesn't miss a beat, though. "Just wondering if I should ask you to Homecoming or if it's already been said."

"Aw." She kisses him on the cheek and points to herself. "You can ask me. Go on," and she motions for him to speak. Troy laughs, and a bunch of our friends, including Greg, fill in the rest of the table. While I shove my food down my throat, I feel Jessyka's fingers on my leg. She strokes them back and forth, creeping them up my thigh until—

I jump and yell, "I'm going to the gift shop!" Many people laugh at me, and although my food is halfway done, I toss everything in the trash and hide in the men's bathroom until it's time to leave.

Chapter 8
Rhiannon

Dad was right.

If I listen to the same songs over and over again, I'll get sick of them, and that is *exactly* what happened.

Down at Tori's basement, I open my CD binder and choose Dad's Mixtape #2. Before I take it out, I read the joke on it. *What do you call a fish with no eyes? Fsh!* I smirk. Sure, it's not the same as when Dad says it, but it's the thought that counts.

Once I hit Play, minor chords boom, and I pump up the bass. "Tragedy" is a song by the Bee Gees with a lead singer who has a high-pitch voice. At first, I slam against the punching bag in rhythm. Each hit is a rush of adrenaline, striking the heavy bag and wobbling with every hit. As I close my eyes, I reimagine January first, but this time, in my favor. Instead of being the victim, I'm a fair match.

I am not vulnerable.

I am not fragile.

I am not weak.

Then, I open my eyes, and rather than simply punch, I dance and whisper the song. "Tragedy" is about a man who has nothing going his way. He's drowning, suffocating, yet he clings to his love. I don't know how it ends, but my *real* story finishes with disaster. The further into the song, the louder my voice becomes. My throat burns from the volume with no sense of melody.

"Rhiannon?" Tori opens the door, and I rip my headset off my ears. "Are you okay? I heard you screaming."

"S-sorry." I shake my head. Apparently, I wasn't just singing off tune, I was sounding like a monster. "I'll keep it down." My cheeks redden, and I stare at my aunt's feet. Her footwear is clunky clogs with two vibrant high socks. When I peer at her face, she smiles, nods, and closes the door. I wait for a minute and then continue hitting the bag without any music being played.

After about ten minutes, sweat floods my armpits, my chin, and my forehead. As I grab my towel, my aunt screams.

It can't be happening.

My blood runs cold, and my face drains of all colors. Shaking, I travel up the stairs, one by one by one. My heart thumps as I creak upward. The only thing I can hear is the beating of my chest and the ringing of my ears.

It can't be happening...It can't be happening...It can't be—

Once I swing the door open, I finally stop, my eyes fluttering. Hank. Although Tori's laughing at him, I can't stop rapidly breathing with my head in a fog. The bile creeps up through my throat. I want to run upstairs, want to grab a paper bag, and want to vomit.

With my eyes closed, I lean on the door to catch my breath. "Sorry, Rhie," Tori says, and when I open them, she sheepishly smiles. "Hank claims to not mean to scare me"—she turns to face him—"but this is ridiculous."

"What can I say? I'm like Keanu Reeves." I give him a blank stare. *Who is Keanu Reeves?* He sighs. "You know, Keanu Reeves? The introverted actor? Man of few words? Oh! This guy!" Hank does a slow-motion bending of his waist backward, waving his hands over his head.

"The guy from *The Matrix*?" I ask. He snaps his fingers and laughs as I grab a water bottle and chug half of it. "Do you come over here often?" My heartbeat slows down as I drink.

He grins. "About twice a week. She'd come to my place except I have a cat, and she's *allergic*." Hank uses quotation marks around "allergic" and glances at her.

"Didn't you and Mom have a cat? Chuckie? Or Charlie?"

"Yes." Tori narrows her eyes. "But doctors say you can develop allergies." He and I scoff at the same time.

"So, are you guys, like, dating? Or something?"

The two of them glance at each other, and his smile widens. "No. She's...not my type." I'm confused. For the past two years, all she talks about is Hank, how wonderful he is, how clever, and how articulate.

When I open my mouth to question him some more, she says, "Dinner's almost ready. Do you mind setting up the table?"

Once I set the plates and silverware, I push in my

chair and wait for the other two to join me. Hank carries a large platter of tomatoes, lettuce, basil, and sour cream while she brings out pita bread and thin-sliced chicken. Everyone serves themselves, and once Tori stares at my plate, she snaps her fingers.

"I keep forgetting you don't eat meat."

She keeps "forgetting," like I'll wake up and magically turn into a carnivore. But I guess being an herbivore was overnight. After everything that happened, I wanted to lose weight right away. So, I claimed to be a vegetarian because I didn't like the way farm animals were treated. I told them, "Did you know some pigs are kept in cages no bigger than their bodies?" I researched so many facts that my parents agreed they'd try to change their diet.

Dad lasted a week, Mom a month.

"Are you almost done with your costume?" Hank asks. "I still have some tiny touch-ups, but mine is practically done."

Tori shakes her head. "I *finally* completed the head."

I glance up. "What costume?"

"Halloween!" Well, that explains the locking of the spare room's door. "For the past seven years, Hank and I have *dominated* the costume field."

Ten minutes later, I barely touched my food. Either they don't notice my lack of appetite or they don't care, but they talk about where they would travel to once they retire. "How about Italy?" Hank asks as he grabs seconds. "Maybe Tuscany? Rome?"

"Rome's too crowded." She pours a second glass of wine. "Besides, you said you wanted to travel somewhere neither of us had been."

"You're making this *very* difficult considering you've been around the world...*literally*."

The tea kettle rings. Hank dashes into the kitchen and grabs a mug. I can hear the pour of the tea into a cup. He sits down, pulls out a flask, and drips a small amount of the liquid into the mug. While they continue to discuss their plans, I stare at the dark fluid, bubbling along the edges.

"Seriously," Finley whispered and dragged his flask onto the coffee table. "You're beautiful."

"Too bad you didn't say that two and a half years ago," I slurred my speech, the words falling out of my mouth. "I had a slight crush on you."

I've rewinded that scene a hundred thousand times. Unfortunately, nothing changed what happened. My eyes space out, and no matter what, so many questions are left unanswered, *can't* be answered. *Why had I said those things in the first place? Was it because I felt I could confide in Finley? Or was it because I was unhappy?* I shake my head. *If I just changed the subject, it never would have—*

Stop.

Just stop.

While I pretend to be intrigued by Tori and Hank's conversation, I grab a piece of pita bread and munch, swallowing the morsel of food. The real reason for my actions and words was because I was tipsy and drunk. That's why I vowed to never drink again.

Then, Tori and Hank laugh, snapping my mind out of its own little world. I force myself to chuckle and ask, "What's so funny?" Tori pulls out her chair, dashes up the stairs, and slams a door, my guess is to use the bathroom.

"I love your aunt's laugh." Her giggle is similar to mine, when I couldn't even breathe because I thought something was so funny.

We glance at each other awkwardly, him staring at his empty plate and me following suit. "You know, I had planned on traveling with my ex," he says, and I eagerly look up. "Yeah. Happened about three years ago." I remember Tori mentioning Hank about three years ago, too, the same time she must have been comforting him about his girlfriend. "I wanted a partner, a marriage, but he didn't want one."

Once I turn red, Hank chuckles. "I'm sorry about that," I say. "What was he like?"

It may have been three years ago, but even now, his face brightens. "Stubborn...*very* stubborn. A monotone voice...definitely had a Dad bod." I giggle, the same tone as my aunt. He exhales and closes his eyes. "Kind, the type of kind you don't find every day. He didn't talk too much, but when he did, I was in awe." His eyes open. "You do that with your questions."

I blush as his smile grows.

"We used to watch *A Christmas Story* every year, reciting it word for word."

Grinning, I say, "I triple dog dare you."

"I can't put my arms down!"

"He looks like a deranged Easter bunny." And with that quote, we chuckle. Dad and I watched *A Christmas Story* every year, and with a memory of the past, my heart sinks. "Can I borrow your phone?"

Hank hands me his phone right away.

I walk into the living room and dial Dad's phone, but

it goes straight to voicemail. Maybe he and Mom went out for dinner. "Hi. Now *you* say something. *Beep!*"

"Hey, Dad, it's me, you know, your daughter. I just want to say..." Say I miss you, say I'm sorry for not calling sooner, say a little joke to cheer him up, whether or not he's having a bad day. "Call me back, or not, whatever. Love you," and I disconnect the call.

Tori and Hank clean the dishes while I close my eyes and meditate in the living room. Every once in a while, they laugh until he sits on the couch next to mine. *So much for peace and quiet.* I stand, but then stop. Normally, whenever she puts in a movie, I run upstairs, slam the door, and either read or watch my own film. Mom had said, "Go easy on Tori. And who knows? You might enjoy her company."

I sit down and read a *Time* magazine.

She scans in search for a DVD from hundreds and possibly thousands in individual cases. Once she spots a particular one, she stands in front of the player, pressing every button on the remote.

"Every time," she mumbles.

"'Every time' what?"

"You would think I would know how the DVD player works." I stand and walk over to the player, grab the remote, and hit a single button. The main menu of *The Wedding Planner* comes on the television's screen. "Beginner's luck," and she sits next to Hank.

I've never seen this movie.

"Oh, Rhie, I got you something," she says, picks up the plastic bag, and hands it to me. With caution, I pull out a daily calendar. This daily calendar has inspiring quotes, tips to make your life easier and better, and cats...so many cats. When I don't say anything, she rambles. "Shoot! I thought you would like it! It was on sale and the salesclerk was so persuasive—"

"I love it." My eyes water. Although she says it was a last-minute thing, I think—*know*—how much time she put into the perfect gift. I smile and glance up. "Thank you."

For the first twenty minutes, Tori recites every line Jennifer Lopez says, and Hank, Matthew McConaughey.

SCREECH!

I peer out the window to witness a car swerving all over the road. Two cars nearly collide, sliding past across, inches away from each other. Then, they zoom by as if nothing occurred. My ears perk up, expecting beeps from their horns, yet it's silent.

"Why isn't there any honking?"

Tori hits the Pause button. "Other than northeast and California, no one uses it."

Hank nudges her. "Yeah. This one time, a guy cut your aunt off, and she beeped the horn. He almost crashed into the building, he was so scared!"

They chuckle and continue the movie. I try to watch the film, but with the two of them talking to the other, I can't concentrate. However, it's not 'cause of their volume (because they're *awfully* loud) or the number of cackles they give (which is three every minute), it's because of the bond they share.

And how I haven't had a good friend in a long, long time.

```
New Year's Day
Xavier's House
   1:30 a.m.
```

"So, I have white wine for Rhie, red for Sadie, a Scotch for Duff, and," Xavier said, snapping a can, "a beer for me." As we clink our glasses, the men gulped a portion of their drinks while Sadie and I sipped our wines.

Xavier wrapped his arm around my shoulder. I rested my head in his nook. When I looked up, I noticed two things: his messy hair (which is a classic sign that he's getting tipsy) and the redness of his ears. He got his ears pierced earlier that week.

I gently stroked his ear. "Are they infected?"

"Just irritated," and he kissed my cheek. "But if they get worse—"

"You'll go to the doctor's?"

He shook his head. "I'll have my mom look at them. One of the *many* perks of having your mom as a manager at Ultimate Diamond jewelry. I got these for free," and he showed off the tiny studs.

The Night at Times Square

The kitchen was half full of people conversing about the New Year's ball dropping. I turned on my camera and took three pictures without them knowing. Then, I scurried to the counter, placed my camera on the countertop, and returned to where I belonged.

Once Xavier and I kissed, I noticed Finley did the same thing with Sadie. She melted with her eyes fluttering. I giggled as he asked, "Something wrong?"

I shook my head. "Only the fact you two look so adorable." I unwrapped Xavier's arm and pinched Finley's cheek. He chuckled and blushed, glancing at the balcony. The condo's stoop was romanticized, full of fairy lights, a circle of expensive outdoors seating, and a fire pit currently out of use.

After Xavier kissed me again, he chugged the last of his beer, saying, "I'm gonna get another one. Do you want anything?" We shook our heads, and he jogged toward the balcony. As he opened the door, a huge gust of wind blew into the condo. Half the girls shrieked due to the draft he let in.

My teeth chattered, and I rubbed my arms while jumping to keep warm. My dress slid down the front, revealing my bra over one breast. I yanked my dress up to my collarbone and slightly hopped with my head lowered.

"Did you see her boob?" Immediately, I stopped moving, perked my ears, and watched Lizzy slur her speech. She wore different clothing, the current dress's length shorter than earlier at Times Square. Although she lowered her voice, her side-eyed stare told me she wanted me to hear her. "I'm surprised she's got a boyfriend, nevertheless a hot one."

My face grew redder and redder, glancing for a quick escape.

"I know, right?" A different swim team girl spoke louder. "The only explanation would be that Xavier likes big women. Otherwise, who'd want a Rhie-no?"

Sadie gasped and turned in my direction, yet I avoided it in fear I'd burst into tears. As they laughed, I grew angry, embarrassed, and sad all at the same time. I hated them and their fat-shaming. And I knew I shouldn't care about what people thought of me, but unfortunately, I did.

"Excuse me," I whispered and shuffled through the girls in the kitchen and the living room and breathed once I hovered over the mantle. Closing my eyes, I felt stupid and betrayed. Last year, I told the swim team how I battled childhood obesity and the kids called me, "Rhie-no." Hearing them using the same word tonight infuriated me.

Then, someone's feet creaked by the wooden planks. But when I turned around, expecting to see Sadie, my best friend, I was surprised at who was there.

"You okay, mate?" Finley stared with a worried crease in his brow. Why was he worried? Why did he think I would just tell him? And why wasn't he here with Sadie? I barely knew the guy. As I glanced past him to see Sadie, she switched from our group to Lizzy's. She bent over her knees and humped the air, twerking to get the girls laughing. My fist tightened. I couldn't believe it; rather than rushing to rescue or comfort me, she stood with the culprit. And she was so happy!

"Rhie?"

I shook my head and faced him. If I was to tell him

my worries about Lizzy fat-shaming me, or Sadie just ignoring my feelings, Finley would roll his eyes and tell me I was fishing for compliments. I mean, our deepest conversation consisted of *The Office* quotes.

So, I just said, "Just cold, that's all," and forced a smile. Nodding, he pulled off his zip-up hoodie and handed it to me.

"Oh, that's nice of you, but..." I've never seen Finley do anything kind. Not only was he giving me a sweatshirt to wear, it was his Hogwarts sweatshirt, a staple in the Duff wardrobe.

"Take it," he said with a grin. "I'm warm blooded, anyway."

I laughed and swooped my arms through the sleeves. It was a little snug, but the hoodie warmed me up. "Thank you." He chuckled and stared into my eyes. I felt a little guilty because I thought he was a total dick.

Maybe this man would be great for Sadie.

As I turned around, she quickly jogged away from the girls and nudged Finley to sit on the couch. She grabbed his hand and dragged him while I waited for Xavier. Once I was back in between the kitchen and the living room, each moment passed. More girls swarmed the kitchen, whispering in my direction. I shuffled my feet and picked at my manicured nails.

How many people did he invite? Where was he? Why wasn't he acting like my protector? The countless number of strangers' stares buried me beneath their questioning looks. I grabbed a beer from the counter, opened the pull tab, and gulped it down.

But the more I drank, the worse I felt.

Then, Xavier wrapped his arm around my shoulder, and I leaned on his and closed my eyes. He smelled a combination of cigarettes and weed, which would explain what took him so long.

"Never leave me, okay?" My eyes filled with water and stung, but I wouldn't let them fall. Although he claimed me as sexy yet cute at the same time, I was worried about my weight and was afraid of him leaving me because of that.

He spun me around and gazed into my eyes. "I'm right here." We kissed for an extended amount of time, leaning on each other and foreheads pressing together. "Feeling better?"

I nodded, linked Xavier's arm with mine, and skipped into the living room. Sadie snuggled into Finley, took out her iPhone, and snapped a picture of her kissing his cheek. However, he seemed stiff and barely smiled with no teeth showing, despite the dog filter.

Once Xavier and I sat down, Finley exhaled, unhinged his shoulder, and sank into his seat. She scooted closer to him and leaned on him. "Well, well, well," Xavier began, and pointed at the two of them. "Aren't you the happy couple?" He grinned and wrapped his arm around my shoulder.

She stared into Finley's eyes. "I've never been happier."

"Awe," and Xavier playfully punched him. "Any nicknames for each other? Me and Rhie are Romeo and Juliet because we met each other in English class. We were partners in William Shakespeare II." He squeezed my hand. "Rhie loves his work."

"I don't know." Sadie turned with a sheepish smile. "Maybe we can combine our names. Like Finley and—" and she waited for his response, the witty combination of their names like, *"Sadley"* or *"Findie."* However, he must be drawing a blank 'cause he grew pale and stared at me.

"What if Duff doesn't remember me? Or worse: remembers the wrong name?"

A lightbulb went off to save the day. "Oh my gosh, Sadie!" I inspected her manicure. "I *love* your nails! They're so much better than mine. Where'd you get them done?" As she beamed and explained where to go, he mouthed the words, "Thank you."

After a small conversation, the immense silence was awkward, even if we had thirty other people in the background. "So, what are you doing on Friday?" Finley asked me with a sip of his scotch. "Wanna hang out?"

"She can't," Sadie said and glanced at me. She was about to say, "because Rhiannon and I are having a movie marathon," when Xavier leaned forward, placed his hand on my knee, and squeezed it.

"It's our anniversary."

"O-oh," Finley said, and smacked his lips. "Another time, then." The boys discussed something, but I wasn't paying attention. The only thing I did was weakly smile at Sadie, whose eyes burned into my scalp. As she shook her head, Xavier noticed the two of us being extremely quiet.

Before Finley could say or ask anything, Xavier interrupted. "Would you like to do a shot?" He motioned away from us.

Finley glanced at me, at Sadie, and back at me. His blue eyes were solemn, which was weird because he had been so happy early in the night. "We'll be here," I said and forced a smile. He wasn't buying it, though, and as Xavier left the room, Finley hovered around my knee before he went into the kitchen.

With a sigh, Sadie shifted her weight, gulped a good portion of the wine, and groaned. "What the hell, Rhiannon?" I swallowed and watched the fireplace crackle behind the glass cage.

"I don't know, Sadie. I tried, I really did, but I don't know, he was so excited for the reservations."

"So, is this how it's gonna be? Me placing second in your life, and Xavier always first?"

I frowned. "That's not fair. I haven't always—"

"Yes, you have!" Sadie yelled, and a few people stopped their conversations to spectate ours.

Lowering my voice, I said, "That's not true."

But at this point, she was fuming. "What about your three-month anniversary? Or what about the time when you ditched me for his cousin's birthday party? Excuse after excuse after excuse!"

I didn't know what to say because everything she said was true. Whenever the two of us were going to hang out, Xavier suggested something different, and I caved, *always* caved. I even missed her grandmother's funeral because of his stupid robotics meet. So, I said nothing as my eyes overflowed with tears.

I was about to open my mouth when Sadie started crying, too. I stopped and watched her leave for the bathroom. Why didn't she say something sooner? I could have made time for her, really, I could have. *That's a lie.* If something comes up in the future, I'll always choose

The Night at Times Square

Xavier over Sadie.

My throat tightened with emotion, and I couldn't breathe, inhale but not exhale, and I could only imagine the joy of viewing the New York City skyline. I pushed through the crowds, pushed through the bathroom line, and entered the balcony.

With a deep inhale, I exhale. Little clouds puffed from my mouth as I walked to the edge. I should have been angry with Sadie, but it was all true. I rested on the guardrail with my head over the ledge. Most nights, New York seemed picturesque, with its million lights scattered among the low-lying sky.

Not now, though.

"You okay?" I jumped and held my chest, my heart thumping: Finley.

"Geez, do you ever say anything else?" I brought my hand to my side. "I'm fine, thank you." He smoked his cigarette with one black puff and snuffed it out with his expensive shoe. Whenever he wasn't wearing a Slytherin or Hogwarts shirt, he dressed nicely, so unlike most guys, he wore khakis, a stylish sweater, and a golfer's hat.

He walked to the rail next to me and shook his head. "No, you're not."

I laughed. "You're right." We stood looking out at our city, the streets still full with crowds. Once I glanced to my right, his fingers on the railing fidgeted. I knew I needed to blow off some steam, to vent, but telling him all of Sadie's flaws wasn't right. So, I remained upright with the wind gently blowing in my face.

"You know," he began and nudged my elbow. "I'm an excellent listener, 'cause I'm British and whatnot."

I turned to face him and grinned. "I don't think that's a thing."

"Oh, it is...that and our wonderful dental hygiene."

I giggled and pushed his shoulder.

"But in all honesty, I can tell something's bothering you."

I bit my lip and glanced away from Finley. "Girl shit, I guess."

"With Sadie?" My cheeks flustered. I wouldn't spill. Recently, Finley and I had become slightly better than acquaintances, but she and I were best friends long before now. "She's a nice girl and all, but..." He shrugged and pulled out of his pocket another cigarette.

After a prolonged smoke, I said, "So, you mean she's not 'the one'?"

He laughed and coughed, so much I tapped his back repeatedly. As he breathed easier, he shook his head. "No, not even close."

"She'll be devastated."

"She'll get over it, believe me," and he puffed some more of the tar. "Earlier when we were on the couch, I said something sarcastic about Kim Kardashian, and she replied, 'Oh my gosh, she's my idol!'"

"Wow," and I chuckled and patted his arm. "I'm so sorry." Finley turned to his right and blushed, and I returned to the railing in silence.

"Now that you know we aren't dating, what did she do?" He wiggled his eyebrows and maniacally rubbed his hands together. We've never hung out one-on-one before, and it's so easy that I'm about to actually pour my feelings out right there. *She's been too whiny, she's too self-conscious and has a one-track mind, and she knew how to make me feel so small.*

But as I stared into Finley's blue eyes, I forced a chuckle. "It's nothing. I...I'm overreacting. *If* I still feel the same way tomorrow—"

"Which is today."

"—I'll text you."

"How..." He swallowed and looked at his shoes. "How about you call me?"

"Sounds good," and we shook hands as the wind died down. The atmosphere was silent. I could barely hear any traffic jams, honking, or swearing. I closed my eyes and listened to the sea gulls singing.

"There you are!" Xavier stepped outside with a chuckle. He wrapped his arms behind me. When he turned me around, he asked, "Is that Duff's sweatshirt?"

I nodded. "Wasn't that sweet?"

"It's a little tight." Xavier immediately blushed. "I mean 'cause Duff doesn't work out, and he barely eats. Not 'cause you're..." His voice trailed off, and he lowered his gaze. I wanted to tell him, "I know I'm fat," but if I kept repeating that phrase over and over again, Xavier would discover it's true and dump me.

Forcing a smile, I said, "I know what you mean," and as fast as I could, I removed the sweatshirt and handed it to Finley.

Xavier put his arm around my shoulders and stepped inside. When we returned to the foyer, a friend of his called his name. He kissed me on the cheek and said, "I'll be right back."

He talked to a group of friends and headed to the kitchen. My guess was to get a giant tub of chocolate chip cookie dough ice cream, leaving just me and Finley in the hallway. Most people had or were leaving, grabbing their coats and heading out the door. I checked my phone. At this point, it was three thirty in the morning, and even the entire condo was still.

"So—" Finley and I both said, and we chuckled.

"You go," and I motioned to continue.

He put his hand in his khaki pocket and remained holding the Hogwarts sweatshirt. "I think I should go." His eyes flickered to Sadie. She lounged on the couch and texted away. Then, she held out her phone in front of her, and smiled wide with glimmering teeth. She must be taking a selfie, or Snapchat.

My phone beeped, and as I checked it, it was from her, reading, "Where r u? I'm lonely" with a sad emoji, although her million-dollar smile dominated the phone's screen.

Once I looked up, Finley forced a grin. "I think you should give her a second chance," I said. "A love of Kim Kardashian isn't the *worst* thing. Come on, the night can only get better."

"It's better if I leave. Nothing good happens past three."

I rolled my eyes. "That's a superstition."

"It's a *true*-a-stition." He nudged my elbow with his. I burst into laughter, leaned forward, and caught myself with his peck. I stared at his thin abs and worked my way to his eyes. Quickly, I turned red.

"Sorry," I said and pulled my hand away.

"Don't worry. Cheers," and he gave a salute.

As he put on his sweatshirt at the entryway, I leaned

on the doorway. Maybe Finley wasn't such a bad guy after all.

Then, the coldness of a spoon hit my arm. I screamed while giggling and leaned in the opposite direction. Xavier swooped me up and spun me around. I nuzzled in his grasp as he turned me around. After we kissed, he said, "It's just the four of us now," and scooped a chunk of cookie dough into his mouth.

"Three. Duff left."

"Aw, really?" He gently placed me on the ground and snapped his fingers. "Does Sadie know?" I shook my head, and he heavily sighed. "Shit...she's gonna be in a *wonderful* mood."

"Are you gonna tell her? Or should I?"

He held my shoulder and inched our way to her. "I'll do it. She's less likely to be pissed at me than at you." We hopped onto the couch, each one of us surrounding Sadie.

Once she glanced around, her beam faded. "Where's Finley?"

After clearing his throat, Xavier held her hand and explained how Finley didn't feel well (lie number one), how he wished he could stay (lie number two), and how he'd call her as soon as he felt better (and lie number three). Sadie sheepishly smiled as Xavier gave her his phone number.

But the second Xavier left to throw away an empty container of ice cream, all Sadie did was lecture me on how I can't trust boys and how girls needed to stick together.

Chapter 9
Rhiannon

Rather than hanging out with Tori and Hank before school starts, I spread my wings and hit the library. On the way there, the main secretary sits at the standing desk, half reading a book and half checking her email.

I stop my path and hover near her, close enough so I can be heard. As I squint at her name tag, I read, "Suzanne." I step forward and say, "Hey, Su-Suzanne." She looks up from her book and tilts her head. I point to myself. "Tori's niece."

She snaps her fingers. "Rhiannon! That's right! Such a unique name."

We shuffle our feet awkwardly. Tori had purchased a gift, the small calendar with a goal to accomplish each day. The first accomplishment is to make a new friend, or at least be friendli*er*.

"What book are you reading?"

She glances at the book and chuckles. "Oh, it's nothing," and slides the novel under her desk, turning red.

When I peek at it, the cover has a black background, a muscular shirtless man with long hair, and a woman with her eyes closed and her mouth in an O shape. A smirk creeps on my face.

"Well, I'm off to the library," I say, and she frowns.

"Good luck."

After passing through the lounge area, the huge fireplace, and up the stairs, I barge through the doors.

Hawken School has everything a student and faculty could ask for. Tori has unlimited art supplies, the wood shop builds advanced machinery, and the science labs create experiments that could literally blow your mind.

Yep, Hawken has everything, except books.

Mini bookshelves, tall empty drawers, and thirty computers. Only one-third of the shelves are filled to its capacity, and half of those books are out-of-date historic. The rest of the books are encyclopedias or dictionaries dated to the early 2000s. When I stand near the librarian's desk, no one's there, only a bell.

Bing!

For thirty seconds, no one shows up. I tap my sneaker repeatedly, glancing at my Salvador Dali watch. His nose lies at the center, and his mustaches are the hands of the clock. When I glance up, a young boy, can't be older than fifteen, plasters on a smile.

"Can I help you?" He flashes his braces. I can't help but stare at the egg leftover from breakfast stuck in his teeth. "Ma'am?"

I shake my head and force myself to look up. "Do you know where the fiction books are? I mean, are *all* of them out?"

He chuckles and gestures to the *magnificent* computer. "We have a million books right here, nonfiction *and* fiction." While facing the computer, he asks, "What book are you looking for? Or better yet, why don't you sign up for our newsletter? It has a book of the week, and you can browse without leaving your desk."

"I don't have a Kindle."

"That's okay! Most of our subscribers just use their phones."

With a deep sigh, I say, "I don't have a phone."

Once again, he chuckles until he sees me draw a blank stare. "Oh...you're...you're serious?" He raises his eyebrows and wipes his brow with a tissue, breathing in and out at a rapid pace. "I-I-I don't know what to say. I-I-I can't help you." He peeks over the counter and lowers his voice. "Are they gonna fire me?"

I lean toward him, smelling his foul breath. "I doubt it."

Turning around, I squint at four books labeled "Fiction" and another shelf labeled "YA," which carries fifteen. I place my headset on and click the Play button. This mix CD is full of instrumental pop songs like "The Sound of Silence," "Landslide," and "Zombie" on Dad's Mixtape #3. At the bottom, he wrote, "How does a taco say grace? Lettuce pray."

My fingers gently touch each book, from the nonfiction biographies to the YA novels. I read each book's summary and place three of them on the top shelf. There isn't a rule limiting the number of books I can carry, but I decide it's better to check out one at a time. I choose *You Will Be Tested*.

The Night at Times Square

The librarian scans and types the book into the computer. "Anything else?" He hands me the book. Before I shake my head, my eyes wander behind the boy. *Greek Mythology, for Beginners.* I point to that book, and he grabs it. "You really don't have a smartphone?"

I ignore his question.

I make it to Mr. Lane's classroom before he arrives. Since I have classical music playing in my ears, I don't need to turn it off. Twenty minutes before class, I open *You Will Be Tested* and read. I'm engrossed in the novel. Page after page after page, I don't think I've read this fast, and before I realize it, the bell rings.

Reluctantly, I slide my novel in my beige backpack and glance around. Everyone sits in the same seat as always, except when I turn to my left, it's Austin.

Was that by accident? Or purpose?

With a final peek, he smirks, and I instantly blush. *Damn it.* "Please stand for the pledge of allegiance," says the announcer. I move my mouth without saying anything. Only half the class speaks, and as soon as the morning announcements finish, everyone resumes their chatter.

Mr. Lane flips through his lesson plans and says, "This unit is about the *brilliant* playwright William Shakespeare. He was a master of comedy"—he laughs—"and tragedy," and he frowns. Zero members of the audience are entertained, though. "The first play we're going to study is the classic *Romeo and Juliet*."

I slouch in my chair with my arms crossed. In the second term of freshman year, my school read the entire play, loving every detail and sonnet. However, in less than a year, I have learned to despise it.

"This play is one of my favorites."

I want to raise my hand and ask him, "Why? It's just a bunch of foolish teenagers rebelling against their parents." But I sustain.

"Okay, everyone should gather in groups of four, the same groups as last time. Fun fact: Until further notice, these will be your groups for the rest of the semester." My face draws pale. *I have to deal with Jessyka for that long?*

As we slide our desks over, each foursome is assigned a sonnet from *Romeo and Juliet*. Our group chooses to do the scene where Romeo beckons to Juliet. The goal is to create something more memorable and easier to decipher.

"Hey, Rhiannon?" As I glance up, Jessyka's smile seems real, but not her eyes. "Can you, like, write again?" She holds up her fingernails. "I just got them done yesterday?"

Is this going to happen daily? Why can't she write? Does having perfectly nails prove anything?

I grit my teeth, take a deep breath, and am about to say in a Victor Frankenstein's assistant's voice, "Yes, master, yes," when Austin reaches toward Jessyka's pen.

"My penmanship is atrocious, and I want to improve," he says, clicking the pen and scribbling on a piece of paper. He stops and stares at me. "That is, if you don't mind."

I swallow and shake my head. Austin writes our four names on the paper, and although it was sweet to volunteer, he does write messy.

"What are we doing again?" Greg asks, his breath reeking in my direction. I hold my nose, the smell making it potent that he smoked pot before class.

"I...erg...wasn't listening?" She scoffs, crosses her arms, and glances at Austin. He looks at her and back at Greg.

"Long story short, make *Romeo and Juliet* interesting," Austin says.

"How are we gonna do that?"

Then Austin looks at me, and immediately, I grin. "'Romeo, where you at?'"

Both he and Greg snort, and Austin jots it down. "That's so great," and he glances up. "Make our rewriting so stupid, Mr. Lane will lose a couple of IQ points."

"Well, if that's your goal—"

"And it certainly is."

"—then absolutely."

We gaze into each other's eyes. I hadn't noticed Austin's pupil on the right is slightly darker than the left. His eye color changes to darker brown, but the amber is entrancing until someone coughs. Jessyka stares at Austin, leans toward his direction, and raises one eyebrow, just one. She pops one of her buttons off, and both boys in our group lower their eyes.

Is she jealous? Have Jessyka and Austin broken up? Or are they dating?

I try to be discreet and hobble my chair away from him, just in case. He doesn't notice. For the rest of the class, I allow Jessyka and Austin to collaborate while I doodle in my notebook.

After three classes, it's time for lunch, and as usual, everyone sits with the same people in the same seat. But I don't mind. Rushing toward my spot, I sit on the highchair and press Play as soon as I'm comfortable. Yet, there is someone giggling, or cackling, over by the huge table. Once I turn in their direction, a group of boys and girls, some standing, some sitting, have their eyes on Austin, including three new girls that I don't recognize.

One of the three literally drools over him.

Everything comes easily for that boy. When he struts around, everyone's eyes follow, and they grin in a trance. He stops walking and leans over Jessyka. She touches his hand with a stroke of her palm.

Yep, definitely dating. How could I be so stu—

Then, Austin backs away from Greg and Jessyka, and right after Troy sits down, she climbs over him and lies on his lap, two hands circling his neck. They make out, and when I'm about to roll my eyes, I notice her peering in Austin's direction. She glares, smirking and almost daring him to do something drastic, although I'm not sure what.

"Rhiannon?" I shake my head, rip off my headset, and glance at the girl with the pink hair, except now it's green. Dressing goth, she wears all black, black skirt, black band shirt, black boots giving her an extra four inches of height. She places a tupperware container and opens it up. The smell is chocolate chip cookies, possibly homemade. My nose sniffs the air as I melt.

I think the girl's name is—

"Brielle," she says and points toward herself. Ever since Sadie stopped hanging out with me, I've had zero friends, especially girls. When two guys argue, they confront each other and get over it. Girls stab you in the back without batting an eye. So, I've been cautious.

"From PE, right?"

She smiles. "The one and only."

The awkward silence hangs between us. She holds a paper bag with a huge grease stain in the bottom, labeled *Brie* with three hearts surrounding the name. Pushing the tupperware container toward me, she smiles. I grab one and devour it. I close my eyes as I chew the chocolate morsel of goodness.

"I'm glad you like it." Brie smiles again as I open my eyes. With a deep inhale, she says, "I just wanted to say...you didn't even know me—well, know-me-know-me—and you still stood up for me. No one's done that before...So, yeah. Thank you." She stops staring at her feet and looks up, glancing at Jessyka's direction.

"Gosh, I hate her," she whispers and immediately clasps her hand. "Did I say that out loud?"

I chuckle and bring one finger up to my lips. "Your secret's safe with me." With a laugh from her, the conversation ends. She looks into my eyes and glances away. Does she want to sit with me? I've put all my walls up, from everyone at this school and the entire state of New York.

When she turns around, I suddenly blurt out, "Want a seat?" I smile a genuine smile and tap the table across from me. "I mean, no one sits here besides me, like, ever."

Except Austin.

I push the thought away. "Two is better than one, right?"

Without a beat, Brielle hops onto the seat and pulls out of her bag a greasy grilled cheese. As she eats, I pull out my book and read. "I read that book three times."

My eyes brighten. "It's *so* good!"

"Right?"

"Who's your favorite character?"

For ten minutes, we return answers to the other's questions without any effort. It's weird, like we're old friends, the way Sadie became friends with me in sixth grade. But Brielle isn't like Sadie at all. Brielle's kind, thoughtful, and doesn't care what others think of her.

I finish my granola bar and toss the wrapper in the trash. While I shake my protein drink, she asks, "How come you don't have a phone?" I tilt my head and turn red. She leans forward. "Hawken is a small school. It's so small everyone heard you don't have one." She chuckles. "Well, not everyone. The lower class of popular society."

I snort and stare at my shake. "I dropped it," which is true, "and I didn't feel like getting a new phone," also true. However, I didn't tell her *how* I dropped it.

Brielle slow claps. "I *wish* I could get rid of mine. I'm afraid I'd get some form of withdrawals."

"Oh, you do."

"Really?"

I nod. "The first stage is denial, the *I don't need a phone* stage. But then you sweat, your texting fingers shake, and in the middle of the night when you would check your Instagram or Facebook, sweat pours from your face, your armpits, and your neck."

"Maybe I'll wean myself off."

"Or cut your screen time?"

"Brilliant!" and we high-five each other laughing. Then, the back of my neck burns, and as I turn around, Austin's smile grows and mouths the word, "Friend?" I bite my lip and nod with my cheeks flustered. Brielle leans away from me, and once she sees who I'm looking at, she sighs.

"Austin may be nice in PE, but he doesn't stand up for others," she whispers. I wonder why that is, why he doesn't stand up for the little guys when everyone treats him like a king. Then again, did I fight a bully back in New York?

As I stare at him, I shake my head, and without meaning to, my lips twitch.

"He's..." The twitch turns into a genuine smile. "He's okay."

She shoots her trash into the garbage, misses, and gives me one piece of advice. "Just be careful."

Chapter 10
Austin

After a long day of swimming practice, Troy and I relaxed, cleared our heads, and traveled for fifteen minutes in Cleveland with ten other people.

One of those ten being Jessyka.

We travel in four cars, driving to Euclid Beach Park. When I find a parking lot, I turn off the car next to the handicap space and wait for the others. Greg leaps out of my car and knocks Mickey Mouse into a puddle: *Splat!* My heart quickens. I move, diving my hand into the gross water and scooping up the mouse. He drips and oozes with soaked leaves and soil. I brush him off and place him on the dashboard.

"Shit, man," Greg says, pats me on the back, and stares at my now disgusting bobble head. He shrugs and glances at me. "I mean, it's just a toy, right?"

Mickey and I have been together since I was ten years old, and every morning, I'd rub his sneakers for luck. My hand hovers over the bobblehead, about to rub his feet before I leave, but looking at Greg, who has no idea about the superstitious habit, I just slam the door.

Euclid Beach used to be filled with people and had an amusement park with a roller coaster, merry-go-round, and Ferris Wheel. It opened in 1921, but due to a decline in attendance and an increase in lake pollution, it was shut down in 1969. The new pier is renovated, and if you step to the edge of the water, you see an amazing skyline.

When Troy parks next to my car, he hops out and slow-motion runs. I reciprocate. "Don't forget meee," he bellows.

My arms are wide open. "Neverrrrrrr." He sways as he continues his path until a gust of air whips him around. "Where are you goinggg?"

"Wherever the wind takes meeee," and he leaps into my arms.

Jessyka rolls her eyes and leans toward one of her friends. "Boys will be boys, I guess." Troy and I link arms. We skip past the metal swings, down the staircase, and into Euclid Beach Park. The pier is elongated with two metal gates hanging high above us. The metal artwork is full of intricate characters, like kids on bumper cars, a young boy licking an ice cream cone, and a little girl pulling a dog behind her. In between the two signs are thick beach chairs, each having one solid color of red, yellow, or blue. At the end, two long benches lie with their seats facing outward.

Even though it's almost October, the air freezes once the sun sets. The girls shiver, and most of the boys chivalrously hand over their coats. Troy points to Jessyka, but she shakes her head despite her chattering teeth.

Greg sits on a bench with a large thermos that's not

filled with coffee. He pours a SOLO cup for each person with plenty left over. Troy brings the mini wine bottles and spews it into a different cup. The ten of us raise our glasses. I say, "Speech! Speech! Speech!" toward him. He hip-checks me.

"To our senior year," he begins, "and shall it be our best year yet!"

"Our senior year!" the five girls screech, and I chug a good portion of the screwdriver. We played a couple of rounds of Never Have I Ever, followed by the drinking game of Kings. Half of us sit on benches while the other half lounge on planks, but during Troy's turn to pick a card, a huge wind gust sends the cards flying into the air and landing in the sea.

"Aw," Jessyka says, pouting. Then she giggles into Troy's arms and snuggles into his grasp. She stares into his eyes and sways.

"Maybe it's best that the wind ended our game." He grabs her drink and places it on the other side of the timber.

After a refill, I walk to the edge of the pier and sit on a bench. The waves crash along the wooden planks with hundreds or thousands of barnacles sticking to the oak. The orange moon is bigger than usual, and it keeps disappearing behind the silver clouds.

"Dude!" Greg slaps me on my back harder than necessary. "A bunch of us are going bar hopping. I got a fake ID from my older brother. You in?" I feel my body getting tipsy. Tomorrow morning, I have to swim at least thirty laps. The screwdrivers were fun, but I'll pass.

I shake my head. He hits me again, and this time, I dodge it.

Once most people leave, I scoot over, so Troy sits next to me. Jessyka lies on his lap and kisses him on his neck. She sucks on the sensitive spot near his pulse, and he moans. The entire time she does this, though, her eyes aren't closed and instead are directed at me.

"Oh!" Troy snaps his fingers. "You didn't tell me about the boxing match a few weeks ago!" He slides Jessyka off his body, and for once, she reddens. I glance at her and then him.

"What about it?" I ask with caution.

"It's no big deal, Strong. Seriously," she says.

"Babe, it's a *huge* deal! I mean, beating every person in boxing on your first try *ever*? That's remarkable! Don't you think so?" My eyebrows raise. First of all, she has worked with a personal trainer who specialized in boxing. Second, she beat one person and then hit an innocent girl; for the rest of the class, she was in the principal's office. "Aus?"

After I gulp the last of my SOLO cup, I slur, "Yeah, she's just like Enyo." Both Troy and Jess blink.

Enyo was the goddess of destruction.

I'm about to explain how I used to be obsessed with Greek mythology in seventh grade when I hear gurgling coming from someone's stomach. Troy jumps to his feet and searches behind me. "Nature calls," he says and taps me on the shoulder. With one last kiss from Jessyka, he sprints to the far-off restroom. I continue to watch the lake and its waves crashing along the shore in hopes she gets a hint. But her hand graces my chin and drags my head to her direction.

"Wanna go on the swings?" Jessyka asks and glances at the distance where they are. I wait for the catch, the pounce, or just a mesmerizing stare. The only thing she does is roll her eyes. "Come on, Chang. I don't bite."

Jessyka leads, and I follow her up the stairs along an outstretched path. On this autumn night, leaves of auburn, macaroon, and tangerine fall along the pavement. The streetlamp brightens once the sun sets, and every few yards, there is a bench and a barrel. Close to the entrance, a large swing hides beneath the awning.

We share the same swing, and as I pump mine, water falls underneath the hinge above. It lands on my head and shoulders. Jessyka giggles, a laugh that I don't recognize, but when I turn to face her, she covers her mouth.

This is the Jessyka who I liked. Before that night happened six months ago, I hated her. So when I bluntly said those not-so-kind words, she shed her walls and spoke to me. It was only that night she was genuine, and just now.

As she slides her hand closer to mine, I drift my body farther on the bench. "I already told you, it's over." She tries to hold my palm, but I sit on my hands.

"Listen, Troy's a great guy and all, but he's not you." She turns and faces me. I reluctantly beckon her call.

"I can't. If he found out about us..." I shake my head and stare at the fallen leaves. "I doubt he'd be okay with me. As long as he's my friend, I'll remain loyal and do what he says."

"If Troy told you to jump off a bridge, would you?"

I scoff. "Depends. How high is this bridge?"

Rather than laughing, Jessyka's smile disappears. "Why can't we start a new life together? We can sneak around for the rest of senior year, and then we'll travel far away instead of going to some boring college. How great would it be to backpack through Europe? Like France or Ireland?"

"I don't want to, okay? Even if you break up with Troy, I'd never date you."

A life described by Jessyka would be messy, and I want my family and my children to realize how much I love them. Growing up as an only child, my parents had so much love in my family. My mom would tease my father, and then he would chase her around the house. Ten years later, they grew apart, grew separate, grew routine.

I vowed never to have a marriage like that.

Then, Jessyka blurts out, "My parents are getting a divorce." My mouth falls to my feet. I've met her parents before, and sometimes, they argued, just like every married couple. I thought they'd make it.

"Jessyka, I—"

She breaks down and leaps into my arms. My fingers caress her skin as her body pulses up and down. I tell her how everything is going to be okay, even though I don't know if that's true. While we hold on to each other, I realize I've never seen her this vulnerable. She's a tough girl, tougher than me, so to see her cry breaks my heart.

When I kiss her forehead, she kisses me through her soaked tears. I know I should push her arm and jump off the swing, but the alcohol takes over. Her kiss, her touch, creates a thirst I can't describe. My hands rise under her shirt's back. Her skin is unbelievably smooth, and as she kisses my cheek, my neck, and bites it, something inside me switches off.

Stop, Chang, just stop.

I leap to put distance between us, wiping her slobber

off my face and shutting my eyes. I feel her staring, the tilt of her face, the curl of her lips.

My eyes remain closed. "It's been *six* months since we slept together, Jessyka! And you don't feel any guilt? Because I do! It's tearing me apart!" Her eyes must be watering because I hear her sniffle. Taking a deep breath, I whisper, "It's not fair to Troy."

"You got that right."

I fling open my eyes, and instantly, my heart rate soars through the roof. I back away from Troy. As I walk, the terrain switches from concrete to grass. I fall and think, *Oh, how I wish to bury myself in a six-foot ditch.* The pissed-off man walks, struts even, and while Jessyka raises her body, she hides behind him.

Coward.

Then he bends above me and reaches my breathing space. His eyes are bloodshot, his breath reeks of alcohol, and his teeth are purple, the color of red wine. My heart thumps against my chest, and I freeze, unable to move any extremities.

My eyes widen as he pounds his sneakers against the soil. He's so upset right now, and I can only laugh and smile, hoping he thinks I'm joking with him.

"Troy—"

He winds up, holding it for a good two seconds, and I do what anyone would do and close my eyes.

I guess I shoulda rubbed Mickey's shoes after all.

Chapter 11
Rhiannon

Something's off.

I sit in the same seat I'm always in. Greg makes some stupid joke to the guy on his right, most other people text nonstop, and Jessyka chews her gum. Although Austin isn't here yet, that's normal. He's probably showering after his morning laps at practice.

But something's *definitely* not right.

When I glance at her one more time, she seems distant, like her mind is elsewhere. Every other day, she talked nonstop, using obnoxious hand gestures with a question mark at the end of every sentence. Today, though, she stares at her desk and picks at her fingers, her *precious* manicured nails.

After the bell rings, Austin walks in and sits. His hat covers his face along with sunglasses, and his T-shirt's back is wet around the neck and the spine. I guess he didn't have enough time to dry himself today.

"What's your excuse this time, Austin?" Mr. Lane

passes the copies of Shakespeare's *Macbeth*. "Can't say it was practice because I saw a bunch of your teammates roaming the halls, so Coach let everyone out with twenty minutes to spare." He taps his shoe, yet Austin still won't respond. "I'm waiting."

"I took a shower after everyone."

"Really?" Mr. Lane raises his eyebrows. "Why?"

Austin shrugs and mumbles, "Argument," and that's it. They stare at one another, my guess because Mr. Lane wants more of an explanation, but Austin refuses to give it to him. Eventually, the teacher shakes his head and resumes passing out copies.

"Mr. Chang?" Austin looks up as the teacher passes out another copy. "Lose it." He mimes removing his hat and sunglasses. Immediately, Austin loses the baseball cap but hesitates to take off his glasses. When Mr. Lane finishes passing out *Macbeth,* he sighs. "Don't make me give you detention for something as minor as a dress code violation."

Austin's dimmed sunglasses glance my way. It's like he's saying something to me that no one else can hear. I smirk slightly, as if to say, "Just get over it." With a deep breath, he removes his glassware, and everyone, including me, gasps.

A black eye.

His eyelid droops down, purple coloring on the lid, like how a young girl overly does her makeup. Below the eye is blue, and farther away are yellow and orange.

His classmates whisper among themselves. "What the hell happened?" asks Greg and leans toward him. "Did you fall down?"

Austin glances at Jessyka, who stares down at the floor. "Something like that" is all he says.

While Mr. Lane does the attendance, everyone gossips. The crowd's noise grows. I get whiplash from all my turning and notice Austin putting his sunglasses back on. Jessyka continues watching her desk and picks at her nails until one of them breaks.

"All right, all right," Mr. Lane attempts to calm the class. "Get into your usual groups, okay? Al— I mean, Austin?" He waves him over while Greg and I turn our desks into a small circle. As I shimmy my desk, I stare at the two of them, Mr. Lane pointing to the black eye.

Austin forces a laugh and brushes it off. He says, "I fell," and he animates the entire scene.

But I doubt that's what *really* happened.

Jessyka, Greg, and I wait for Austin. Once he sits across from me, I wait to write down a few notes. Austin was the ringleader last time, and I suspect him to do the same again, except he won't look up.

Well, if no one else will do it, then...

"So, has anyone in our group read *Macbeth?*" Austin and Jessyka refuse to speak, so I glance toward Greg.

"Uh, I saw the movie? Does that count?" I slap my hand against my head, and Austin chuckles. "What?"

I turn in their direction and ignore the football player. "Austin? Jessyka? Did either of you read it?" I glare at Greg. "And *not* just watch the movie?" I haven't read it, but I know the gist of it. The king kills his father, and he sees the ghost throughout the play. Shakespeare isn't my thing, though, especially *Romeo and Juliet*.

Austin and Jessyka stare at each other, like they've

forgotten me and Greg are here. She mouths the words, "I'm sorry," and Austin slouches in his chair.

For the next thirty minutes, I run our group because no one else is willing to. I actually want to do well in this class. So, I force my group to participate, ask the questions, and even make Jessyka talk more than three words. Mr. Lane walks around the room and hovers around my group. When I turn around, he smiles.

At the cafeteria, I have my prepared lunch of a protein shake and granola bar and sit in the usual spot with the usual person. While I eat, I glance around the cafeteria when I see Austin. He has his hood over his head and hovers over his tray of food. Once he slouches to his table, he stops, and his eyes grow wide, his face draining of color. I watch him as Troy stands and lets out a loud scoff.

"You've *got* to be kidding me," he says, shaking his head. "Sit anywhere *but* here." He wraps his arm around Jessyka. She freezes the moment he touches her skin.

Greg nudges Troy's shoulder and points to Austin with a hefty laugh. "Come on, Strong. Me lunch table es su lunch table," and he pats the empty seat. "Chang's got a black eye from a fall Friday night, and—"

"*That's* what he told you?" Troy asks and shakes his head, glaring his piercing eyes into Austin's soul. "How about he was having an affair with *my* girlfriend!" Greg's mouth drops, as does mine. Troy picks up Austin's tray and tosses it across the cafeteria's floor, splattering the lunch everywhere. A little sauce stains a few screaming girls.

Greg turns to face Austin. "Not cool, Jackie Chan, not cool."

Austin shakes his head and says, "That's not what happened. If you just let me explain—"

Troy raises his body so they are eye to eye. Although they are around the same height, Troy doesn't have the usual swimmer physique, having massive chest and arms. I wonder if he could beat Greg in an arm-wrestling match.

Then, Troy steps closer, his eyes narrowing down at what appears to be a tiny boy. Austin cowers and loses three inches of height. If he were a dog, he would've had his tail between his legs. His eyes glaze over without blinking, his body quivers, and he breathes in and out at a rapid pace.

I don't understand what is going on at the moment. Why isn't he moving? Why isn't he talking? *And why am I stepping forward?*

An unspeakable force pushes me out of my seat, and for all I know, the two boys have already forgiven one another. Brielle calls my name, but I can't explain it and have to keep going. I shuffle and push through the crowd of people with their iPhones recording the situation. When I finally reach Austin, I stare only at Troy. His face is redder than Hot Cheetos screaming at the scared boy. I step in between them, and Troy instantaneously stops.

"Can I talk to you?" I glance at Austin and back at Troy. "Alone?"

Confused, he asks, "Who are you?"

The next thing I know is Troy and I are standing five feet apart, his mouth agape. My hand shakes, my nails are picked at so much they bleed, and my eyes sting. Looking around, we're in an abandoned science classroom with the lights off. I have no idea where I am.

Did I black out again?

Every once in a while, my mind goes dim like I'm on autopilot, and with Troy's stare, I realize I probably told him something I shouldn't have. Gently, I sit in a chair and lay my hands on my knees. It didn't occur to me how out of breath I am, and as I press two fingers on a pressure point, a strong heartbeat pulses. I close my eyes, hold in my breath, and exhale. I do this three times. When I finish, I open them to find Troy sitting across from me.

Just lie. Tell him you're joking, brush it off, and walk away. Tell him you don't care about Austin, and he can do whatever he pleases. But I'm not gonna lie, even if he's a somewhat stranger to me.

"This happens sometimes," I whisper. My voice is hoarse, raspy, and painful. "The blackouts."

Troy nods, but he's still staring at me. "Is it true? I mean, what you said during the blackout?"

I break the trance and watch the far wall of the science room: a skeleton wearing a witch's hat, four sinks with a Costco-size soap, and a sign reading, "Fair Play." Before I answer, it occurs to me there's no way of knowing if it's true or not, what I told him, or how I told him.

I say the only thing I can. "Probably."

He doesn't make me explain and rather tells me he can keep my secret. For a full minute, we sit there until the bell rings. Slowly, he pulls out his rolling chair and stands. Before he leaves, I force a chuckle.

"Hey, Troy?"

He turns around.

"Where are we?"

After a few blinks, he bursts into laughter, that odd sound reminding me of Goofy. He motions me to join in, to reciprocate, egging me on to mimic him. He leans closer, and a crease in his brow deepens. So, I fake laughter, fake joy, fake a giggle.

I hate this, the longing of a good laugh; I haven't had a good laugh since Finley's stupid comment.

Perhaps he realizes I can't giggle, or thinks that I'm embarrassed for not knowing which direction to go for my next class. Nevertheless, he motions me to follow and says in a kind voice, "I'll show you."

Maybe...just maybe, I made another friend today.

```
New Year's Day
Xavier's house
  10:00 a.m.
```

Just look at his face.

I stared at the guy whom I adored. I brushed his hair behind his ear, no longer was it red, and stroked his cheek. His mouth opened wide, like I bet a spider could easily become his breakfast. Every once in a while, he snored with no sense of the rhythm. Sometimes he was consistent while other times it was random. He even cleared his throat in his sleep.

My head beat with a slight pulse, a sign of a hangover. I knew I should've brought my water with me. The hangover will be gone by noon, though.

Glancing around, I saw his room was the same as always. Maybelline sat on his nightstand, his black-and-yellow sneakers propped against the foot of the bed, and a stuffed Slytherin snake was on a nightstand. He got it from Finley.

Xavier was always a Gryffindor.

I played with my new necklace in one hand, removed my fake eyelash with the other, and tiptoed to the adjacent bathroom. After I opened the mirror cabinet, I unscrewed a cap, swung a huge amount of mouthwash, and swirled it in my mouth, spitting into the sink. I applied the necessary makeup discreetly, not wanting Xavier to realize how much time and effort it took to look pretty.

Once I scurried back into his bed, I laid in bed and gently kicked him. He groaned, and I mimicked him. As he opened his eyes, he grinned. "How do you look so sexy in the morning?" With a sheepish smile, I shrugged and pretended to be half-asleep. He wrapped both his arms around me. "What time is it?" I stretched to the Star Wars alarm clock and held it near him. After he read the time, he mumbled and hid beneath the covers. "It's too early."

"It's ten o'clock," I said, yanking the covers from over his head. "We've practically wasted the day." Although I giggled, I internally sighed. We were wasting the *entire* day away, and because I've been up since eight thirty, I was annoyed. He kept shaking his head, his eyes fluttered as he was about to fall back asleep. *That's it.* Using both hands, I shook his stomach, or muscular abs. "Xavierrr."

He shut his eyes tightly. "Coffee," was all he said. "Coffee, coffee, coffee."

I leaped out of his bed, slid into his slippers—which were far too big—and shuffled to the door. "I'll make you scrambled eggs, too." Then, he opened his eyes and smiled that special smile.

As I closed the door, I flicked on each light switch in the penthouse as I passed and picked up the trash that had accumulated during the party. Xavier's parents returned from the Bahamas tomorrow, so I wanted to make the house as clean as possible. And since they barely used the kitchen, I had to leave it spotless.

Once I was in the kitchen, I turned on the coffee maker and sang, "That's Amore," by Dean Martin. I scanned my clothing. It was all Xavier's, even the underwear that I made him promise were clean. Checkered red-and-black pajama pants, two different patterned socks, and a robotics club shirt that was a little too tight. I measured my waist with my hands and sucked in the flab.

Five pounds, Broderick. That's all you need. Xavier will still have what he likes about you. You'll have more confidence.

Making coffee doesn't take much time, but I opened my phone and scrolled while waiting, anyway. By scrolling Instagram and Facebook, I caught up on everybody's news feed by the time the machine stopped.

After I grabbed another mug for Xavier, I poured two cups and was about to enter his room when there was a knock at the door. I placed both down and jogged to the entrance with my braless breasts flying with each step.

Yep, definitely need to lose five pounds. I'll start today, new year, new me.

I yanked open the door and was confused. Finley? He hastily scanned from my oversized slippers to my head and back to my chest. "What are you doing here?" we both asked.

We laughed as he walked through the entrance. "My New Year's resolution starts today. I want to gain weight."

I punched him in the arm. *Lucky bastard!* Having not enough weight was a dream of mine! The two of us walked to the kitchen. "Xavier promised to begin weight training. Did he tell you?"

"Nope," I said and sipped my coffee. "Why are you training? The Mr. Asshole competition isn't until October."

He grinned. "Ha, ha, *hilarious.*"

"Why are you training, though?"

He shrugged and grabbed another mug. "Chicks dig the whole muscular vibe, I guess." Finley gulped his coffee and winced, probably because he scorched his tongue. He peered at the tile, noticing how filthy it was from last night. "Besides, I...I kinda like someone."

I placed my mug on the counter. Was it the girl from science class? Or the one from Spanish? Maybe even Sadie, and he was just too drunk to realize it last night?

My eyes lit up, and my hands rubbed against each other, but he held up one finger. "*Not* Sadie," and he laughed. I snapped my fingers and continued drinking my coffee.

"Does Xavier know?" Finley shrugged. I smiled, grabbed Xavier's coffee, and scurried to his room. I knocked twice and slowly peeked in. "Xavier?"

He lounged on his stomach, mouth opened wider than ever, and snored. If he were a volume setting, he'd be set to loud...*very* loud. I laid his full coffee mug on his nightstand. The liquid spilled over the edge, landing on Maybelline's two front paws.

"Shit," I whispered and dabbed her arms with the bottom of my shirt.

Once I closed the door, I found Finley standing in the kitchen with an empty cup. He stared at the same floor tile, lost in thought. Slowly, I grabbed my camera, turned it on, and snapped a great photograph. His head shot up, and he blushed.

"I wasn't prepared for a picture," Finley said.

After I turned the camera off, I placed it on the ledge and laughed. "Those pictures are my specialty." I poured two more cups of coffee and opened the refrigerator. "You like cream and sugar, right? Two of each?"

"How'd you know?"

I leaned across the kitchen table and smirked. "Believe it or not, I actually pay attention." As he added cream and sugar, we switched from the kitchen to the living room. The fireplace was off, and I attempted to turn it on, but Finley shook his head and patted next to him on the couch.

He rubbed his temple with one hand and poured something else into his mug. Was that vodka? "Whiskey," he said and handed it to me. "Want some?"

I was about to say, "no thank you," but then I remembered drinking in the morning almost instantaneously cures my hangovers. I smirked and took it. After I poured the whiskey, I placed it down, took my phone out of my pocket, and scooted closer to Finley. Using Instagram, we clung to our mugs and captioned it *#hairofthedog*.

"Where's Xavier?" As he placed the flask back into his pocket, I tagged my photo under Finley, Xavier, and Sadie, just for good manners. Was she gonna be pissed she wasn't invited?

"He's hibernating." We laughed as I put my phone away. I turned on the television and searched through the streaming channels to bide our time. While I did this, Finley's phone blew up with a *Beep* every three seconds, although he ignored it. "Who's texting?"

He sunk into the chair, gulped his mixture, and showed me his phone. "Sadie's been texting me all morning. I don't even remember giving her my number."

My phone beeped once, and I knew who it was and how upset she was because she wasn't asked to attend our little get-together this morning. I stuck my hand in my pocket and turned it to silent.

He tossed his phone to the other side of the couch. I slid down toward the middle cushion. "Don't get mad, but Xavier gave it to her."

If it were possible, Finley sank even more.

"Figures," he mumbled. I reached for his phone and turned it off. He lit up, laughed, and held up both arms. If Sadie found out that I turned it off, she'd be more mad than she already was. "I won't say a thing."

We stared at each other for a second, and then my eyes drew to the television screen. "Hey," and I nudged him. "How about this?" The British version of *The Office*. "You can relate to it, right?"

"Can you relate to someone who lived and breathed California air?"

I chuckled. "I guess not."

"I've never seen it, though."

"Well, then, that makes two of us." After I chose an episode, I drank the rest of my cup. Finley handed me the flask and unscrewed the top to egg me on. Back and forth, we chugged our whiskey until my cheeks reddened and my bones went numb.

As soon as we both finished, his eyes glazed over. He squinted, so much that his eyes watered. "Do you need glasses?" I asked.

"Actually, I've needed glasses for the past three years. But I don't want to be called *four-eyes*."

"Well, I think they'd make you rather dashing," I said in the most British accent I've given.

"That wasn't half-bad!" The two of us giggled as I hit the zoom button on the remote.

Finley stopped laughing, leaned back in the coach, and sighed. "I can't live with Xavier." I blinked a few times, slid toward him, and turned down the volume. What was he talking about? "Last night, my dad told me we're moving sometime next year. To Ohio."

I didn't know if they were real tears or if the alcohol was doing its job, but Finley's eyes watered and refused to glance in my direction.

"Hey." Squeezing his hand, I smiled. "Ohio's not as bad as everyone says."

And that was the truth. Before I began high school, I would look forward to the yearly trip to Cleveland.

"Besides, now I have another reason to visit my aunt."

He faced me with a wide grin. "Really?"

I nodded. "Do you know where he's stationed?"

"Cleveland."

Punching him weakly in the arm, I said, "Even better. We're practically neighbors."

Then, I faced the television and turned the volume

up for the rest of the episode. For its entirety, I watched the show, but I could tell Finley stared at me, a smile stretching from cheek to cheek. He must feel relieved that he has at least one friend next year.

At the end of the episode, I hit Pause on the remote and sat up straight. "It's not nearly as good as the original," I said while I stared at Ricky Gervais's stoic face. Then I heard a giggle coming from Finley's mouth. Either he was buzzed, or I said something incredibly stupid.

"Rhie," he said, and I turned to face him. His entire face was bright red, even his hands. "This *is* the original." I blinked a few times, and then I couldn't stop laughing. I don't know why I was giggling, perhaps it was the fact Finley was British or the fact his giggle was so cute.

Finally, our laughter subsided, and our tears were wiped. "Well, shit. I guess what they say is true; America is the fattest country *and* the funniest!" Finley howled at that comment as I grabbed the flask and swung it above my head. I drank just a few drops.

Then I faced him. His expression turned to something more serious. "Does..." He giggled, and I touched his shoulder to reassure him to go on. He glanced away but remained smiling. "Does America have the most beautiful women?"

I burst into laughter and pulled my hair back behind my ears. "I doubt it. I think that's Scandinavia. You know, 'cause of the blond hair and blue eyes."

"Naw, it has to be America." Finley swung the empty flask. "You're in it."

Snorting, I rolled my eyes and nudged him. "Ha, ha, good one." Boys only liked me because of my personality, besides Xavier. Even then, he's never called me *beautiful*, only *hot* when we discussed my weight and *cute* whenever I said something clever.

"Seriously," Finley whispered and dragged his flask onto the coffee table. "You're gorgeous."

"Too bad you didn't say that two and a half years ago," I slurred my speech, the words falling out of my mouth. "I had a slight crush on you."

I giggled until I glanced up, his eyes lowered to my lips, and for a split second, I closed my eyes. Finley must have leaned into my breathing space because I could smell his morning breath. Then he kissed me. It all happened so fast, the mixture of coffee and whiskey, the stubble on his chin, and his tongue in my mouth.

My eyes flew open. I pushed him off me. What is he thinking? I'm Xavier's girlfriend! Finley's probably drunk, and he didn't mean to exchange our saliva. It must have been the look on my face that caused him to look away.

Before I could say anything, I heard heavy footsteps, so thunderous my mug on the table vibrated. "What the fuck?"

Finley jumped off the couch and stumbled onto the rug. My eyes widened and my mouth dropped because I didn't recognize his voice. This Xavier had a lower tone, bloodshot eyes, like he was coming out of his body.

I've never seen this side of him before.

As he stormed through the foyer, he swung his arms like a mad man, knocking my camera off the ledge and onto the floor, smashing it into a hundred pieces. I gasped, covered my mouth, and watered my eyes. I stared at Xavier, yet he ignored me. He didn't turn around, didn't say sorry, didn't give a shit. My precious camera, the one thing that I adored, was utterly destroyed.

At that moment, it was like a piece of me was broken, too.

But I snapped into reality and focused on the task at hand. He approached us closer and closer until I stepped in between the two boys.

"It's not me you're mad at," I said the rehearsed lines through my tear-soaked eyes, the ones that gave me control rather than his bipolar disorder. Yet, unlike the times before, Xavier's demeanor didn't change. "Let's-let's go for a walk and-and-and calm down."

But he wasn't listening to me.

Finley stepped backward and fell. "It was an accident!" I yelled. "I didn't mean to—"

"I know *you* didn't mean anything to happen," he growled and pointed to the tiny guy. "*He* did."

Finley shook his raised hands. "I can ex—"

But Xavier wanted no part of that. He pushed me out of the way, and I slammed against the mantle. I winced from the pain as six framed photographs fell in a domino effect.

Finley attempted to escape and scurried to the entrance door on his hands and knees. Xavier grabbed the boy's shirt with one hand, turned him level with the floor, and punched him in the face. Instantly, Finley's nose spurred blood, his right eye blackened, and he gasped for air.

"Xavier!" I screamed and began sobbing. "Stop it!"

It was no use. Finley stumbled, fell hard on the rug, and shrieked. He breathed in and out at a rapid pace with dilated eyes. When he tried to stand up, Xavier pounced on him and hammered his face over and over again. At one point, Finley grew unconscious. This monster kept throwing punches into the floor.

Pow!

Pow!

Pow!

"Stop it! Stop!" My voice was hoarse from the repetition and volume of my words. But this guy was a person I didn't recognize: glazed-over eyes, the black-and-blue of his knuckles, messy hair like Einstein or mad-man Frankenstein.

I remained staring at the two boys, frozen in time. I couldn't stop my boyfriend from practically killing Finley, but I knew some people who might. As a final hope, I pulled my phone out of my pocket, and with a shaking hand, dialed three numbers.

"Nine-one-one, what's your emergency?"

A yank of my necklace brought me backward. I dropped my phone, breaking it with a shattered screen. Xavier pulled my necklace until it broke. I stumbled and fell onto the brick of the mantle, face-first. My chin throbbed and blood oozed onto the floor.

After a flutter of his eyes, Xavier turned around, picked me up, and held me by my throat. He lifted me up off the rug and slammed my back against the fireplace. "X...Xavi—" It was like he didn't *want* to listen to me as his grip tightened. I wheezed, but nothing happened.

I couldn't breathe.

Xavier clenched my neck, and I tried to leave and wiggle out of his grasp. He wouldn't let go. I tried to inhale, kept trying, trying, trying; nothing escaped.

I couldn't breathe.

I couldn't breathe.

"Say something!" he cried, mucus falling all over my neck and body. I hit his arm, his fist, and at one point, his face, but my punches were weak. Xavier must not know how strong he was. As my arm fell to my side, I struggled to stay conscious.

"You're...you're gonna kill her," Finley weakly replied, like he was having trouble staying awake, too. My sight faded in and out, blurs filled my vision. I stared at Xavier, pleading him to do something as I was about to...to...to—

Then something snapped in Finley. He screamed. "You're gonna kill her, Xavier! You're gonna kill her!" The normal Xavier returned, blinked multiple times, and loosened his grip. I gasped.

And the last thing I remember was falling onto the fireplace, my head smashing against the concrete bricks, and Xavier's black-and-yellow sneakers remaining still.

Chapter 12
Austin

For the past week and a half, I've been in hell. Because Troy is our captain, he has forced me to do extra laps, suicides in the pool, and even clean the locker room.

That's right, the locker room. After practice, I wait for everyone to shower and change into their clothes. Then, my grunt work begins, scrubbing the stalls and sweeping the entire room until it's spotless. And that's on a *good* day. If Troy feels like it, he "accidentally" spills a Gatorade, like we just won the Super Bowl. "You know what to do" is all that comes from Troy's mouth.

However, I deserve it...a hundred percent.

Today, though, I decide to skip the morning practice and get some carbohydrates to strengthen myself for the first meet. Once I grab a healthy breakfast of Cheerios, grapefruit, and orange juice, I pull out a chair at the kitchen table and eat. I glance out the kitchen window and squint at the hired gardener. He stretches, hops on the lawn mower, and gets to work.

The Night at Times Square

I stop eating to watch him evenly cut our front yard. Dad used to do it, but once his job took too much time, he hired people to do everything: the lawn, the pool, the house, *everything*. It's a shame because he loved yardwork.

Dad loved keeping China's spot clean on The Cultural Garden, too.

As if on cue, he walks into the kitchen and frantically peeks in all the cabinets. "Where did I put it?" he mumbles and opens the refrigerator. "I doubt I would put them in here..."

"You should put them in the bowl." I grab his keys next to my cereal and jingle them. He turns around, notices my presence, and takes them. "That's where everyone else puts it."

"One of these days, I'll remember. Your mother nags about it all the time and—" He stops talking and swallows. "Don't you have...that thing? In the morning?"

Obviously, communication skills are not our strong suit.

"Swimming, yeah," I say and munch on the cereal. "I have a meet today."

"Oh." We stare at each other, not knowing how to do this. Every second that goes by makes this more awkward. Finally, Dad walks to the coffee machine and turns it on. "Good...good luck."

"Thanks," and I continue to eat. He stands by the coffee maker with his toe tapping away. I rarely see him not wearing a tie, button-up shirt, slacks, and work shoes. Even now, he looks like he's ready for an interview.

The percolator stops. Dad pours his coffee into his gray mug, taking it black. Right when he's about to leave for his office, I ask, "Dad?" He stops moving, turns around, and waits. I don't know why I'm doing this, maybe because it's my senior year and nostalgia kicks in, or it's the father-and-son bonding we never truly had. "Do you want to come to my meet? I mean, I'd invite Mom too, but she's away, so..."

"Oh-oh." I caught my father off guard because he literally stumbles and grabs a chair. "Wa-when?"

"After school? Around three thirty?" He ponders for a second and lowers his eyes to the floor tile. My heart sinks, and suddenly, I'm not hungry anymore.

"I'll...I'll try my best." My head shoots up, my grin widening. "I may not make it because I have to get my baby inspected." Ah, his *precious* Tesla. Last time I asked him to use it, I got a lecture about why I'd never, *ever* get the chance to drive it. I'm pretty sure if he had to choose me or the car, he'd choose the latter.

"You can always take an Uber."

He snorts. "I'd rather walk."

When I'm about to give him the details of where the pool and parking are located, he practically sprints into his office. Still, I can only hope, right?

Since it's a home meet for Hawken School, our fans fill the stands to its capacity. A few students paint their faces red and white. Some girls create signs to cheer on our team. Jessyka holds a glittery poster reading, "We are STRONGer than you!" and paints a star on each cheek. Ever since Troy confronted me, their relationship has

The Night at Times Square

been passive aggressive. This afternoon, she clung to his hand with no reciprocation.

During stretches, I glance at the stands every two seconds and search for Dad as the spectators fill the stands. But once the whistle blows, my hope for having my father here becomes diminished. I shake my head and focus on Coach.

I have to concentrate.

Troy divides us against our opponent, three swimmers per race. There are four races: freestyle, backstroke, front stroke, and the butterfly. For Troy, he swims the freestyle, and I swim the backstroke. Neither of us swam in the third race, so I'm eager to see how the junior swimmers do.

All three of us win our races. When it's time for the butterfly, our swimmers are a junior, Troy, and me. Since we already won our meet, the opposing coach suggests they end the competition. But before Coach says yes or no, Troy steps forward and replies, "We *have* to race." He's still fuming with anger, I know that, but shouldn't we celebrate our victory?

He bumps my shoulders, his way of signaling a challenge. I open my mouth to explain what *exactly* happened and how it was just one time, thinking Jessyka and Troy had split. But he won't hear it. As he glances in my direction, he looks at me with a snarl.

My fist tightens. Maybe it's the adrenaline or it's the fact I'm sick of apologizing every day, but for once, I *have* to win.

Stepping up onto the diving board, Troy puts on his goggles and nose plug and flaps his arms to become looser and more flexible. I do the same. My skin burns from his stare. However, I won't look at him anymore.

"On your mark," the announcer says. We step to the board's edge, gripping the front with two hands and one foot. The second foot remains outstretched back on an upper lift. I close my eyes as the crowd silences.

You can do this.

BEEP!

We dive into the water, and a cool temperature hits me. I soar through the water for as long as possible. When I reach the surface for my first breath, I don't see anyone; I'm in first. I glide my arms through the pool and move faster and faster. My feet kick harder than ever, and despite Troy's tactics of making me have longer practices, he's only strengthened me.

At the opposite side of the pool, I submerge, somersault, and push my feet against the concrete edge. I can't even see Troy's splashes, something I've always been able to do. With a smirk, I increase my intensity, no longer caring about my form or equal breathing. I can sense the space between us increasing. He must be exhausted and frustrated and—

What if I let him win?

I slightly slow down my pace, make my form sloppy, and think it looks like the usual fatigue. But as I glance at Coach, he must realize my mistake. "Keep going, Chang! You're gonna break the school record!"

Although having my legacy written down below my name would be a wonder, I can't. I'd rather have Troy's forgiveness than a plaque. More and more lethargic, I see his splashes by my side. With ten feet, we're neck and neck. Once I reach the wall, I don't outstretch my arms and hover over the pool's edge.

I stare at the pool wall and try not to smile. *This is it, Chang. Troy will grin, hold out his hand, and ask, "Are you coming?" just like old times.* However, when I turn to the stands, none of them believe I actually lost, and rather, they know I lost on purpose. Only a few fans clap, one of them being Jessyka, but the rest of them go silent, whispering to their neighbor and shaking their heads.

As my heart sinks, Troy swims to the lap divider and rips off his goggles. I prepared for every reaction, except anger. "Seriously? Did you think letting me win would solve all your problems?"

I swallow the chlorine water and don't say anything because yes, yes that is *exactly* what I thought. He scoffs and squirts water out of his mouth.

"Think again."

He has been a team player who always shook his opponent's hand, even back when we started as freshmen. Not this time, though. He storms off into the locker room, no hands shaken and no congratulatory speech. Jessyka skips down every other aisle bench and runs toward the locker room while she carries her high heels.

The crowd disperses one by one as I float, staring at the arena's ceiling. When I flip to face Coach, there is one person left in the stands: Dad. Our eyes lock, and I hope, *pray*, he'll say something to me to ease my humiliation. But he glances away, raises in his sleek-cut suit, and leaves.

Coach and I sigh, both because of our disappointment. With his outstretched hand to help me out of the pool, I shake my head. I don't care about the empty stands, or my silent father, or everyone witnessing the argument between Troy and me.

I just swim.

Lap after lap, I realize what a stupid mistake I made. Of course, Troy wants to beat me, but fair and square. I could easily move on, befriend new people, and party with fresh buddies. But since eighth grade, we've been close, confiding in one another. I'm kicking myself for that one night six months ago.

After thirty laps, my fingers are pruny, and the lukewarm water turns to ice. I hop out of the pool, grab a towel from the rack, and wipe my head. My teeth chatter despite the friction from the towel.

When I turn around, one person remains. Jessyka walks down the steps until she's five feet from me. She wipes her face, leaving a smudged red stain on her cheek. With one step forward by her, I take one step back.

"Well, you win," she says, scoffing in the most animated way. "We broke up." She waits to hear the usual comforting speech, just like I did on the pier, yet I stare blankly with a lump in my throat.

"Wha..." I swallow. "When?"

She forces a laugh. "A few minutes ago, actually. He was ranting about you, and suddenly he stopped and asked, 'Aren't you gonna say something?' I guess no answer was not the *best* answer. But it doesn't matter, not really." She holds my hand. My pruny palm doesn't clasp hers, the same way Troy acted hours ago. "We can *finally* be together, Austin."

Neither of us says anything. I assume she wants me to comfort her, possibly hold her in my arms, and ask, "Will you go out with me?" I used to daydream of her saying those exact words. I'd imagine traveling anywhere on the planet, from simple Cleveland to China or Australia. I'd imagine walking through the halls while holding hands, and I'd imagine her having a meal with my family, the *whole* family, at the dinner table.

Those wonderful images are just that: a fantasy.

"Jess, it's over." I step back and tighten my towel. "Really."

She sighs with a slight chuckle. "I figured, but hey, at least I tried, right?" She walks up to me and kisses me on the cheek. "That girl, Rhiannon?" she asks, shaking her head and gazing at the high ceiling. "Well, do you remember when she pulled Troy aside? Apparently, he won't tell me what she said, but it must have been memorable. Our relationship started to decline after that."

Rhiannon and I have only known each other for a few weeks, but every interaction, every *single* one of them, is indescribable.

"Anyway..." She gazes into my eyes. "Goodbye, Austin."

"Goodbye, Jessyka."

I stand and watch her leave. She turns around to look at me three times, and when she's finally through the double doors, I exhale and squat on my knees. It's a new chapter in my life, not being labeled as freshmen, sophomore, junior, or senior, but it's more of the significant events. I believe this moment was one of those. And with Rhiannon's help, I got rid of someone toxic.

I dash to the locker room, change into my clothes, and sprint to the car with my body still smelling of chlorine.

There's someone I have to thank.

Chapter 13
Rhiannon

I'm listening to my Walkman as I punch the bag in Tori's basement. This is a routine now; she cooks while I get my anxiety levels down.

Left, left, right.
Left, left, right.
Left, left, right.

Sweat drips from my forehead, and the back of my neck is soaked. The washer spins and shakes with the detergent moving like a bobble head. I try to forget everything happening during the past week and focus on the punch bag.

Then, my music stops. I need a new CD. After I replace the disc—Dad's Mixtape #4—I hit play, and the song "Mystery of Love" by Sufjan Stevens resumes. I hit the punching bag, but stop and close my eyes. One hand on the piano plays the same lick repeatedly, while the other instruments boom. Monotone voice soothes me with his soft sound. It reminds me of Simon and

The Night at Times Square

Garfunkel. I tap my foot, raise my hands, and dance.
DING DONG.

Unlike before, though, I don't stop and find myself lost with the rhythm. I picture Mom and Dad taking me to Coney Island. Dad knew the owner. We had the entire place to ourselves. It was February, so all the rides were closed. The only thing we could do was play games.

I hop and fling my arms all over the place. The second time the chorus plays, I sing along with the lead.

"I didn't know you sang!" Tori claps. I rip my headset off, immediately hitting stop.

Turning bright red, I bite the unclasp strap and yank off each glove, placing them next to the detergent on the washer and adding a sweatshirt to my attire. "I don't."

"It sounded like you—" She stops mid-sentence and stares up the rickety stairs. "Anyway, you have company."

Maybe Brielle came over for dinner. She asked if I had plans tonight, and I told that I had a family dinner. It wasn't a *complete* lie, but it wasn't the whole truth either, considering it's just Tori and me.

Jumping every other step, I expect to see Brielle with homemade cookies fresh from her oven. Once I reach the top of the stairwell, I freeze. Austin? What is he doing here?

"I'm so honored to meet your friend," Tori says and closes the basement door behind me. "He told me he had something to share with you and then he could leave, but I told him, 'Nonsense!'"

My eyes scan Tori, Austin, and back to her. "What's going on?"

She laughs. "I invited—" She points at him.

"Austin."

"—Austin for dinner. You don't mind, do you?" I'm so confused. Why is he here? Why is Tori acting like he's an old pal? And why is he *here*, in my aunt's *house?* I open my mouth to protest when she opens the bottle of wine and places three glasses on the counter. She pours herself a full glass and two miniature ones, handing Austin a Pinot Gris. Once she hands me a glass, I shake my head.

"I don't drink, remember?"

"That's right. My apologies," and she pours my wine into his glass. "But I still don't see why you're a vegetarian."

Austin looks at me. I instantly blush *again*. "You don't eat meat?"

I'm not gonna tell him everything about me, so I shrug, grab a water bottle from the refrigerator, and chug it, thinking how weird this is for me and for him. I mean, it's got to be weird for him, too, right? We stand awkwardly while Austin sips his wine, picks up a coaster, and places it on the counter.

"I'll help you set the table," he says.

As he holds three plates, Tori says, "What a gentleman! We should have him over all the time." I roll my eyes and notice him chuckling. "Your parents raised you right."

"Actually, we never sit at the table. Mom's got her plate in the home office doing some doctor stuff, and Dad paces on the phone the entire meal. Our housekeeper cooks dinner for us."

My first instinct is *spoiled brat,* but I bite my tongue. I shouldn't jump to conclusions if I barely know the person.

"We live right there." He points to the mansions across the stream as I turn to gaze out Tori's window. There's a long, steep path down to the shallow river, and once you cross it, it's quite the hike up the mountainous hill. It must be a great workout, though.

He lays the plates, glasses, forks, knives, and cloth napkins down for the three of us. Then he drags a chair from the table and nods for me to sit. Hesitantly, I oblige, and he pushes my seat against the table. I sit with my feet dangling above the rug and lean toward the kitchen. They whisper so I can't comprehend what they are saying.

The only thing I can figure out is the word *potential*.

Austin whispers some more, and Tori laughs as she enters the dining room. Tonight's dinner is haddock with a side of mashed potatoes and asparagus. My aunt is an excellent chef, but when she places my plate, I tilt my head. The haddock is cut in thirds, and the mashed potatoes and asparagus are half a serving. She only cooks how much she and I will eat because she hates leftovers. She's laid food out, so there's enough for Austin, too.

After she presents dinner to him and me, she brings the wine bottle over. "Another glass?" She points to his cup. He glances at me for a second and shakes his head.

The three of us eat in silence. One would expect an awkward presence with the noiseless munching, but I kind of like it. I devour the haddock, not liking certain foods to be cold, and wait for the others to catch up. The mashed potatoes are smooth with no lumps. I add so much butter Austin chuckles.

"You can never have too much butter," I say in a Julia Child voice. Tori nearly chokes from laughing so hard at my impression.

Once we finish, I clean up the table and wash the dishes. My aunt doesn't have a dishwasher, so everything is washed by hand, and because Tori cooks, I clean. I scrub the plates first. A hand touches mine, and as I look up, Austin slides over. He clutches the washed dishes and dries them.

Ten minutes later, he grabs his coat as I guide him to the door, but Tori jumps from the reclining chair. "Stay!" We halt and look at her. "Have you seen this movie? I mean, I've never seen it before, but it *seems* like a good one." She waves him over and points to the empty spot on the couch by me.

He places his jacket on the coat rack. "It is," he says and sits down. I plop on the solo couch and glance at the screen: *The Wedding Planner.* I raise my eyebrows. Tori's *totally* lying, and there's no way he's heard of this romantic comedy.

Halfway through the film, Tori yawns three times and stands. "It's time for me to go to bed," she announces and stands. Austin's about to get up when she waves him down. "Stay until the end." Right before she climbs the stairs, she winks at me. My cheeks flush. I want to crawl into a ball and roll under the couch.

After Tori leaves, we continue watching the movies again until I hear a loud gurgle not coming from me. The curve of my face stretches. "Hungry?" I ask, and he sighs of relief.

"Starving."

I hop to my feet. "I got just the thing." Once I run to the cabinet, I grab two family-sized bags of chips and hand them out for him to choose. He does and chows down the salty goodness of Cool Ranch Doritos.

As we watch the movie, my gaze switches from staring at Austin to the sewn tapestry reading, "Fore Play." I point and ask, "How come here it is spelled F-O-R-E, and at school, it's F-A-I-R?"

He laughs and leans forward. "Senior prank."

My eyebrows raise. "Really?"

"It was during my freshman year. 'Fair Play' is our school's motto, the golden rule if you will. So, a bunch of the seniors screened the special font, framed about twenty copies, and displayed them everywhere in the building. It took about two hours to notice that *every* sign was now risqué. Some teachers loved it"—he points to the glass casing—"while others did not."

He stares at me, like he's expecting me to laugh, possibly snort, but I can't. I force a chuckle and turn to face *The Wedding Planner*. We continue to eat as much as we can until our munching stops. Then Austin turns down the volume so it's barely audible. "Remember on the first day of school when Greg told you to smile more?"

I nod. Of course I remember. I insulted Greg before I realized how I broke the popularity-codes' rules.

"How...how come you don't? I mean, I don't think I've heard you laugh before. Like, really, *really* laugh."

That's because I haven't laughed in months. I used to be the bubbly, happy-go-lucky girl who could create this sense of ease just with a curl of my lips. But that was before.

So, I hold my breath and shut my eyes. "I can't laugh." My eyes open and lower to the rug. I assume he would scoff, roll his eyes, and possibly leave Tori's house. However, when I raise my eyes, he grins and rubs his hands together.

"Challenge accepted."

"I didn't say *you* couldn't make me."

"You might as well have."

His smirk becomes wider and wider, yet my mouth's edges don't move. I'm so confused; sure, we may have had our moments, especially at the museum, but still. Why does he want me to laugh? Why is he flirting, if he is? And why— "Why do you care?"

I almost tell him, "Never mind," when he says, "Everyone deserves a good laugh." That phrase can be taken in many ways with a chuckle or an exclamation point. But his smirk morphs into something more genuine, sincere, kind.

"Okay," I say, "but we need some ground rules. Number one, no tickling. That's basically cheating."

"Got it."

"Rule number two, I can scoff or smile, even chuckle. You have to make me full-out laugh. Like pee-my-pants-I-can't-breathe."

"Understood."

"And rule number three, I hate fart noises, so if you bring your elbow to your mouth, you're disqualified." Austin snaps his fingers while I walk over to him and stick out my hand. "Deal?"

"Deal."

I return to my seat and cross my legs. Austin stares at the ceiling, my guess is he's contemplating how he will pull this off.

"Okay," he says. "A guy walks into a bar—"

"Nope. Has to be clean. And we all know 'a guy walks into a bar' only ends in racism, sexism, or derogatory nonsense."

"You're making this difficult."

"Oh, believe me, I know."

I can't tell if I'm flirting or if he is.

"Okay, what game do the Greeks play? *Hydra*-go-seek!" It must be the puzzled look I give him that causes a soft sigh. "You know, *hydra,* giant sea monster? Nine heads? It's in a Greek mythology book." I'm wondering if he's a nerd or not. "I mean, my *dad* likes that kind of thing. But me? Nope...Nope, nope, nope."

Although I nod, his geeky side is shown. I like it.

"April showers bring May flowers, and what do May flowers bring?" He claps and presents jazz hands. "Pilgrims!"

I snort and flip my ponytail.

"You never said I couldn't tell a dad joke."

"True."

He leans forward, as do I. The curl of my lips turns into a wide smile, and he reciprocates. "What do you call a fish with no eyes?"

At the same time, we say, "Fsh."

"That was one of my best tricks." I wiggle my eyebrows and lean back. However, Austin's face turns stern, like the fact I knew the answer made this silly little game more serious.

"Austin isn't my name," he says, and I tilt my head. "Austin is my middle name, but on the first day of eighth grade at Hawken, I begged the dean to change it."

"How come?"

He stares into my eyes. "As a kid, my name was one reason I got made fun of. That, my crooked teeth, and my *resemblance*"—he uses air quotes—"to Jackie Chan." He stares at the ceiling and then returns to my face. I scoot to the edge of the chair.

"I needed a fresh start at Hawken School. New clothes, new style, new teeth." He smiles wide, and damn, that is some gorgeous orthodontic work. "And a new name. Or middle name, but still." He breathes in, as do I. My heart pounds louder than his. "I've...I've never told anyone this before, including Troy."

"Then why me?" The words fly out of my mouth, like I can't control myself.

"You said you can't laugh. Well, I'll tell you what my real name is." I wait, and he fills the air with suspense. He knows I want to hear it. Before this moment, I wasn't feeling anything, almost numb. So, the fact anyone can do that to me is surprising.

"I'll tell you. I will. It's, well—"

"Spill it out!" I scream, and then I cover my mouth. I'm about to apologize when he closes his eyes.

"Alvin."

There's a beat of silence, and my grin turns into a scoff. "Like...like the chipmunk?"

"Yep, that's why I got made fun of; because of a stupid rodent."

"Did they ever go 'ALVINNN'?"

"Constantly."

I suck in my lips and try as hard as I can not to giggle. "Did Simon make fun of you, too?"

The Night at Times Square

His smile is wiped. "Fleetwood, stop it."

I giggle. "At least your middle name is not Theodore because, oh gosh, if you were fat, I can only imagine the *torture* you'd be put under."

"Rhiannon, stop."

Then, I burst into laughter. The fact he's acting so serious makes me giggle even harder. My obliques, my stomach, and my back hurt. But at this point, I'm not laughing at Austin's real name; I'm laughing and crying and sobbing from the tiniest detail that I couldn't laugh before.

And it feels so, *so* good.

At one point, I giggle so much I fall onto the carpet and literally roll on the floor with my eyes closed. "It's-it's-it's not you I-I-I'm la-la-laughing at." I can't breathe, and I can sense Austin lying down beside me, his hand holding my side. But what surprises me is how I'm not pulling away. As I continue to pulse my body, I move closer, and slowly, I can breathe and relax.

We lie like this for a while, him stroking my puffy sweatshirt. Austin has no idea why I couldn't laugh, why I froze in the gymnasium, why I took Troy to the side during lunch. With such a small gesture, Austin gave me the ultimate freedom.

Then I open my eyes and touch his soft cheek. Unlike Xavier, Austin's face is smooth, although it was well past five o'clock. He closes his eyes and gives a soft moan. When he opens his eyes, he smiles, and this time with his orthodontic teeth.

"Thank you," I whisper. "Seriously, you don't know how much that meant."

He has to be puzzled, but he nods. "You're welcome."

His eyes drift to my lips, and he leans forward. My eyes grow wide. I scramble, wiping the soot from the ashes off my sweatpants.

"I-I'm tired." Lie number one. "I-I-I have to go to bed before my aunt yells at me." Lie number two. "Besides, I need a good night's sleep since I have a test tomorrow." And lie number three. I don't know why, but I'm jittery, my hands shake at my side, and despite the warm fire on an early October night, I shiver.

What is wrong with me?

"I'll see you in class, then," he says and hovers for a hug, but stops and leaves, not remembering his jacket. I scurry to the small window next to the door and pull open the curtains. I stare at his walk, skipping down the miniature staircase and breathing into his hands to keep warm. He stops moving and glances at the house. I thought he might be upset because I ended our evening so abruptly. When he turns around, he has the biggest smile on his face.

He sees me. As he hops into his car, I close the shades, biting my lip. My smile may not be as wide as Austin's, but it's more significant.

Much more significant.

Chapter 14
Austin

"Please," I say and rub my eyes. After an hour of waiting in the main office, three interruptive phone calls, and twenty minutes of a lecture, my guidance counselor, Mrs. Bruno, isn't budging. All I'm asking for is a simple class switch! "It's *literally* moving to the next room, from Mr. S to Tor— I mean, Ms. Benner."

Raising her eyebrows, she jots down some notes. "And how does that make you feel?" she asks in a monotone voice.

I lie on the full couch. "The first term hasn't ended yet. I still have two weeks before our classes are locked." I sit up and sink into the couch with my posture going astray. "So? Can I *please* switch?"

Of all the guidance counselors in all the schools, Mrs. Bruno had to walk into mine.

She remains calm, and a slight smile comes on her face. "Why do you want to switch?"

"I need some challenging courses." I practiced my speech in the car so I could remain calm, keep eye contact, and make her believe the biggest lie. "Photography and drawing, those courses are somewhat boring, to be frank. I need a place where I can *thrive*, so I can *grow* as an artist and a person." I straighten my back, widen my smile, and bat my eyes, hoping that will win her over.

But for the first time, she smirks. "That's not the *real* reason you want to switch, is it?" She closes her notebook and slides it into her desk's drawer. "I'll tell you what. I will switch your classes *if* you tell me the truth."

My mouth flies open and my knee bounces vigorously. My hand pushes my hair back on my forehead. *Tell her the truth? Are you serious?* There is no way I'll—

"I slept with my best friend's girlfriend." The words come out of nowhere, and staring at Mrs. Bruno, her mouth catches flies, too. "But to be honest, I thought they had broken up. It's not an excuse, though. I'm trying to be the bigger person and leave her toxic environment behind. I need a fresh start." I should ask to switch out of Mr. Lane's class too, or at least change groups, but being with Rhiannon is good for me.

Mrs. Bruno removes her glasses. "Why didn't you say so?"

She picks up the phone and dials the secretary's number.

As she hangs up, she slides out of her rolling chair and stands. "Follow me." We walk through the hallway, through the lounge area, and to the art studio. She halts her high heeled walk and knocks on Mr. S's door. He immediately answers her.

The Night at Times Square

"This is a surprise," he says, and out of the corner of his eye, he sees me. "Something wrong?" While they converse, I peek into the classroom and notice Jessyka glaring my way. She chews her gum to cover up the stench of cigarettes. With the tilt of her head, she smirks and waves me in.

Not today, toots.

Mr. S pats me on the shoulder, and my focus is back to the adults. "You always were the most animated kid here, but I understand why you want to leave." My face draws pale.

"You-you do?" I ask with a tiny squeak at the end of the sentence.

He nods. "You want to be bold! Daring! You need Ms. Benner to show you the way! Have you ever used a potter's wheel?"

I sigh, relieved that not *everyone* knows about what happened. I can feel Jessyka's stare burning into my neck, but I won't let her win.

"Actually, no." I grin. "I never had the pleasure of having Ms. Benner as a teacher."

"You'll like her."

After we shared a handshake, I follow Mrs. Bruno into the art teacher's room. In between the two art rooms, there's a little office where Mr. S hangs his sweatshirts and Ms. Benner her coat. They must answer emails on their computers, and one monthly calendar hangs on the wall. When I'm about to push through the door to enter the art room, I stop and stare at the beige backpack on the floor and smile. That must be Rhiannon's.

"Ms. Benner?" Mrs. Bruno knocks and pushes the

door open. My mouth hangs. I've never been in this classroom before with four potter's wheels, three kilns, and five tables. There are hundreds or even thousands of art pieces, some finished, some halfway done. A giant fluorescent Marilyn Monroe hangs above the back of the room.

Mrs. Bruno smiles as I close my mouth.

"You have a transfer student from Mr. S's class. Do you know Mr. Chang?" She presents me to Tori.

"Of course." Her smile widens. "Take a seat." I turn around and wave goodbye to Mrs. Bruno. While Tori describes the different clay glazes, my eyes search for a stool, half of the class members I don't recognize because they're junior or sophomores or both. On the right, Greg sits next to—

Shit.

I pause my steps, and Troy turns around. "You've *got* to be kidding me," and he doesn't lower his voice.

"Strong." She snaps her fingers. "Please pay attention."

As she continues her lesson, I glance at each table and do a double take, a smile creeping on my face. Rhiannon sits alone in the far back corner, blares music in her headset, and doodles in her notebook. I don't think she realizes I'm here. When I sit down, she gives me a side-eye until it becomes clear who is sitting next to her. She lowers her headphones around her neck.

"What are you doing here?" Her warm voice is calm and effortless, and damn, it takes every strength in my power not to stare at her lips.

"Need a fresh start," I whisper. Our elbows touch. I

The Night at Times Square

don't know if she feels it considering the layers of fabric on her arm, but my bare joint grows goosebumps. Turning her notebook page, she draws dots, about ten by ten. Once she's complete, she connects two and hands me her pencil, nudging me to do the same.

We play the dot game when Tori lays a piece of clean paper in front of me. "Do you want one?" she asks her niece. She shakes her head, turns the page, and starts to draw again.

With an hour left in class, I sketch from my imagination. Maybe I'll sculpt the human figure, similar to *The Thinker,* or a sculpture of my idol Michael Phelps. It's been fifteen minutes, and I filled up the entire paper. When it's time to pick an idea, I turn to see her paper, frowning. She just doodles.

"Fleetwood." I point to her paper. "Those aren't ideas."

She smirks. "Thank you, Captain Obvious." Her hand lowers to the notebook, and she glances up. "That's the beautiful thing about being related to Tori. No matter what I create, she'll give me an A." She chuckles and continues to doodle. As I peer at Tori, she stares at her niece. I remember her telling me Rhiannon had potential; she just needs a little push.

My eyes wander around the classroom. Two boys finish cleaning the potter's wheel. I leap out of my chair, and Rhiannon purses her lips. "What are you up to, Chang?" I hold my outstretched hand, encouraging her to follow, yet she doesn't budge. I bring my hand to my side.

"I've only seen people use the potter's wheel on YouTube," I say, and she snorts. "Have you ever done it?"

Her eyes draw to the wheel and stare at the blank base. For about thirty seconds, she closes her eyes and repeatedly presses the invisible foot pedal. Her fingers shake, and as I peer at her lips, the top bites the bottom. She flutters her eyes and blinks. "No, I haven't," and she continues drawing.

Rhiannon just needs a little push.

I place my hand again, this time, in between her paper and her face.

"You really are persistent, aren't you?"

"I'm actually not...Most of the time."

She gives a slight eye roll and a sigh, but when she realizes I'm not going anywhere, she hops out her chair and follows me to the opposite side of the art room. Although I focus straight forward, Troy's stare might have daggers in it.

We place our notebooks on both stools so that we've claimed the potter's wheels. Once we run water and cut our clay slabs, we sit across from the other. Rhiannon wets the tile center and looks up. "Do we need smocks?"

"You're right," I say and stand. As she's about to join me, I shake my head. "I'll get it for you." She lowers on to the stool. I jog to the smocks and grab two of them off the rack. After I turn, Troy is right there, inches from my face.

"Why the hell are you here?" His voice is cold, his fist tightening. I close my eyes. Is he gonna punch the other eye this time? "Well? I'm waiting."

"I'm sorry, I asked to get switched from Mr. S to this one because—" I pause and gaze up. "Anyway, I forgot you're in this class."

The Night at Times Square

Troy scoffs and tosses the air back to me. "Just stay away from me," and he stomps off. Once he sits down, I can breathe again, my shoulders relax, and my back hunches.

With the apron's strings dangling on the walk to the potter's wheel, I untie the fabric until I drop both to the floor. Rhiannon's sweatshirt sleeves are rolled up. The front of her sweatshirt is covered in dry clay. She effortlessly dips her delicate fingers into her plastic cup and switches the speed on the wheel.

While I lean against the wall, she concentrates, sticking her tongue out to the side. Her clay is immaculate as the slab turns into a pot. The thickness of the pot's sides are spot on, and she raises the vase slightly, the walls coming up to create intricate details. As she dabs some more water, she slows the wheel down and adds design features. A few spectators gather around her. One student whispers, "Holy shit."

But Rhiannon tunes out everything except the vase. I would bet that if there was a fire drill, she'd stay right where she is.

Tori's gentle hand taps me on my shoulder. "I knew it," she says.

Rhiannon stops, sucks in her belly, and blinks a few times. After she looks up, her cheeks redden as she stumbles out of the potter's wheel. She stares at her piece of clay and collapses the vase against itself.

"I'm-I'm sorry," and she removes her sweatshirt and tosses it on the floor: the muscularity of her arms, the pronounced collarbone, the length of her neck. Her T-shirt has a picture of a pipe, and written are the words,

"Ceci n'est pas une pipe" over her breasts. "Do you have an extra sweater?" she asks Tori.

She nods, and Rhiannon slams Tori's office door.

I stare where she stood, wondering who this girl is. Her aunt is an excellent sculptor, and I knew Rhiannon loves—*loved*—photography. But I just assumed she couldn't go above and beyond the normal expectation of art.

She's incredible.

I sit in front of the office door, mindlessly texting and scrolling through random social media sites. I type the words on Rhiannon's T-shirt in Google translator: "This is not a pipe." Clearly, it is, but I'll ask her what it *really* means. As the bell rings, I jump and pace. The knob turns, and my heart pounds against my lungs, tossing my stomach. However, it's Mr. S.

"She already left," he says with a weak smile. "Wearing *my* sweatshirt."

Once I reach the cafeteria, I forget about my lunch and walk toward Rhiannon's spot. I don't sit down. A smirk appears on her face.

"So, 'This is not a pipe'?" My cheeks hurt from smiling so much. "Please, *please* explain."

Rhiannon jumps down and holds the bottom of the Cleveland Cavaliers sweatshirt. With a deep breath, she pulls it off. I catch the glimpse of skin under her shirt.

"Ceci n'est pas une pipe," she says and points to herself. "It says that because it's *not* a pipe, rather it's a *drawing* of a pipe." I chuckle and nudge her, noticing how her arm grows goosebumps the second our skin collides.

"Fleetwood, about today...in art," I start. She adds her

sweatshirt back to her attire. I take a deep breath before questioning when someone plops in the chair next to me and sighs. Brielle's not exactly my biggest fan in the world, but she's one of Rhiannon's friends. Smiling, I give my hand for Brielle to shake.

She gives me a head nod, but as she opens her lunch bag, she grabs the tuna sandwich and whispers under her breath, "Dipshit."

Rhiannon tries not to laugh and shoves her granola bar in her mouth.

"Nice talking to you, too," I say and turn to an empty seat at a different table.

"Why don't you sit with us?" Rhiannon asks, and I spin around. She's looking at me, so is Brielle.

"Only if I'm welcome."

The ball is in her court as me and Rhiannon eagerly wait for her answer. Once Brielle nods, I drop my backpack and sit across from the two girls.

After practice, I'm finally home. This is my routine: shoes off, backpack down, television on, and into the kitchen for dinner. I grab a plate and serve buffet style, picking up the chicken, broccoli, and penne.

Yet, when I'm about to leave the kitchen, I stop. Over and over again, day after day, each family member eats dinner alone, Dad standing in the kitchen, Mom sitting in her office, and me lounging in the living room.

That *was* part of my routine, except I don't want it to

be anymore.

While I sit at the table and eat, Dad's stare burns my back. As Mom runs down the stairs, she halts abruptly. "What's wrong?" she asks, holding the back of her hand to my forehead. "Fever? Flu? Covid?"

"I just want to eat here," I say and shrug my shoulders. "That's all."

She stares at me and smacks her lips. *Please, Mom, come join me. It'll be so much fun eating a delicious meal made by someone else in the awkwardness of dinner.* After she grabs her plate, she stops and contemplates, glancing at me and at the stairs, where she has a lot to do in her office.

Mom doesn't choose me.

I sigh and continue to eat while Dad talks on the phone. But then, he brings his plate over to the dining room table and stands there, lingering in the room. Although he hasn't said two words to me, he eats his entire plate rather than the usual half.

Baby steps, Chang, baby steps.

The next day, I skip before school practice and sit next to Rhiannon, or what will become her seat. I sit in Mr. Lane's class, dwindling my thumbs and constantly glancing at the clock. The second hand makes a loud *Tick! Tick! Tick!*, and as the minute hand moves, I grow eager, grow nervous, and grow fidgety compared to my usual self. I haven't been able to stop thinking about the creation on the potter's wheel and how easy Rhiannon made it seem.

Just when I pull out my phone, Rhiannon appears, stops moving, and blushes. "You skipped practice," she says, not asking.

"Ye-yeah. I did."

"What's wrong?"

"Art class, I..." It's my turn to redden and begin to watch the one tiny ant crawl near my sneaker. "I wanna know. But only if you want to tell me. Otherwise, we can have a debate on who is the best actress in Hollywood."

"Meryl Streep, of course."

I chuckle and turn beside me. Carefully, she places her beige backpack down and turns her chair so we sit side by side.

"If you couldn't tell, it wasn't my first time using the potter's wheel." She lowers her gaze and picks her fingernails. "I took a pottery class early junior year and loved it. I signed up to take Pottery 2. But—" She stops abruptly, breathes in, and stares at me. "I've...I've had no desire to create art, so..." She fades into the distance and brings up another wall again.

"I'm so sorry for pushing you, I—"

"No!" She laughs. "Don't apologize! I should be thanking you." When she peers downward, I do the same. Her hand clasps over mine, and we both freeze, wanting or *needing* to hold the other one's hand.

Once Mr. Lane opens the door, we separate, and Rhiannon holds her hands beneath her seat.

"Anyway," she says with a smirk and looks up. "Don't think it's gonna be the usual thing, okay, Chang? Doodling is fine with me." Unzipping her backpack, she reaches inside and pulls out a novel. She starts to read, but peeks at me. "For now."

"For now..." My lips curl. "I'll take that."

For the next thirty minutes, we secretly flirt. I mimic

the crossing of her legs, and she mocks the constant leaning back of my chair. At one point, I hold her chair at a forty-five-degree angle, and she shrieks *really* loudly. I bring her chair down on solid ground, both of us bursting into laughter.

"Ahem," Mr. Lane coughs, but I'm still chuckling.

Rhiannon leans toward me. I can smell her strawberry shampoo. "You're gonna get me in trouble," she whispers, brushing her hand against my arm. "What's next? Skipping class? Only people who didn't believe in the *importance* of education skip school." Then, she sits back in her chair with her eyes not leaving mine.

Yep, she's definitely flirting.

The bell rings. The announcer says, "Please rise for the pledge of allegiance." Rhiannon shoots up before anyone else and recites the pledge, loud and bold. She turns around and sees me trying so hard not to laugh. She steps back and nudges my arm. I turn red and wonder, *Why doesn't she keep her hand there?*

As she sits facing forward, her mouth gapes, and she turns a ghostly white. Her breathing becomes deep. I bring myself forward, but she shakes her head and hides behind her copy of *Macbeth*. I'm about to say something when Mr. Lane claps twice. Everyone silences.

"Ladies and gentlemen," Mr. Lane says. "We have *another* new student, today!" He turns to face the new student: fair skin, nose and ear piercing, lanky with a little belly falling over his khakis, and Slytherin sweatshirt over a polo. His glasses constantly fall from the bridge of his nose, and his brow has a permanent snarl that says, "I'm better than you."

While Mr. Lane questions where this guy lived, hobbies he partakes, sports he plays, and his favorite author, I grin and glance at Rhiannon. Yet she sinks lower into her chair. What is going on with her?

"Well, even though the only books you've read are by J.K. Rowling," he says and frowns, while half the class giggles, "we are happy to have you join the Hawken School family. I introduce—" He holds his breath and means to be suspenseful. When no one is gripping their chairs, Mr. Lane sighs. "Finley...Finley Duffy."

Chapter 15
Rhiannon

This can't be happening.

The second I see him, I go numb, ringing in my ears, sweating palms, and shaking fingertips. Although Austin talks to me, I stare at Finley. He still looks similar, yet different. He pierced his nose and cartilage, got a snake tattoo along the forearm, and his gut tells me he still drinks. But as he glances in my direction, he doesn't recognize me.

Thank goodness.

Since the last time I saw him, I chopped off my hair to shoulder length and dyed it a more natural color instead of the highlights I used to have. Plus, I've lost thirty pounds, even if I don't show it off because of my baggy clothing.

Mr. Lane introduces Finley. He pulls an ear bud out and waves once. He smiles for a moment, but then he returns to his stern face. "You can sit in the back next to Jessyka." When my eyes follow his path, Finley drops his

The Night at Times Square

mouth and shakes her hand, his eyes moving to her breast.

A true connection, for sure.

"I love your accent," she says.

He chuckles. "Why, thank you. I've been perfecting it since I was a young lad."

Jessyka giggles at a deafening volume, causing the entire class to turn around. While Mr. Lane reviews the difference between past participle and perfect participle, she chews her gum louder and louder, laughs when it's appropriate, and as Finley rolls up his sleeves, strokes his hairy arm.

"Where'd you get that?" She holds his arm and traces his tattoo.

"Have you ever seen *Harry Potter?*"

I roll my eyes and face forward. He used to be fascinated by the *Harry Potter* book series, and during sophomore year, he claimed his hero to be Draco Malfoy. He couldn't wait to turn eighteen and get a Dark Mark tattoo.

"So," I hear Finley from behind. "Who should I get to know around here?" My heartbeat quickens as I sink in my chair and lower my head. *This is it, Rhiannon. Jessyka will say something about you, and he'll put two and two together.*

"There's no one here but me." Jessyka inches her way, practically on top of his chair.

He chuckles. "Yeah, that's what I thought." He scoots his chair closer to her if it's possible, whispering, "Want to give me a tour, then? 'Cause I'd hate to get lost on my first day."

Apparently, Sadie is *completely* out of the picture.

Jessyka and Finley continue to flirt, and I practice my grammar, remaining silent the rest of the class until it ends.

Then, I bolt out of there.

All day, I check to make sure Finley isn't in any of my classes. He struggles in math and science, so having honors in those subjects is a blessing. When it comes time for lunch, I sit in the bathroom stall and wait around till it's time for my last class. However, as I walk into my last block sculpture, Finley is there.

I sneak through the stools, the pottery benches, and in Tori's office. After I shut the door, I sit in her chair, lean my head against my knees, and breathe, breathe, breathe.

This can't be happening.

Well, I started to believe a new, fresh beginning was all I needed. I have friends here, two or three, but still. I was going to be happy. But now? Now I'm not so sure. Maybe I'll return to my online schooling, graduate with my GED, and—

Knock, knock, knock. My head shoots up. Should I hide? Should I run? Or should I just do nothing?

"It's me." I exhale, and my blood pressure decreases the second Austin beckons. "Can I come in?" I raise, trudge through the mounds of loose-leaf paper, and open the door. He stands erect, but he's jittery. His hair looks greasy, like he's been sweating too much today. "Can I talk to you?"

As I glance at Finley, he already made a ton of friends, one of them being Troy. I nod and close the door as soon as Austin enters. When I glance at him, a worried crease appears between his eyes. He presents me with Tori's chair, and I take it. I didn't realize how much effort it took to not buckle my knees.

Austin paces back and forth, my eyes following each

The Night at Times Square

step. "Did...did I do something wrong?"

I'm taken aback, literally leaning backwards with eyes blinking. Before I answer, he continues.

"I mean, you were super quiet in homeroom and English, and I couldn't find you at lunch." He stops pacing and laughs. "I can be stupid, idiotic, and even an asshole at times. But something told me it wasn't all my fault, right?" With a deep sigh, he brushes his hair back. "What I'm trying to ask is—"

My eyes light up; he's worried about me?

"Austin." I stand and touch his warm hand. He gazes into my eyes, and I blush and glance away to my sneakers. "I..."

Should I tell the truth? I should be able to confide in him, like how he confided in me about his real name. But I can't.

I force a chuckle and step backward. "I'm just not feeling well, that's all. I don't have a license, and my aunt can't leave today. Some faculty meeting, or whatever." I'm sort of telling the truth because Tori does have a meeting, and seeing Finley for the first time in ten months makes my stomach hurt.

A moment of silence fills the atmosphere. I swallow hard and pick at my nail. When I look up, Austin outstretches his hand. "I got just the thing." I stare at his palm and hover mine over his.

But hastily, I whip my hand behind my back and say, "Let's go." All I need is fresh air, or a cup of soup and saltines. No matter what, putting a hall in between Finley and me sounds like a dream.

Austin pulls the door open and motions me to enter the art room. "Hey, Tor— I mean, Mrs. Benner?" Tori turns around with a smile. Everyone's working on their clay pieces, and most of the kids, like Finley and Troy, listen to their headsets. "Rhiannon and I are going to the cafeteria. We'll only be gone for like twenty minutes." She nods and resumes helping a student with his sculpture.

The hair on my neck stands. Someone's eyes bury into my back, and goosebumps crawl all over my body, even though I have on two layers of clothing. Like an invisible force that I can't describe, I turn around: Finley. As my heart quickens, he scans me and stares into my eyes. A frown forms, and like the snake tattooed on his arm, he tilts his head with his tongue slightly out.

"Rhie—" Austin tries to call me, but I pick up the pace.

Out of the art room, I hault. The hallway sways, and I cling to the side of the wall. Am I going to pass out? Once I move past the tissue-paper dress, I slide down the wall and hide my face. My head pounds, the front of my skull hurts, and my stomach shoots against my back and through my throat.

Someone sits next to me and hovers his hand over my shoulder. At last, my head rests in Austin's nook. He wraps my body with his. I've never noticed how massive his arms are, or how large they are compared to mine. For a few moments, I shut my eyes and simply breathe. The goosebumps disappear, my neck hairs subside, and my hands stop shaking.

When I open my eyes, his hand covers mine. I look up, and although he doesn't know what's going on, he's calm. My eyes water, because ever since the whole fiasco with Xavier, I never thought a person would take care of me.

"Do you feel better?" he whispers. I intertwine my hands with his. I don't notice the few people roaming through the halls or the assembly happening in the nearby auditorium. I can breathe, like I've just started running all over again. He does, too, and slowly, he picks up his shaky hand and lays it on my cheek. I gaze into his eyes and somehow, nod, a sheepish smile growing on my face. Is he going to kiss me?

Then, the auditorium doors swing open, and the students pour out. The number of people in that cramped hallway is claustrophobic. Austin jumps to his feet and helps me up. "Well," he says in that Austin way, "maybe you just need some soup, saltines, and a large glass of water."

He nervously chuckles and waves me over to follow.

Once we reach the cafeteria, we sneak back behind the ovens and into the cafeteria workers' office. A lady who is always smiling looks up. "What a surprise!" she says and jogs to Austin to embrace him. She wears a black shirt with a brightly colored font reading, "Autism Awareness." This woman's smaller than me, thinner than me, and has shorter hair than I do. She glances in my direction.

"Oh, I'm sorry," Austin says. "This is Allison."

We shake hands, but she stares at him with wide eyes. When they don't realize I'm watching, she mouths the words, "Another girl?" and raises her eyebrows. He blushes in an instant. Before she has the chance to say, or mouth, anything else embarrassing, he switches the subject.

"Do you have a cup of chicken noodle soup? With saltines? I think I saw some yesterday." He looks toward her lunch bag. She pulls out a large Tupperware container.

"You don't mind if this is heated by a microwave, do you?" she asks while walking to her office.

I glance at him and then at her. "You shouldn't give up your lunch for me."

"I don't mind at all!" She turns around. "It's Friday, and that means I have to go to my second job in twenty minutes at Austin's house." I must give her a puzzled face because she laughs. "Twice a week, I clean the Changs' house and cook dinner for three nights in preparation. They are very generous, don't worry about it."

She pulls out a container of chicken noodle soup, lays it flat in the microwave, and presses the button for two minutes on high. We each grab a tray, a pack of saltines, and two waters. As I walk to the cafeteria, I see four other students studying.

Austin and I sit at our usual high table and eat our food. Although my insides are wonderfully warm, my fingers still shake, so a little of the soup falls to the table. I don't look up, but somehow, he senses something's up.

"Feeling better?" he asks.

I'll be better once I get home.

"Yeah." I force a smile. "Thank you."

It's silent again, the heating vent turns on, and warm air is right above my scalp. I close my eyes. "What's your favorite vacation?" Austin asks. My eyes fly open.

"What?"

"Of all the places you've been to, which was your favorite?" His smile makes me turn to Jello as he leans forward. "Listen, I can tell you're not okay, and I know it's none of my business. It's just—"

"Cape Cod," I say, quickly. "My favorite vacation

spot was Cape Cod."

His cheeks twitch. "Really?"

"Yes." I mimic his actions with the curve of my face growing. "Is that amusing?"

"N-no. Not at all."

I sit back in my chair and slurp some more soup. The shake of my hand subsides, my shoulders relaxing. With one hand on each side of the bowl, I gulp the soup down and slouch in my chair, my feet dangling high above the floor.

"Second question," Austin says, "and this one might be tricky. What's your favorite memory?"

I ponder for a moment because there are so many options. The first time Xavier and I kissed, or when Sadie and I skipped school and got free matinee tickets for *The Hunger Games* marathon. Or even my first day of school at the Bronx High School of Science, when everyone greeted me with open arms.

But then I think of another memory.

"I was five years old. My parents took me to an art museum. I...I remember how big everything was. We wandered around for hours until we entered a photography exhibition. At one point, I stopped walking and stared at this photo. It was of the Golden Gate Bridge, fireworks in bright color, but everything else was black and white. Even though I was five years old, I was so moved, I cried."

I chuckle. "My parents were so embarrassed, apologizing to all the guards. But one of them, an older gentleman, smiled, and said, 'If a photograph touched your daughter's soul, then great things will come from her.'"

I haven't thought about that photograph since the Cleveland Art Museum, when Austin showed me a photograph, even if he hadn't heard my story.

As I stare at Austin's hand, it's inches from touching mine. This time, he swallows and says, "I didn't know you were so passionate about photography."

My hand slides onto my lap, my gaze following. Should I tell him the truth about everything that happened in New York? My eyes shoot up and look straight at him. Out of the corner of my eye, a bead of sweat falls from his hair.

"Austin," I say. "I need to tell you some—"

"Rhiannon?" a voice asks, one that isn't Austin. My blood is drained from my face, and I close my eyes. Maybe if I can't see him, then he'll walk away. My whole body shakes. A hand touches my arm, stroking it, although I still quiver. When I open my eyes, Austin's eyes grow wide.

"Is that really you?" No one will forget a British accent in the middle of Ohio, that's for sure.

"He's from our English class, right?" Austin glances behind him and then at me. "You guys know each other?"

I try to nod, try to say yes, try to do anything, yet I can't move. I stare at Finley as he grows closer. With only ten feet between us, I leap into the air and lean against the wall. He stops moving.

Somehow, I ask, "What are you doing here?"

Finley steps back, but his eye contact remains with me. "I was actually given the option of living with my dad or staying in New York, with Xavier. He begged his father to allow me to stay. I don't know, after everything that happened, I..." His voice trails into the distance, like it's too painful to mention what occurred between us.

"Anyway, I didn't recognize you. How much weight did you lose? You look great."

My throat swells and suffocates me, just like New Year's Day. A million questions come to mind. Why didn't you come to my defense? Why didn't you tell everyone about how much of a monster that guy had become? And why are you still his friend? However, my brain isn't working.

My breathing becomes rapid while Finley backs away. He doesn't leave, though. He has to be told to leave, still unable to decide on his own terms, searching for the best way out of anything. Then, I glance at Austin and hope for him to come to my defense. All he does is blankly stare with glaze over his eyes.

When I face Finely, I breathe in and notice another figure joining us. "Is something wrong?" Troy jogs over, and this time, he's standing between Finley and me. He whispers, "You okay?" I can't even make a cohesive sentence, and with a beat of silence, he steps in front of me. "You need to leave, *now.*"

Troy has a good four inches of height on the little man. Finley cowers beneath the other guy and backs up. He's about to exit the cafeteria when he spins around.

"I'm sorry," Finley blurts out. "I should have done something. When the police came to question me about New Year's Day, I told them Xavier and I fought, and it was mutual. I didn't press charges because, I don't know, we had been friends for so long."

Troy doesn't seem fazed by this new information because I must have told him *much* more than I anticipated. However, Austin's mouth drops.

"I only dated Sadie to make Xavier happy. A month

into our relationship, it ended, and the three of us went our separate ways. I couldn't tell you how they're doing if I tried." Finley seems genuine, like he's turned over a new leaf. He never was a bad guy, and if the circumstances were different, we'd probably be dating. "But, rumor has it, Xavier didn't pick Ohio State or NYU. He attends Cleveland State. But hey, Cleveland has like four hundred thousand people, right?"

He may be chuckling to lighten the mood, but there's nothing funny about living in the same area as the man who almost killed me.

The bell rings. The swarm of students fill through the cafeteria to reach the fireplace and exit the building. Troy steps back, and when Finley turns around, I grab his shoulder and stick my hand in front of him. He shakes it.

I watch Finley until he blends into the mob and disappears. Once I spot Troy, he gives me a single nod and looks behind me. As I turn around, I realize Austin never moved.

"You coming to practice?" Troy says this as a question, but Austin remains still, unmoving, and in a trance. "Chang?"

As if someone snapped their fingers, Austin shakes his head to clear his mind. He still looks into the distance and wobbles like he has been punched. Before following Troy, Austin reddens and says, "I'm sorry," and sprints away.

Chapter 16
Austin

As a warmup, some guys lift weights while others stretch, swim easy laps, or write a quick essay they forgot was due the next day.

Now, I shower.

The scalding water burns my face, my fingers tingle, and my neck blazes. I don't wash my hair or use soap, but just stand there, close my eyes, and let the water fall onto my bare skin. I try to meditate, wishing I'd forget about what happened between Finley and Rhiannon by erasing it from my memory. Yet it returns, and I have to analyze every detail.

After ten minutes, the hot water turns lukewarm. I turn it off and wipe my face with my hand. I slap my cheek a few times and concentrate on practice.

Rather than jog, or sometimes sprint due to my lack of punctuality, I mope, trudging toward the bleachers and sitting at the first available seat. Everyone's body is drenched, a sign that warmup already occurred. I place my towel next to me. "Glad you could join us, Mr. Chang," Coach Desjardins says. "What's your excuse this time?"

Rhiannon stared at me with fear written between her eyes, pleading for me to do something. But what did I do? I froze, my breathing was at a rapid pace, my heart skipping. The whole scene turned dimmer than before.

"Mr. Chang?" When I look up, everyone focuses on me. My heart pounds against my chest, my breath unsteady. I swallow, close my eyes, and breathe. As I open my mouth to say something sarcastic or even the truth, I become mute.

"He was with Ms. Benner," Troy quickly replies. "She wanted to discuss the proportions on his latest sculpture. I guess she thought it was impossible to have a penis *that* small." He forces a smirk. The guys laugh, and one junior slaps me on the back. Coach sighs and continues with the meeting.

Why would Troy make an excuse for me?

"Next week is against University School. The fastest swimmers in the league attend there, and their best swimmers compete with ours. Although they have an undefeated record, so do we." He rambles with enthusiasm. I try to listen and try to become engaged, but it's no use.

Rhiannon's fingertips shook. When she was about to say something, Troy stepped forward and stood between her and Finley. Her face and her shoulders relaxed, and she watched her new protector take over her defense.

Coach claps loudly. I flinch. "Let's get into the normal group." The team files out. I watch from the

The Night at Times Square

sidelines as they gather in a circle. Troy leads a team stretch, standing in the middle, and everyone else sprawls out. Once they switch stretches from their hamstrings to their quads, Coach snaps his fingers and beckons me to his side.

I force myself to stand. Although my legs quiver, I pretend to have the confident manner I always have. Coach sees right through me, though.

"I don't know what's going on with you today," he says, and when I open my mouth to tell him the truth, he raises his hand, "but I don't want to hear it. You can stay or leave. It's your choice."

I'm taken aback. Can't he tell how important this is to me? Sure, I slacked over the past three years, riding on pure talent with little effort, but still. This year, I've focused on speed, endurance, weight training, and worked my ass off.

Rather than saying that, my throat dries. When Coach breathes in to continue the lecture, I sprint on my toes to the furthest spot away from him.

After the group stretch, we're divided into teams of four, but the order is different; the anchors swim first. Once I hop onto the springboard, I add my goggles and nose piece and wait for the first call.

Cough...cough...COUGH!

When I turn to my left, Troy demonstrates the proper right-before-you-race stretches, the arm stretch, flap the wings, and reach for his toes. I want to be a fierce competitor and mimic him, yet I can't because there's too many things going on in my head. He stands straight and nods, almost encouraging me to do the stretches.

Reluctantly, I do them as the whistle blows. I bend down with one foot far behind my arms.

"Get set," Coach says. The six of us bend. When I peek at the opposite end of the pool, my face draws pale.

Rhiannon and Finley?

With a blink of my eyes, they vanish. I shut my eyes to help forget about what happened today and wait for the bell.

BEEP!

I leap into the pool, but rather than concentrating on my form, I just do the butterfly stroke. My mind tries to be clear, tune out everything except this race, *only* this race. I use workouts to lessen my stress level, and up until now, it has never failed me. Yet, my mind is forced to draw attention back to the cafeteria and the mistakes I made.

I shoulda protected her.

I shoulda stepped in front of her.

I shoulda asked Finley to leave.

But it was Troy who did that, not me. I close my eyes and swim, pushing through my arms on the front stroke and kicking whenever my arms move behind. Faster and faster I swim, and I realize I'm in the lead. Coach screams, "Keep going!"

It's no use, though. Rhiannon is all I can concentrate on. What exactly happened between her and Finley? What charges didn't he put on Xavier? Why was Troy stoic while I was blindsided? Did Rhiannon like him—like, *like him,* like him? The answers remain unknown. I'm pissed and frustrated and I shut my eyes tighter and tighter, hopefully pushing the thoughts to go away. But Rhiannon's eyes, the look behind them.

They read one thing: *failure*.

I failed her. No matter how I look at the whole situation, I failed. I couldn't protect her, couldn't demand that Finley leave, couldn't *save* her. My eyes sting as tears well up behind the goggles and I push myself to swim faster and push and push and—

I crash into the wall. My fingers slide in an awkward angle against my palm. My hand shoots pain to my wrist, and I immediately dive under the water. As I sink six feet down, I open my eyes and see the rest of the swimmers continue without stopping. Once I reach the bottom, I scream, so much my lungs and my throat hurt.

For about a minute, I sit on the bottom of the pool until my lungs burn from the suffocation. I can't stay underwater anymore, despite wanting to. I shoot up, leap out of the pool, and barge to the starting line.

Coach jogs to me and opens his mouth to speak, but I talk first. "No, everything is *not* okay," I snap and pound on the tile until I enter the locker room. I see my bag in front of a locker and lift it off the ground, slamming it on the concrete floor. A few items fall like contact solution, sneakers, and ripped jeans. As I kick all three, they slide through the aisle. That wasn't satisfying enough, though. I search for more things I can destroy—trash barrels, paper towels and tissues, sanitizer, liquid soap, and shampoo—but nothing helps.

Then, I sprint to the mirror, wind up my fist, and before I know what I'm doing, smash it against my hand. The entire mirror shatters, glass falling to the sink, countertop, and floor. When I stare at my hand, my knuckles are red on the bone while the surrounding area is yellow and blue. I open my palm. A piece of glass sticks out. I yank it and rinse the cut, wincing from the sting and the pool's wall. After I wrap an ACE bandage, I lean on my hand against the counter and lower my head. Water drips from my trunks and my hair, forming a tiny puddle.

Breathe, Austin, breathe.

Finally, I enter the pool, and as soon as I glance at Troy, he jogs toward me and says, "I left the last lane open for you." His hand hovers above my shoulder, but he lowers his hand to his side and walks to the rest of the team.

So, I do what Troy tells me to do: swim. I don't use goggles or time myself, I just freestyle, back and forth, back and forth, back and forth. At one point, practice ends, and everyone else leaves. However, I still swim until my fingers are pruny and my body's temperature drops. After I close my eyes and float, I turn right-side up and blink a few times.

Rhiannon?

She stands at the bench and walks toward me. With about five inches from the pool, she bends down and hovers her hand above the water. Her hand shakes, her skin turning paler than normal. She scrambles to her feet, runs back to sit on the bench, and holds her chest.

Is she afraid of water? Doesn't she know how to swim? Wait, wasn't she a competitive swimmer?

For the length of the pool, I doggy paddle while she stares. I hop out of the pool and sit next to her without grabbing a towel. I'm shivering, but it's no longer 'cause of the temperature.

"It's...it's why I don't swim anymore," she says. "It's

why I don't eat meat, and it's why I'm staying with Tori, in Ohio." She looks at me. Her hand hovers near mine.

"Because of Finley?"

She draws her hand on her lap and scoffs. "Believe it or not, he wasn't my biggest problem."

I place my hand on hers and squeeze it. She doesn't look at me, but she does blush. "Rhiannon," I whisper. "What happened?"

And then, she tells me.

```
January 3rd
 Hospital
11:00 a.m.
```

At eleven o'clock, the nurse walked in the hospital room, removed my IV, and patted me like a dog. "You're all set, little one," she said and slugged her way to the next room.

Was I still little?

Mom put on her coat while Dad rolled the wheelchair forward and back. I stood on the floor and wobbled two steps in my grippy socks. She guided me to him, and they each grabbed one of my hands, lowering me onto the cushion.

Before Dad moved us through the hospital, he clutched on the push handles. "Do you want to stay one more night? For observation?"

I wished I could smile, wished I could give him a reassuring laugh, wished I could crack a joke. But the only thing I mustered was, "The doctor said three days for a concussion is enough." Dad stared at me for a second and then pushed me out of the room.

The Night at Times Square

The wheelchair squeaked, and because of this, I bumped every three seconds. *Ga-Klunk...Ga-Klunk!...Ga-Klunk...!* I winced as we stopped at the front desk. A different nurse told my mother the instructions to wean me off the pain medication, although I rarely took it. Dad held my shoulder to encourage me that everything was going to be all right.

I doubted it.

Mom received some paperwork, jotted down a few notes, and gave her signature to the nurse. My mother turned around. I barely recognized her: unkempt hair, black circles beneath her eyes, sadness in her lips. Even though I'd been in and out of consciousness, now that I saw her, she looked like she lost five pounds.

Which, I'd also lost. I thought accomplishing my goal would do wonders for my self-confidence, but it did nothing.

After she stuffed the paperwork in her large purse, she put on a façade and asked, "Ready to go?" Her voice sounded weak and tired as she rubbed her eyes beneath her glasses. I wanted to say, "Of course, Mom," "I love you so much," or "Thank you for everything." However, I just nodded and slouched in my wheelchair.

Ga-Klunk...Ga-Klunk...Ga-Klunk...

The automatic doors swished open. My father halted my wheelchair. As my gaze remained down, I watched the weeds sprout between cracks on the sidewalk.

"What the hell are you doing here?"

My head shot up. All the blood from my head drained, and I wanted to vomit. Xavier looked as *wonderful* as Mom for his lips cracked along the smile lines. Dad let go of my chair and stomped his feet. Xavier stepped back on his toes, quiet like a phantom. "I-I-I know you don't want to see me," he said, cowering from my father.

"You're lucky Rhiannon didn't press charges against you. Do you realize that? You coulda been in jail!" The only reason for that was I just wanted to never see Xavier again, and I knew that wouldn't happen in a court battle.

"Please let me explain—"

"Did you strangle my daughter? Did you toss her on the brick floor? Did you almost *fucking* kill her?"

Xavier's eyes filled with tears, but he didn't say anything, only cleared his throat.

"That's what I thought."

I leaned toward the left side of the wheelchair, farther away from Xavier as Dad returned and rolled me down the sidewalk.

Two years and three months I've loved this man, two years and three months I adored him, two years and three months gone in one instant.

Once I hobbled from the wheelchair to the car, my fingers shook while I buckled myself in. Mom stared at me the entire time. I glanced at the driver's seat. Dad's fist tightened on the steering wheel, watching Xavier paced and carried a bouquet of roses, a box of chocolate, and an envelope with my cursive name.

Then I unbuckled myself, slid across to the driver's side, and placed my hand on top of Dad's. He spun around. Right now, a smile would cause pain in my mouth. My father's eyes shed many tears because being a great, wonderful dad meant being a protector, and he must have felt like he didn't accomplish that. But I was the idiot, not him. I laid my head on his hand, and he did the same. Part of me wished he would walk straight to Xavier and punch him in the face and groin, but part of me just wanted the entire thing to go away.

"He's not worth it," I whispered.

"Okay, Fleetwood." Dad kissed my hand. "Let's go home."

As we pulled into our driveway, he scurried to the passenger-side door and held it open for me. I glanced at my house, but it wasn't the same. The shutters and front porch were duller, the immaculate lawn dead, and my window's sheen faded.

With reluctance, I hopped out of the car and held Mom's arm all the way to the house, up the stairs, and into my bed. She tucked the blankets in and kissed my cheek. She was about to close door when she said, "Let me know if you need anything," leaving the door agape.

Three more days passed, yet the only thing I had done outside of sleeping was use the bathroom. The first time that I gazed into a mirror since the incident I drew pale: one eye swollen shut with blue coloring, three stitches on my lower lip, my neck bruised, and an ACE bandage wrapped around the top of my head. My one normal eye watered.

That's why there was a giant poster board covering the mirror.

As I lay in my bed, I heard a *Ring* at the main entrance.

Someone opened the door, and a high-pitch voice cheerily questioned both of my parents. A lower voice, must be Dad, said something muffled. The high-pitch voice laughed. There was a small conversation between the two.

"Please?" the high-pitch voice pleaded. "I have to see that she's okay."

With a sigh, Dad said something and walked away, probably caving or giving up. Many footsteps climbed the stairs. After a beat of silence, a knock was heard on my door. I didn't feel like answering anyone's beckon, so I shut my eyes to fall asleep.

"Rhiannon?" the voice asked over the creak of the opening door. Immediately, I sat up and barely recognized her. This highlighted-blond girl wore high heels, bangs, and a spring dress flowing slightly above her knees. She sheepishly smiled and drew pale once she saw my complexion.

I squinted and whispered, "Sadie?" She nodded. I leaped to my feet, ran to her, and squeezed while hysterically crying. I expected her to return the warm embrace, saying things like, "It's gonna be okay" and "We'll get through this."

But nothing came from her mouth.

Once I released her hug, we sat on the bed as I held her hand. "You didn't answer my calls. It went straight to voicemail," Sadie said. The crease of her brow deepened.

"The doctors said to wait a week. That's why I haven't been in classes." A slight pulse beat against my head. I rubbed my temple. "Besides, Xavier broke it when he..." I turned away. *Does she know? Did she hear what happened? Has she talked to Xavier?* No, no, that couldn't be

The Night at Times Square

it. He's probably expelled.

"Are you getting a new one?" Is she here to cheer me up? Did Mom call and tell Sadie what had occurred? Or maybe she brought the homework assignments I missed?

So, I just swung my legs back and forth against the bed. The hospital admission wristband hung on my arm days later. I glanced at her with those blue eyes. "How are you, really?" she asked me. She *had* to know. *Did she learn about it through school? Did Mom immediately inform her right when it happened? Or are there rumors already?*

I forced a laugh. "Awesome...Totally awesome."

Her stoic face remained. As she picked up her purse, she searched for objects, and pulled out two things. I expected to see some books or notebooks, but to my surprise, it was Maybelline and my necklace. I grabbed the giraffe and held her tight. Her two front paws were a dimmer brown, as if the giraffe had been scrubbed away for hours. I teared up as I asked Sadie, "Where did you get these?"

She fidgeted on my bed and lowered her head, unable to keep eye contact. "Xavier." I remained quiet and shifted my weight. Then she smiled and glanced up. "He feels terrible, absolutely terrible, Rhie. You should have seen him a few days ago...such a wreck. The only thing I could get him to eat was chocolate chip cookie dough ice cream," and she chuckled.

I frowned. *I don't care about how he's doing.* "You're...you're talking to him?"

"Of course. Why wouldn't I?"

My eyes widened. "Excuse me?"

"He's my friend, too." She tried to hold my hand, but

I snatched it away, sliding back to my headboard. "You *really* should talk to him. My boyfriend and I are worried about you two."

"Your boyfriend?"

Laughing, she nodded and said, "Finley," and rolled her eyes. "Duh!" She motioned behind the corner, and after a beat, he appeared. His nose was covered by a cast, his right arm was in a sling, and both eyes were so puffy they looked like he had been stung by a thousand bees. Compared to what he looked like, I just got a papercut. Finley gave a quick wave with his dominant hand and stepped back.

If I recall, he wanted nothing to do with her and made fun of her. It struck me as odd how one person can feel one day, and then do a one-eighty the next.

But that's what I did, wasn't it?

"I'm sorry about this," he said. "It was a...misunderstanding."

Misunderstanding? A misunderstanding is when students think they can't divide by a bigger number. A misunderstanding is when parents forget to pick up their kid from soccer practice because they thought it ended an hour later. And a misunderstanding is when two girls date someone at the same time and they didn't realize they fell for an asshole.

What Xavier did was *not* that.

"A misunderstanding," I repeated and glared at Finley. He grew paler than usual, inching his way to the door.

"What are you thinking?" Sadie asked.

Did Xavier tell Sadie exactly *what happened?* She must

not know; he probably told her I fell down the stairs.

However, when I was about to set the record straight, she whispered, "I know about his bipolar disorder." My mouth dropped to the floor. *He musta told her the watered-down version, about how he dialed nine-one-one, about how he rushed the paramedics to the door, about how he held my hand in the ambulance, despite the fact that no one was allowed in the vehicle.* "I know *everything*, Rhie."

I swallowed hard and cleared my throat. "You, you do?"

She nodded. "I guess some boys can't handle their liquor, amirite? I mean, come on. Why else would Finley have kissed you?" and she laughed. Finley just stood there with his eyes glued to the rug.

Sadie's words stung worse than any hornet. The fact she wasn't comforting me, the fact she was treating the whole situation like it was no big deal, the fact she was not by my side made me question *our* relationship.

"What are you thinking?"

My mouth remained shut. I wasn't thinking about Xavier or Finley or the hospital, I was thinking about my best friend being something I wasn't aware of. She was siding with the guy who nearly killed me. When she realized I wasn't talking, she stared out the window.

"He's outside, right now."

I spun around and narrowed my eyes. "Wha...what?"

"I knew your mom wouldn't let him in, and Xavier's afraid of your father, so..." She chuckled. "He doesn't want this thing between the two of you to be awkward at school."

A beat of silence passed. No *Just kidding* was uttered.

I brought my hand to my mouth because I didn't want to vomit. Once my bile settled, I glanced at her. "He's not expelled?"

"No?" She blinked, and a snarl crawled on her face. "Why would he be?"

"Cause he tried to—"

"It didn't happen on school grounds." Her voice was monotone, matter of fact, emotionless. My heart beat against my chest as my mind spiraled out of control. I hugged Maybelline to my knees and rocked back and forth, back and forth, back and forth.

Why wasn't he expelled?

Why wasn't he expelled?

WHY WASN'T HE EXPELLED?!

My tears fell to the comforter, my breathing quickened at breakneck speed, and the walls and ceiling and floor spun. I shut my eyes, hoping to calm myself.

Then Sadie scoffed. "You're being a little dramatic."

My eyes flew open, and suddenly, everything stopped moving. Her cold voice made me realize that this wasn't working. It doesn't matter the facts—I could sit here and tell her *my* side of the story—but she wouldn't care. I stared at my best friend one last time.

"Get out," I whispered and lowered my head. Even though she didn't quiver, Finley bolted out of my room, down the stairs, and probably out of my house.

She laughed. "Come on, Rhiannon—"

"Get out."

Sighing, she rolled her eyes. "You should talk to him, at least for closure." My blood boiled in my veins. This was my best friend. Sure, I had small acquaintances and could easily move over to a different group to hang out with. But what if they all flocked to Sadie, and left me behind? Was it really worth it starting over? "Rhiannon?"

I snapped.

"Get out!" I screamed and pointed to my door. "Get out, get out, get out!"

As I sobbed, she closed her mouth, stood up, and walked out of my life without a second thought. I held Maybelline in an attempt to make myself feel good, but it wasn't working. Not only was I betrayed by the guy I loved, I was betrayed by my best friend, too. Then again, hadn't I ditched Sadie often? A double standard? I was always canceling our plans without a second thought. That's why she didn't care about me, but rather switched to a different group of friends.

If the roles were reversed, would I have done the same?

Then I glanced at the floor where my necklace lay. After I tossed Maybelline, I picked up the necklace, walked toward the open window, and dangled the piece of jewelry. I heard the three of them, joking and laughing as if they'd been tight forever. Without a second thought, I tossed it outside and shut the pane, not watching to see where it landed.

Chapter 17
Rhiannon

It's a gorgeous, beautiful Saturday morning, and what do I do?

I pace, so much I think I'm going to end up walking through the floor and land in my aunt's kitchen. I stare at the cord phone and continue to walk back and forth in front of the mirror. On the dresser is Hawken's library copy of *Greek Mythology, for Beginners*. I slightly smile because I've been studying it, every once in a while.

Fine, every night before I fall asleep.

Shaking my head, I stare at the floorboards. Should I call Austin, or should I just wait to see him until Monday? I told Austin everything that night at Times Square: the ball dropping, late partying into the night, spending the morning with Finley, the disaster occurring, and leaving Sadie. Austin didn't know what to say or do. So, I sprinted out of the pool in fear of his reaction.

The sky turns into an ominous gray, and being the third weekend in October, the temperature drops from a

The Night at Times Square

nice sixty-five to thirty-eight.

Biting my nails, I stare at the phone, taunting me with its silly soundless ring. The butterflies of my stomach have returned, the flipping and somersaulting. But it's a good stomach pain because I was afraid I'd never feel it again. Last time, Xavier asked me out, took me to dinner, and kissed me first. I don't know why, but I want to explore someone on my own terms. What's better than asking someone else out?

Okay, it's not a *date* per se, just a casual getting-to-know-you. It's not a date, it's not...Not. A. Date.

With a deep inhale, I stop moving, pick up the phone, and dial his number. I only wait for two rings. "Austingoahead?" he greets with one word, followed by a yawn. When I open my mouth, no sound comes out, and no words form. It's like by the whisper of his voice, I turn to mush.

What is wrong with me?

"Hello?" he asks again.

I resume pacing, yank on the phone's cord, and drop it. *Shit*. Scrambling, I reach down to the ground, playing hot potato with the phone and hoping he hasn't hung up.

"H-hi, Austin," I stammer a little, *damnit*. "It's Fleetwood. I mean Rhiannon." I smack my head against my hand. Could I be any stupider?

He chuckles and says, "I expected a two-one-two number to be calling. Did you get a phone recently?"

"Don't laugh." I grin just talking to him. "But I don't have a cell phone. This is Tori's house." A beat of silence is passed between the two of us, creating nervous energy. "Hello?"

"Sorry. My mouth dropped. Come again?"

"I wanted a new start."

"I'm surprisingly jealous. I mean, up until this point, I'm rarely seen without it."

As we chuckle, the melodious laugh makes my knees quiver. But there it is again, the awkward silence. I can practically hear a pin drop.

"Well—"

I talk at the same time as him, and we both become quiet. "You go first," Austin says.

Closing my eyes, I blurt out, "Wanna go out?" At first, he didn't answer. Sweat falls from my brow. "I mean, I kinda sorta want to see the city, and when I woke up this morning, my aunt left, and I don't have many friends, well, one or two, but—"

"Rhiannon?"

I shut up, open one eye, and close my mouth.

"When should I pick you up?"

"Now? Well, like, fifteen minutes? If that's okay?"

"I'll pick you up in about two minutes." Two minutes? Is he Superman? Or does he secretly drive an undercover cop car with the sirens going off? "Sounds good?"

I nod and close my eyes.

"Hello?"

"Sorry, I was nodding."

He laughs as we hang up. I dash down the stairs, drink a cup of tea, and am about to pour myself another when the doorbell rings.

Butterflies bang against my chest as I swing open the door and blink multiple times. I don't recognize him. His large, thick glasses, his sweatpants and sweatshirt of opposite colors, and when he smiles, I notice he has a retainer.

I peer left and right outside of the door. "You stalking me, Chang?"

He laughs and points. "I live right across the pond."

"Ah! That's right! I almost forgot." Then, I toss my arms in front of my teeth. "Do you need that, or..."

He licks his lips and curses. "Okay, so I was asleep before you called. And I completely forgot about the retainer and my contacts."

"I think they look cute on you." The words fly from my lips, and I immediately shut my mouth.

"Really?" His smile widens. "I always thought they were kinda dorky."

"Dorky is my middle name." My cheeks blush. Before I can make a fool of myself, I ramble. "Do you want to come in? I actually have to brush my teeth. Feel free to have some tea, or a cappuccino, but I dunno how that machine works."

Once he steps into my aunt's home, Austin slides out of his sneakers with socks labeled as right and left. I scurry up the stairs and brush my teeth as fast as I can. But after I rush down the stairs, I see him staring at the glass case with twenty photographs inside.

I stop walking and watch him. He squats down, pressing his hands gently upon the glass of the wooden case. The photograph he lingers the longest is of me at ten years old. My bangs are too short, my hair lopsided, and my braces have broccoli in them.

"Disney World," I whisper. "The picture of my

family. It was the first time we'd been there."

"That's a good picture," Austin says, turns around, and smiles. He removes his retainer, places it inside a plastic bag, and puts it in his pocket. "Especially of you." My cheeks flush as I stare down at the tile. Is he complimenting me?

No, he's just being polite.

"Should we get going?" I hope to change the subject and put on my coat. I notice there's a gel pen in my pocket, although I don't feel like taking it out.

He nods and follows me out of the house and into his '07 Honda Civic. This car reeks of a mixture of cheap body spray, weed, and sweat despite using an air freshener. The seats look like a dog bit through the cushion. I try not to show my amazement of the vehicle, but I can't help it. Austin's car is the opposite of most of the cars at Hawken.

When I glance up, he laughs and points to his vehicle. "I know it's not much, but it's all I could afford. To everyone's amazement, I bought Jeff with my own money."

My smile spreads, hurting my cheek. I don't know if I'm smiling because I'm impressed by his work ethic or because he calls his car Jeff. It's so cute!

As he unlocks the car, he asks, "Where to first?"

Wherever you go.

Ew...EW! That phrase is so gross I'm surprised I'm not getting sick. "Whatever" is probably the coolest-*ish* thing I can say. Once he hops into his car, I gaze at the heavens, wondering if I made the right decision to come on this Cleveland adventure.

We decide to skip the highway and travel on back

roads. He shows me the Euclid Beach Park and explains how, way back when, it used to be popular and had an amusement park. But this place was abandoned until 2020.

My stomach growls a little too loud. I sink in my seat, hoping Austin didn't hear it. However, his lips quiver. We cross over West Cleveland to East and park on the left. There are two buildings on one side and a tiny shop on the other. He parks next to the smaller of the two.

"I'm starving," he says, but his stomach doesn't growl. "Do you wanna grab something to eat? Here maybe? It has bomb sandwiches." I freeze and stare at him. "I mean, if you want to, that is. Like, we don't have to go in. We can go anywhere. McDonald's, even." With a beat, he pleads, "Please say something."

I smack my lips, nod, and am about to open the door. "Wait here."

I raise my eyebrows and lean back in the car. He opens my door, and I just blink. I always thought this was too old fashioned, like a 1940s movie. In black-and-white films, it has the women waiting by the door, expecting the men to open the cars. So, like the movies, I step out and lead us into the shop.

With a *cling* of the chimes, three men glance in our direction. All three yell, "Austin!" It's like the *Cheers* bar where everyone knows his name.

"The usual?" The oldest of the three heads toward the salami when Austin shakes his head.

"I think I'll have something new, Frank."

"Are you sick?" Frank brings the back of his hand up and places it on his forehead. "Fever? Flu? Covid? Geez, your generation is making *my* generation sick."

Austin laughs. "I've already had my shots. I'll— I mean, *we'll* look around."

The oldest man raises his eyebrows. "Oh...it's a *we*, is it?"

"Ye-yeah." He swallows and turns red. "This is Rhiannon."

"Like the—"

"Fleetwood song," Austin and I say at the same time.

"Wow." Frank chuckles and stocks some boxes. "You two are already finishing each other's sentences. Good for you, Chang." I turn around and act like I'm not paying attention to them. However, when I glance from my right eye, Austin mouths the words "Shut up" with a smile. As I gaze at the display deli cases and the pre-wrapped chocolates, I'm shocked at their prices because they are so low! I kinda want to buy the whole store.

Then something catches my eye, and I drift toward the case. The bakery section calls my name. Only, I've seen nothing quite like this.

"Pistachio," says Austin.

"Is it baklava?"

He nods, and I scrunch my nose.

"I've had that before. It's just...the green is throwing me off."

"Ah, so, you're a virgin?"

I spin around, my cheeks turning red.

"I-I-I mean, for the pistachio baklava." He quickly adds, "You know what? I'll get us two." As he orders two pieces, I stare at his face, which must be blushing more than mine.

Two sandwiches and two pistachios later, we exit the

small, wonderful store and sit outside. It's around eleven o'clock. The clouds break away revealing the sun, and I regret bringing a down coat. We set up on a tiny picnic bench with no one around.

Austin opens two sandwiches, a turkey club and a toasted tomato-paneer sandwich. He may think about choosing the latter, but I crave the club.

The mayonnaise oozes on the sides, so much that part of the condiment falls onto my napkin. I try to seem calm and eat neatly, but with one bite, my eyes dilate. I moan. The turkey and lettuce and mayo and tomato and bacon—oh, the bacon, how I missed you—combine to create a perfect sandwich. I wolf it down.

Then, the baklava. I stare at the morsel of food, like it's taunting me, saying, "Try the green stuff, it's delicious." I shut my eyes and sniff the buttery dessert. With a deep breath, I take a tiny bite of sugary syrupy, like a pistachio energy bar. The world is brighter and sunnier. I eat the baklava piece by piece, stuffing them into my mouth.

My eyes remain closed as I savor the last bite. When I swallow my food, I open my eyes. Austin stares at me, and I blush because I forgot he was here. I grab a bunch of napkins and try to clean myself up. The baklava is so sticky my hands are like glue.

"Here," says Austin and hands me two wet napkins. After he tosses our trash away, he's about to have us leave when I tap the bench in front of me. Cautiously, he looks around, and I bet he's thinking, *What's her plan?*

What *is* my plan, anyway?

I stick my hands in my pocket to feel something like

a mechanical pencil, realizing it's something else. I grin and say. "Give me your hand." He carefully extends it to me. Out of my coat, there's a gel pen. He rolls his fingers into a fist with the thumb hidden. I bite the cap, place it on the table, and sketch the New York skyline on his hand.

"Did you always know you're meant to be a swimmer?"

He laughs. "And I thought this wasn't an interrogation." But he doesn't answer.

"I'm serious!" I chuckle and continue to draw, waiting to hear what he has to say.

"The answer to your question is no. It was a few weeks ago, actually."

I stop sketching and glance up. "Really?"

He nods. "To be honest, I never took it seriously. I mean, I'm good at it, but it's a natural talent. It wasn't until Troy put in all that summer work I realized he was my competition." When the word *Troy* is said, his brown eyes peer down and shield me like a knight.

"Hey," I whisper. "I'm sure he'll get over this." Austin's eyes remain shut, and I glance at his hand. It's on the table, palm facing upward. With a deep inhale, I slide my hand to cover his.

His head shoots up. His eyes water, but he remains staring.

"Everyone makes mistakes."

And then, we talk and touch the surface-level of our lives. He tells me about how his favorite color is gray, about how Halloween is the best time of the year, and how he never got the chance to have a pet because he's allergic to fur. I reminisce about all the unique places I used to photograph, about how I've seen the movie *Up* hundreds of times, and how instrumental music calms me. From twelve o'clock until three, we hold each other's hands. Sometimes it's silent, while other times we laugh so loud that other people glance our way.

When it's time to leave because Austin has a late practice, we grasp our hands the entire ride home. Once we pull into Tori's driveway, it takes every ounce of strength to leave him behind.

Chapter 18
Austin

My alarm goes off every morning, but today, I'm doing something different.

Every morning for the past three weeks, I have woken an hour prior to our regular practices to swim, *just* swim. I've done twenty laps: five butterfly strokes, ten freestyle, and five breaststrokes. I usually take my shower before everyone else

However, today, I choose to return to my *old* routine of weightlifting. I lift some dumbbells, increasing the bar by ten pounds. Half of the team is in the equipment area, and once they spot me, rumors spread *fast*.

"Is he serious?" Troy whispers to his friends. "Give me a break. If only—" He keeps talking, loud enough so I have to listen despite my being across the gym. It's like he never worried about me. He wants to egg me on so I'll punch him. If I did that, I'd be kicked off the team, and the only time we'll cross paths is at lunch and art.

The Night at Times Square

My fist tightens. As Troy's stupid smile stretches, I'm afraid I'll do just that. Two weeks ago, he was so kind and worried about me. But with every practice, he became a little meaner. I guess as soon as he realized everything was back to normal, he switched places.

When I close my eyes, I stroke my thumb over my pressure point. I tune out everyone, put on my iPhone's playlist, and resume lifting the forty-five-pound weights. I usually listen to heavy metal music for my workout, but this time, I listen to instrumental pop music on YouTube that Rhiannon recommended to me. I've never listened to this type of music before. While the playlist moves forward, my mood shifts, and my shoulders relax. It may not be the ultimate pump-up-the-volume song, but I'm calm, serene even.

Once I glance in Troy's direction, he frowns, along with half our team. Does he want me to be miserable? Does he think he's losing some battle? Does he *actually* hate me? Standing erect, I stare at him until he looks away.

I want to talk to him, maybe explain how everything happened one time and why I kept it a secret. However, what would I say? *Hey, man, I'm sorry for having sex with your girlfriend. No hard feelings, right?* He'd hate me forever if I said that. I shake my head, grab new weights, and lunge with thirty pounds in each hand.

At lunch, I grab a sandwich from the cafeteria's line. Above me, a huge banner reads, "Halloween Homecoming 2022" in black and orange font. The class council decided that rather than the usual gowns, they'd have a spooky atmosphere. So on Saturday, Halloween night, everyone will wear their costumes. I purchased my costume the day it was announced: Mike Myers, *Halloween*. Hopefully, Troy doesn't recognize me.

I walk past his table and notice Finley among them. When he notices me, he gives me a head nod and resumes talking with the rest of the crowd. I speed up and land on Rhiannon and Brielle's table. Rather than the usual books, the two of them giggle. My smile widens. "Do you need me to settle an argument *again*?"

"Yes!" Brielle slams her fist on the table. "Which movie is scarier? *The Nightmare Before Christmas* or *Coraline?*"

"Well, I'd hate to say this, but I've never seen either."

They glance at each other and then stare at me. "Seriously?" Rhiannon asks, raising her eyebrows. "Wow...you were deprived as a child!"

Although I shrug, my grin stretches. "I don't know what to say. My mom thought they were *too* scary when I was little, and my dad doesn't like animated films. He says, 'You can't draw emotions.'"

"Haven't you seen *Up?* It's impossible not to cry at that," Rhiannon says.

"I have seen that movie, but I didn't cry. As far as I'm concerned, the computer animator did an okay job."

She picks up a tiny piece of her granola bar and tosses it at me. Then, Brielle whispers something to Rhiannon, which she laughs at. I blush and stare at the table.

I know Brielle doesn't like me. For the last four years, I never said hi to her in the hallways or classrooms. Troy and Greg joked about her crooked teeth until she got braces, but I was silent. It doesn't matter if I wasn't the culprit of their teasing; the fact I didn't say anything makes

The Night at Times Square

me just as guilty.

"Are you guys going to Homecoming tomorrow night?" I ask and try to change the subject.

Brielle snorts, shoves a cookie in her mouth, and stares at the table. When I peer at Rhiannon, she shakes her head. "Tori and Hank are going out, so I'm handing out candy." The way she gives me her information tells me that even if she was free, she wouldn't go.

"Yeah," Brielle says, and I am forced to stop gazing at Rhiannon. "My college buddies and I are going to watch a live version of *Rocky Horror Picture Show*. Have you seen that?"

I dunno what that is, never mind what a "live version" ensues.

Rhiannon sighs. "I saw the movie, and, I'm sorry, it's not that good."

Once again, Brielle slams her fist on the table. "You *have* to see it live! There are actors, toast flying everywhere, people doing the conga, the works!" She makes a pouty face. Rhiannon laughs with a smile stretching, and with that smile, my stomach does a somersault. I can't stop staring at her.

The showing off of her perfect teeth.

The corners of her mouth.

Her lips—

A slight cough is given by her. As I glance toward her hand, she doesn't hover over mine, but rather she grasps it. "You okay?" she whispers. It feels like we're the only two people in the whole school. I stare into her eyes—brown, like cinnamon—and my eyes draw toward her lips. She draws back and turns red.

"Anyway," I say and shake my head, "any idea what your aunt and Mr. S have planned? The art department has amazing ideas for Halloween."

"I'm not allowed to go in the spare room between August and Halloween. They posted a sign: 'Do not enter until Halloween Begins!' But I'll see what their costumes are tomorrow."

"I bet it's characters from *Alice in Wonderland*," Brielle says.

"Weren't they that last year?" I ask.

"So? It was *so* popular! I think they'll do it again, except more grand."

I shrug. "We'll see on Monday."

"I know!" Rhiannon shrieks and bounces in her seat. "Do we wear costumes, too? You know what? I don't even care. I'll dress up as Samara from *The Ring*."

Brielle leans forward, and in a creepy voice says, "Seven days." They laugh.

We continue to eat, and with five minutes left for lunch, Brielle leaves to grab something from the vending machine, leaving Rhiannon and me. My hand hovers close to her. For the past two weeks, every day we flirted, brushed our hands against one another, and played footsies. But since our Cleveland trip, we haven't hung out outside of school. I'm super awkward on the phone because I'm afraid to say something stupid. Her not having a phone is so difficult. If she owned a cell, we'd text nonstop, I just know it.

"Hey, Fleetwood?" I whisper and adjust my glasses. "Can I come over tomorrow? You know, to help hand out candy?" My heart thumps. A single drop of perspiration

The Night at Times Square

falls from my head.

"Aren't you going to Homecoming? The *end of an era*?" She uses quotation fingers and wiggles her eyebrows, mocking me with slight flirtation. I scoot my chair closer, and she leans forward. Our hands nearly touch.

"I'd rather hang with you." With a beat, I stammer. "If-if-if that's okay."

She blushes and for once looks at my lips. It takes everything in my power not to make out with her. "Okay, Chang," and her eyes lift to mine. "But only if you bring Reese's Peanut Butter Cups."

I stick my arm out. "Deal."

After school, the swim team spreads apart for an individual stretch. First, the goal post, the goal post rotation, straight-arm swing, hamstring streamline, and high hurdle stretch. Out of the corner of my eye, Troy stares at my movement. Each time I switch to a different stretch, so does he.

Coach blows his whistle, a signal to swim three laps as a warmup. Simultaneously, we all dive into the pool. I stay behind Troy, who sets the pace for everyone else. I watch his stroke as he switches from the freestyle to the butterfly. We finish our warmup and climb the bleachers with me in the middle and him upfront.

"Now," Coach begins. "Let's see who to pick for a race."

His first choice is Troy. The other swimmers raise their hands like it was a trophy being handed out. Coach picks four more competitors, leaving him with a sixth swimmer. Ever since I pretended to lose my race against Troy, I avoid races with him.

Somehow, I stand. As soon as I do, all the other hands lower. "Six," I say. Troy inhales to protest, but I hop down the bleachers and stand on the middle platform. I hear his sigh, followed by heel-toe slamming without a word of complaint. He knew the old me, lack of caring, lack of motivation, lack of giving a shit. But that's not me anymore.

He steps up onto the diving board, as do the other four swimmers. Each of us lowers our goggles. "Hey," I say, and his snarled face glares in my direction. "When you come up to breathe, your neck needs to stay just above the surface." He blinks, like I didn't just give a minuscule piece of advice. He faces forward, but his side-eye remains staring. I bend at the waist and flap my arms, outstretched as a last-minute stretch. He does the same.

Coach says, "On your mark," and everyone bends at the start. Yet I could touch the ceiling. "Get set." Now I lower on the diving board, and rather than closing my eyes as always, they're open.

BEEP!

The six of us dive into the pool. My legs push away through the water, hands in front of my head. When I come up to the surface, my face barely moves. I submerge, my knees and my feet kicking as hard as I can. My arms circle. I swear I'm truly flying. Once I spin at the edge of the pool, my shoulders feel like jello.

"Keep going, boys!" Coach yells. My body does everything automatically, my palms reach to the opposite side of the pool, my elbow outstretches, and my head submerges. With a side glance, I see Troy, neck and neck.

And for three more strokes, I inhale, close my eyes,

and reach for the wall.

"Holy shit," says one of my teammates. I open my eyes and glance at the scoreboard. Although I won, both of us hit a personal record. I blow bubbles under the water, and he mimics me. At the same time, we spit, rip off our goggles, and float above the pool.

The team and I had regular practice, dry land and swimming for about an hour and a half. During Coach's daily speech, I pull a notebook out of my bag and jot down the advice. I submerge into the pool for a cool-down lap, followed by floating as I wait for everyone else to leave.

But when I flip on my stomach, Troy grins, holds out his hand, and asks, "Are you coming?"

Chapter 19
Rhiannon

"Trick or treat!" yell five children at Aunt Tori's doorstep. Behind them, two adults stand—a man playing with his phone and a woman taking a million pictures.

The children wear different costumes, like Spiderman, Darth Vader, Elsa and Anna, and an older girl with dogs and cats glued to her elaborate robe. I tilt my head, and the girl sighs.

"It's *raining* cats and dogs," she says and points from head to toe with a scepter. I grin and give her twice as many fun-size candies. She skips down the miniature staircase. "Thank you, ma'am!"

After adjusting my witch's hat, I shut the door and walk to Austin, sitting on the same couch. Wearing a clown nose and now ever-present glasses, he scans the cable menu. "I've seen this one five times in the past week," he says and points to *Hocus Pocus*. "Does your aunt have Disney Plus?" I shake my head, grab a blanket, and spread it over my legs.

The Night at Times Square

Austin stares at my blanket and then his sweatpants. Does he want to share it with me?

"Okay, children!" Hank's voice bellows. "Close your eyes! *No* peeking!" I cover my eyes with one palm and wait. But I move apart my middle and ring fingers.

"On three," Tori says. "One."

"Two."

"Three!"

I drop my hand and my jaw. Tori's the mayor in *The Nightmare Before Christmas*. She wears a towering hat with its point right below the ceiling, a dark cloak, a ribbon reading "major" on her collarbone, and a giant head, one side happy and the other sad. Well, not sad, more like terrified. Hank plays the Oogie Boogie Man from the same movie, complete with dice, intricate tan stitching, and yellow-and-black tongue.

Austin and I glance at each other, both of us still have our mouths open. "Well?" asks Hank. "What do you think?"

At the same time as, "Awesome!" by me, Austin asks, "Who are you?"

Tori's eyes grow. I burst into laughter. "Sorry," I say, "he doesn't know true artwork when he sees it." I wink at him and look at the two adults before me. "It's amazing. Really. You'll definitely win the contest. Seven times in a row, right?"

"Good memory!" Hank high fives lme. "If we win, we'll celebrate next week." He glares at Austin. "Not you, though."

He acts appalled. "What did I do!"

Hank points to him. "You know what you did." I

don't know if Hank's being serious, but I glance away and try not to giggle. Tori pats him on the shoulder, links arms, and motions toward the door. They trudge through the doorway, making their way down the outdoor steps, and waddle until they reach the truck.

At eight o'clock, Halloween's trick-or-treating ends. I close the front door, feed the fire, and run upstairs. "What're you doing?" he asks.

"You'll see!"

I hastily scan the movies in the upstairs cabinet in the spare room. After I climb over mounds of construction paper, I search through the DVDs, but it's not there. When I reach the bottom of the stairs, Austin stands with his hands behind his back, smirking.

"I bought this at the mall this morning. Our minds must be linked or—" He pulls out a DVD: *The Nightmare Before Christmas*.

"Yep, definitely conjoined at birth," I say.

"Nope, nope. We are not at *all* related." He quickly adds, "I mean, my parents wanted to have *one* child, not two."

I shrug. "Maybe we are."

"I think we look a *little* different."

"I suppose," I say and shrug once again. When I am about to walk to the kitchen to make popcorn, Austin gently hip-checks me. I spin around and point at him. "Be careful, *Alvin*." His grin is wiped

"You wouldn't."

"Oh, I *so* would."

Once I pull open the cabinet and press the buttons on the microwave, I slap my face repeatedly. Does Austin like me? Are we flirting? Or are we friends and nothing more? Peeking around the corner, I watch him trying to understand how to use Tori's DVD player. Half the time, she can't even do it herself. I lean on the doorway, and I cannot help but stare at his bu—

Beep! Beep! Beep!

I jump at the sound of the microwave and gently tap my face. *Snap out of it, Broderick.* As soon as I pour the popcorn into the bowls, I walk into the living room, only to see Austin smacking the DVD player. I plug in the two sets of Christmas lights, one white below the television and the other multicolored above the fireplace.

"Excuse me, sir," I say and place the two bowls of popcorn on the coffee table. I grab the remote and glare at him. "Don't you have any manners?" and I raise one eyebrow. Austin steps forward, and out of the corner of my eye, his hand nearly brushes against mine. Before he finds something clever to say, I press one button. Instantly, Jack and Sally from *The Nightmare Before Christmas* fill the screen.

"That's not fair." Austin huffs and sits down, grabbing a bowl and tossing the blankets over his legs.

"What's *not fair* about it?" I do the same, grab the other bowl, and pretend that throwing the blanket over my lap and his is the most normal, nonchalant thing I can do.

We've never sat this close before. I want to lay my head on his shoulder, but I can't, not yet, anyway, because I still can't believe anyone like Austin would like me. I bring my eyesight toward the screen, even if I could gaze into his brown eyes for days.

I swallow and ask, "Are you ready?"

Austin crosses his legs, the right over the left, and says, "Aye, aye, Captain."

For about half an hour, all we do is watch the film. At the end of, "What's this?" Austin says that this one is his favorite song. *Mine too,* I want to say, but I refrain from anything that might be construed as "needy."

Once the three little children kidnap Santa Claus, Austin pauses the movie. Instantly, my heart rises in my throat, and my breath becomes unsteady.

"Troy and I are friends again." He chuckles and waits for a response. *What is he talking about?* "Wa-wa-well, not *friends*, but we are on better terms." My internal self snaps her fingers.

"Really?"

He nods. "Turns out, all I had to do was try."

"That's great!" I scoot my body toward him, and so does he.

"Yeah, and I don't drink anymore *at all*. I do my homework, get great grades, and go to bed at a decent hour."

I pat him twice on the head. "Such a good boy."

"Don't mock me, okay?" He smiles and glances away. "I...I wanted to let you know that I, I mean, you..."

He trails off, and it's my turn to squirm. His arm hovers over me and finally he wraps it around my shoulder. I lean on him, forgetting about what we were talking about, forgetting about a previous life I once had, and forgetting about the movie we were watching.

He leans over and kisses the top of my head. I sink even more into his grasp.

We watch the rest of the movie in silence. I play with his fingers, and he strokes my biceps. This is nice, *so* nice. In fact, I want to bawl because I didn't think anyone would see me the way Austin does.

Should I kiss him right now?

When we finish the film, I glance up, and he gazes down. He stops caressing my arm and places it on my shoulder. I stare at his brown eyes, and as he peers down at my lips, I do the same. They're bigger than I remember, his being bright pink. I suck in all the surrounding air and close my eyes.

"You're still up?" Tori asks, jiggling her keys on the other side of the door. We separate and pant. Once Hank and Tori enter the house, both have their costume heads off.

Austin and I glance at one another, a deep red coming on his face, and I assume mine. Tori smirks and waves her hand. "Don't mind us," she says. "We're just going downstairs," and she holds an unopened red bottle.

I hear her maneuver her way through the dining room, the kitchen, and down the cellar's stairs. "We won, by the way." Hank grins. I stare blankly, and he rolls his eyes. "Teenagers," he mutters and glances at Austin. "I guess I'm taking you instead of Rhie." Then he scurries along Tori's path.

I turn toward Austin. "Did I miss something?" He chuckles and shifts closer to me.

"The whole reason we're watching *The Nightmare Before Christmas*."

I burst into laughter. "I completely forgot!"

"Well, I think we should just watch it again."

"Oh, really?" The curve of my lips twitches.

He nods. "To be frank, I wasn't really paying attention to the second half."

"Me neither."

"Do...Do you want me to stay?"

Without hesitation, I nod, and after I rewind to the part where we stopped focusing, I hit the resume, but we aren't nearly as close as we once were. During the film, he opens his mouth multiple times, yet each time, he won't say anything. By the fifth time, I hit the Pause button.

"I can tell you want to know something. But I'll tell you what, Chang, it better be good." Laughing, I am sorta loving this, but the stare in his eyes tells me he's serious.

"What's..." He trails off and can't even look at me. I wiggle in my seat, and although it's pretty chilly in this room, a bead of sweat falls from my brow. He peers into my eyes, and once again, I think he's going to kiss me.

I hope so.

"What do you like to do?"

"I..." A lump in my throat forms, unable to find the words. *What do I like to do?* I lean against the couch. "You," I whisper. My head shoots up and turns a deep shade of red. "I-I-I mean, hanging out with you."

A sheepish smile forms across his face as he intertwines his fingers with mine. "What else?"

"I don't know..." We stare into each other's eyes, and I glance away. "Reading...I'm fascinated by a great book." A smile creeps on my face. "And music. My dad has incredible taste. He made me some CDs of different genres. Every time I listen, I find myself wanting to dance."

The Night at Times Square

"Really?" He places his hand on my chin and drags it so we're eye to eye. "I didn't know you danced."

"If there's another dance at school, I'll challenge you to a dance-off." I grin. "It'll be just like the movies, everyone clapping, forming a giant circle, cheering us on. Well, cheering *me* on. 'Cause, you know, I'm awesome and whatnot."

"It's a date."

Giggling, I snuggle into his breastbone. His heart and mine beat as one. He holds me close and kisses me again on top of my head. I close my eyes with a soft moan. Austin has an indescribable scent that has to be cologne.

"What's your passion?"

"Oh, you know," I say and open my eyes, "to be the next Meryl Streep and win an Oscar. When I deliver my speech, I'll thank all the little people and tell everyone to follow their dreams." I bat my eyes. But when I look up, Austin's face is stoic.

"Seriously." He stops moving his hand and places it on the couch. "Your passion used to be photography, right? I know your ex destroyed your old camera, but did you buy a new one?"

This fun little game turns into something serious, too serious for my liking. My fist tightens. "No, Austin, I did not," I say, half truth, half lie, because my dad did.

"Then what is it? What do you love?"

"I don't know."

Why is he asking me all these thought-provoking questions? Why is he trying to have a heart-to-heart conversation? Does he think by talking to him, suddenly everything will go back to normal?

"You have to know."

Please, stop talking.

"You can have it again."

Please, stop talking.

"Tell me, what's your plan? After high school? Do you want to go to college? Do you want to dive into the photography business?"

Please. Stop. Talk. Ing.

He wraps his arm around me. For the first time tonight, I freeze. Why won't he just drop the subject? "Rhiannon, what do you want to do?"

And that's when I snap. Pushing him away from me, I stand. "You wanna know what I plan to do after graduation?"

He jumps, a smile coming on his face, eager to hear an answer, but as he's about to hold my shoulder, I back away.

"I plan on leaving." That smile vanishes, with his mouth parting. "Yep. Either to Montana or Alaska or maybe the Grand Canyon." The corners of my eyes swell up with tears, and I glance away. "I'm sick and tired of everyone asking that question, 'What's your passion?' Because, to be completely honest, I don't have one." *Not anymore.*

"But you had one, once."

"I already told you. My dream was to live in New York, become a gallery owner, move in with him, get married, have babies, live happily ever after!" I raise my voice higher and higher. "My parents and my aunt care about where I go in life, but that's it."

But my parents have given up on me, sending me

away, sending me 450 miles away, because they can't deal with me. How long will it be before Tori gives up, too?

"You have *everyone*. Your parents, your friends, your coach, hell, even *Troy* wants you to succeed. Now that you're friends with him, you won't want to hang out with me. I have no one!"

I wait for three seconds, praying that he says, "That's not true," but the only thing he does is swallow and lower his head. With that, I give a slight gasp with tears falling. I wipe them away and mimic his movement. My breath is unstable, trying to keep my composure and not sound like the little girl in that gallery.

"I...I have no one." I'm realizing if I had him leave when Tori and Hank came home, this conversation never would've happened. "You don't even know me."

Austin can't look at me. "Maybe I don't know you that well, but I do know you enough to realize you're not living up—"

"To your potential," we both say, and with those three words, Austin becomes insignificant. His voice is monotone, just like everyone else's: Mom's words, Dad's words, Tori's words, the guidance counselor's words, Austin's.

"Like I said, you don't know me." My eyes burn as I cross my arms and point to the door. "I think you should leave...you-you should leave." We stand with neither of us inching away. He inhales, as if he's about to say something, but he closes his mouth. After he sighs, he puts on his jacket, takes one last look at me, and leaves.

I stay at this exact spot with the movie still paused. When Tori and Hank scurry up the stairs, they halt and then walk cautiously into the living room. "Austin left?" she asks.

"Yes," I whisper and wipe the tears from my eyes. Her hand hovers on my shoulder, but I back away. "I'm going to bed."

"Rhia—" she begins. I'm not listening, though. I sprint up the stairs, enter my room, and fall onto my bed. My walls build up again, possibly for good, as I toss and turn into the nightmare of a holiday.

Chapter 20
Austin

Rhiannon's words ring inside my head.

"I have no one."

When she kicked me out of Mrs. Benner's house, I sprinted to my car, branches breaking beneath the ruffling leaves. As I fumbled with the keys, I stopped. What if she wanted me to come back? But once I turned around, my heart sank; she was gone from the window. I stared at the same spot, the one where I could see her face that one time I saw her at Mrs. Benner's. She wasn't there, not this time.

And that's why I'm skipping school today.

After I take my glasses off and lay them on the nightstand, I lie on my bed and gaze at the ceiling fan spinning faster and faster, although it's on a slow setting. The Flash action figures glare at me, like they're saying, "I'm not mad, I'm disappointed." I glance away and watch my blank television. The sound might as well be black noise with the light shooting from the screen. I've been right here for two days, but nothing satisfies my hunger or thirst.

I keep replaying the scene because it happened so quickly. One moment, we discussed our futures, and the next, she wanted me to leave.

Then Mom scurries up the stairs, her feet almost inaudible. As she passes my room, she backtracks and scans my body over the covers. "Austin?" A crease forms in her face. "Are...are you okay?"

My skin is like ice covered in goosebumps, and my teeth chatter. I'm naked, minus my boxers, and my lips are cracked without water to soothe its thirst. I don't want anything to make me feel better, though.

When I don't answer, Mom flicks on the light switch, turns down the television's volume, and sits on the edge of the bed. She grabs the bundle of covers and lays them like a cocoon over our bodies. I close my eyes and remember how Mom used to tuck me in before she said good night.

Grabbing my foot, she tickles my toes, and I laugh like the little kid I used to be. Once I glance at Mom, she scoots to the headboard of the bed and sits up straight. I do the same and rest my head on her shoulder. We watch television for so long. I hate to admit it, but I even snuggle into her nook despite having half a foot on her.

"I have an idea," she says and motions to the door, but I remain still. She jumps off the bed and runs down the stairs. I change into my clothes and stop at the top step. As she turns around, she smiles up at me.

I hop down the stairs two at a time, land on the

The Night at Times Square

wooden planks, and glance at the dining room table. There are four chairs aligned, one of them being Allison's. Mom backtracks and links arms with me.

"Shall we?" She squeezes my arm and looks my way. Maybe Mom is trying to become a better colleague, better friend, better parent, or it's the guilt for those ten years when she became isolated due to her work. Nevertheless, she's trying.

I tighten her grip. "We shall."

We reach the kitchen with Allison wrapping an apron around her waist and humming a little tune, something I recognize.

Mom and Dad brought me to China's spot on the windy road. She had a boom box, and he had a picnic basket and blanket. With each on opposite sides, they flew the blanket into the air and laid it flat, not a wrinkle out of place. I remember my action figure The Flash, the only one I owned, and I made him soar through the air like he was running so fast. I was, what, six? Peanut butter and jelly sandwiches, juice boxes, and salt and vinegar chips were gourmet for me. The mouthwatering food kept getting caught in my palate expander.

I played with The Flash, Dad ate his sandwich, and Mom drank from a juice box, laughing for hours upon hours with the song "Moon River" playing from the boombox. When the song switched to something more upbeat, Dad screamed, "Who wants to play Trashketball?"

My hand was raised. "Me! Me! Me!"

Mom grabbed three barrels and spread them out ten feet apart. She put her hair into a long ponytail while I grabbed my gardening gloves. Dad kicked off his shoes above the freshly cut grass, his dirty right sock having a hole in it.

"On the count of three," I said and hopped with excitement. "One, two—" and Mom sprinted to the middle, picked up a piece of trash, and returned to her basket. I huffed. "Not fair! You cheated!"

Allison yelps, holds her heart, and immediately turns red. I shake my head to focus on what's going on. "Mrs. Chang," she says while fumbling with the pan and peeking at the clock. "Am I late? Was there a special request? My phone died during the day, so I'm sorry if that—"

Mom raises her hand, and Allison closes her mouth. "Actually, I wanted to learn."

She blinks. "Learn what?"

"How to cook."

Allison's mouth drops, and her hand closes it. I slide into the chair at the kitchen's island.

As she grabs the salt and pepper, Mom says, "I'll have to apologize for my cooking skills ahead of time. There was a time *eons* ago"—she looks at me—"when I was halfway decent at cooking."

"What was your favorite meal?" Allison asks.

Mom freezes and stares at the ceiling. Then she smiles, and I know what she's about to say. Simultaneously, we reply, "Cutlets."

Allison laughs. "Well, I guess today's your lucky day." She leaps to the other end of the counter and reaches inside her bag for thin slabs of beef, breadcrumbs, parmesan cheese, and eggs.

At first, Mom hovers over Allison's chef-esque work, whisking the eggs, dropping the beef in the batter, and patting it in the spiced breadcrumbs. Once she places the cutlet on the plate, she turns on the burner. She nods in

The Night at Times Square

Mom's direction, staring at the naked meat with her fingers shaking.

Allison pours the vegetable oil in the pan. "I'll peel the potatoes, and you'll start the cutlets?" she asks. Mom closes her eyes, her fingers moving through the motions. Faster and faster, she grabs a piece of beef. When I was little, I always loved this part of the process. It was like she was a composer with her orchestra playing for the Cleveland Orchestra.

As I watch her work, my mind finds Rhiannon. She had glanced away before she snapped, her face had turned stern, and she froze. At the time, I was aloof as to her feelings. I should have stopped talking and changed the subject. If only—

Dad shuffles in his white Gucci socks, loosens his tie, and talks on the phone. Mom places three cooked cutlets on a plate and waits for him to see. The second he realizes she helped prepare our meal, he halts, but the person on the other line rambles nonstop. She turns around and beams. Allison and I watch the two of them.

I wish he would say, "I'll call you back," hang up the phone, and sit at the table.

However, when the stranger asks, "Tao? Are you there?" Dad shakes his head and exits the kitchen without any food. My heart sinks, and my head lowers to the table. All I can do is stare at Mom's smile dropping. She just waits for him to return until Allison touches her shoulder.

Mom jumps and snaps, "I need to get back to work." She grabs a cooked cutlet and bites into it. She winces from her tongue touching the scalding meat. "This is burnt. *Great,*" and she runs through the doorway.

"Sorry," Allison whispers and turns the burner down. I should say something, either to Mom or Allison or both. No words come from my mouth, though. I pull out the chair and stare at the space where she stood. She has to realize Dad loves her, right? They grew apart while I just watched from the sidelines without a care or coping mechanism.

But I want them to be together.

I hop down from the stool and grab two cutlets and a spoonful of mashed potatoes. When I walk and am about to climb the stairs, I see Mom moping on the couch. I place them on the side table and sit next to her. She lies her head on my shoulder and closes her eyes.

I stroke her shoulder as she gently weeps. With her free hand, she covers her mouth. She mustn't want me to see her cry. Everyone, and I mean everyone, breaks down every once in a while. So, I peer down at her while she glances up. I nod, letting her know that it's okay. Then she sniffles and lets the tears fall on my shirt. I close my eyes and hold her tighter.

We didn't say anything for a while until Mom's sobs turned into the occasional sniffles. I can hear the kitchen sink run, Allison scrubbing away at the grease from the pan. She hums a tune, and I recognize the song: "Get Low" by Lil Jon. I chuckle, tap my foot, and bobble my head to the beat, singing along, word for word. Mom sits up.

"Those are the lyrics?"

I smirk. "Mom, it's a classic."

We snort and laugh and tears fall from her eyes and mine. When her crying subsides, I stand with my arm outstretched to her. The two of us pick up our plates, make our way to the dining room table, and scarf down the food.

After we say goodbye to Allison, we enjoy dinner together, but Rhiannon is all I can think of right now. Maybe I pushed her too hard, maybe I'll open up the conversation about her future on a different day, or maybe I won't mention it again.

Tomorrow, I'll go to school, apologize, and hopefully, she'll hug me, hopefully she'll say, "It's okay," and hopefully, *hopefully,* she'll forgive me.

Chapter 21
Rhiannon

It's been three days since Austin and I fought, and because of this, the house phone rings for the fifth time today, including right now.

On the second floor, I snuggle underneath a blanket, tucked so tightly I resemble a burrito. Even if I wasn't mad at him, I still couldn't answer the phone. Tori's voice on the answering machine comes on. "You've reached Victoria Benner. I'm probably casting in the studio and cannot come to the phone right now. Just give me a little jingle, and I'll get back to you. Ciao Bella!"

Beep!

My ears perk up, and I turn down the volume on the television. A loud mouth breather waits. "Are you there?" Austin waits four seconds. "Please pick up. You're probably drinking tea, or eating popcorn and a protein bar." I glance at the tiny side table: an empty mug, crinkled cellophane, and half-eaten popcorn bag.

How does he know?

"Rhiannon, I want to say I'm sorry." He sighs and waits for a response. But I won't give it to him. "Okay, so I guess you're still mad at me."

You got that right.

I pick up the remote and prepare to turn up the volume. "Do you remember the first day we met? I was running late for practice, and BAM! We crashed into each other. Well, not into each other. It was me, knocking into you, so..."

I turn around and stare at the cord phone hanging on the wall. "Anyway, I just wanted to say, you're right. I shouldn't slam into other people's business, like I did when we first met." He waits, possibly for me to pick up the phone. He sighs again. "Just...Call me back," and after another five seconds of his mouth breathing, he hangs up.

I should forget about his words, forget about him, and forget about going back to Hawken. My aunt, my parents, the guidance counselor, they said the same thing, but Austin's voice is the only one that stays. When I claimed to be sick for the second time this morning, Tori glared, but since she had to leave for a conference, she didn't feel like fighting and left. First my parents didn't know what to do with me, then my guidance counselor didn't, and now, neither does my aunt.

For the twentieth time, I watch a movie, turn the volume on mute, and attempt to fall asleep. But my mind is restless.

You're not living up to your potential.

I sit perpendicular to my bed with my hand shaking. My eyes wander over Tori's artwork, so many sculptures, so many paintings, so many mono prints, sketches, and bronze pieces. Her passion is art, whether it's flat or three dimensional. As I bury my head in my hands, I wonder, *Why can't I have it again?*

I have to try.

Tossing the blankets, I stand, dashing down the hallway and down a second staircase to the cellar. Where did I put it? Somewhere low? Or up high? I peer up, my eyes scanning old memories stashed away: sleek dresses, fitted jeans and crop tops, puzzles of New York's boroughs, and a shoebox full of photographs.

Then, I stop searching. When I stretch to the tallest box, my fingers touch the side and drag the trunk until it falls to the ground. Dust covers the top. I blow the sand away from an untouched camera, Fujifilm X-T4.

"Open it," said Xavier. He slid the package across the table with his dirty hands, unable to be cleaned, no matter how often he scrubbed them.

This was our third date, one week since he asked me out. This hole-in-the-wall restaurant, Vinegar Hill House, was unique. Tiny, the walls were divided into two, half was white wood and the other half was a musty green with hung artwork. The candle flickered in the center of our table. The rustic atmosphere made me feel at home.

For dessert, we shared a single blueberry pancake covered in maple syrups, falling fruits, and mounds and mounds of butter. Although we're already stuffed, we wolfed it down. With a last bite, I laid my fork and clasped my fingers over his. "I told you already. No gifts on my birthday."

He kissed my hand. "Take it, please." His free hand passed a present across the table. The bow was as big as the rest of the gift, the corners tucked to hide the wrapping, and the present was bright orange and blue, my favorite colors. As I glanced up, he was more excited than I was.

I tore the middle of the gift and ripped the wrapping paper apart. Once all the paper fell to the floor, I flipped it over. My eyes grew wide. "Are you serious? How—"

"I get forty percent off since I work at Best Buy. Plus, the manager loves me, and gave me an extra fifteen percent." He held his hands in front of him. "And some extra hours in the shop, since I don't work there anymore."

"Xavier, it's too much!"

"Babe, you're worth it." He stroked my hand, kissed it, and nudged me to open the gift.

The camera's box was simple, all black other than the white "X-T4" written in the center. I opened it with ease, like it was meant for me. As I lifted the camera, my knees bounced, my grin widening. I turned it on, set it to portrait mode, and focused the lens on Xavier. He stared out the window. With a flash, his smile dropped. "Don't take my picture!"

"Why not?" I asked and played footsies.

I placed my camera on the table, and he picked up his wooden chair and slid it next to mine. Our eyes locked. He brushed my hair behind my ear, leaned forward, and with slight hesitation, he kissed me. We held it, and when we finally released, I smiled and wiped my lipstick off his mouth. "Best. Birthday. Ever."

When I arrived home that night, I searched for the price of the camera: two grand.

Dad bought the same camera as a going-away present, though I didn't open the box. I simply said, "Thank you," and stored it beneath my bed until we left for Tori's. Even then, I only have it now because he packed it when I wasn't looking.

I stare at the camera, but it doesn't carry the same

excitement as before. I keep waiting and waiting, hoping the inspiration will come again. Nothing happens, though.

I have to try.

With a deep inhale, I open the box, letting the packaging fall to the floor. I flip it over and turn it on. The screen remains black. When I scan the instruction manual, it says it needs one hour of juice before it will turn on.

Well, I guess Xavier thought of everything.

After I plugged the camera in, I set a timer for one hour and sit, watching the little red light flashing. Whenever my eyes wander, I force myself to focus on the camera. Unlike the first camera I received, no excitement, no spark, no need, nothing. Photography used to be a wonderful hobby, so wonderful I was hoping it would become a career someday. My favorite thing to do was find joy in unexpected places, rather than boring, stereotypical smiles.

The first time I could see a future in photography was on my first day as a wedding photographer's intern. Peter was in charge, wearing a short, black button-down shirt, and having many tattoos. Most were elaborate, like the Celtic Cross sleeve, while others were ugly, like the shark on his bicep.

Xavier begged Peter to let me come along one time to see how talented I was. When Peter asked me to see my portfolio, I reddened because I didn't have one.

"Look." He unloaded two cameras, one was new, and one was old and beat up, living on its last leg. He handed me that one and rubbed his eyes. "Just...Don't mess up, all right?"

At Saint Augustine Catholic Church, spectators sat in the pews, reading pamphlets for the wedding. While Peter discussed with the groom, my hands shook, picking up the delicate camera and

The Night at Times Square

taking many test shots of the cathedral. Hundreds of candles backed on the high counter, roses and lilacs laid in front of the altar, and chandeliers hung above the aisle. On the left and right of the altar, intricate stained glass filled the walls. Most were of Jesus, but some were of nature, like three calves drinking from a pond.

"Broderick!" Peter snapped his fingers. "Get ready." I wanted to say, "That's what I'm doing," however, my lips remained closed.

The pews were filled with people, jam-packed beneath the arched ceiling. When the band played, Peter squatted, clicked the shutter button a hundred times, and stared at the back of the church. The mother of the groom, mother of the bride, and eight bridesmaids wore crimson tulle. Then everyone rose, and Peter shuffled so he focused on the bride. No one glanced at the groom, except for me.

I snapped three shots of the groom, his eyes watering. As the bride revealed herself, he clasped his hand over his mouth and smiled.

The perfect shot.

A few weeks later, Peter called. He said of every shot he took, nothing compared to the groom's emotional picture. For the entire summer, I loved every wedding I photographed, and at the end of August, he said he'd be more than happy to write me a recommendation letter. And I had planned on it.

Had.

The timer rings, and I stare at the camera. What if I don't remember how to use it? I keep telling myself, *I have to try, have to try, have to try*, yet I can't move. The alarm rings again, and my eyes flutter, letting go of the trance. As soon as I turn the timer off, I step in front of the camera, turn it on, and close my eyes. My finger presses the shutter button and snaps a picture.

When I open my eyes, I frown. This photograph is out of focus and angled peculiarly, my finger half covering the lens. My hands are clammy, so I have to wipe them on my pants. Then, I photograph twenty pictures: a unique marionette, Maybelline, a doll house, and Tori's sculptures. I'm rusty, and although a few of the last batch are halfway decent, nothing is working.

"What's the point?" I say with a sigh of defeat. As I lower my arm, my palm is so sweaty, the camera slips through my fingers, tumbling on the floor and stopping at an old, wooden case. *Shit!* Did I break it? I may not be enjoying the one thing I used to love, but my dad paid an arm and a leg for it.

Please...please, don't be broken.

Squinting, I trudge on the carpet, squat next to the antique box, and open it. Hundreds of different colored paints lie, some new, some with a few strokes of paint left, and everything in between.

My lips twitch.

Running back down the stairs, I glance every which way until I spot a canvas. I grab it, sprint up the stairs, and pick up the case, continuing to the middle of the backyard. I lean the canvas against a bronze sculpture and unfasten the paints. With the black, I stare at the beige canvas.

On January tenth, I walked into my kitchen and stopped to see my guidance counselor. As I sat at the kitchen table, my neck was still bruised, and my eyes still swollen, my hand shaking on my lap. Mrs. Zwirek smiled, a smile that said, I can't save you.

"We're worried about you, Miss Broderick," she said all the right words, like a rehearsed speech she'd practiced on the drive over. "Everyone misses you."

She may be expecting a smile from my side of the table with the words of reassurance. I gave her nothing, though. There's no point in

The Night at Times Square

playing pretend on my behalf.

She dropped the smile. "Principal Lyman and I coordinated a new schedule for you as soon as you feel prepared to return." She slid one piece of paper over to me, but I didn't glance at it. I stared at her face as the sound faded.

What if I was never ready?

Mrs. Zwirek's mouth kept moving, yet all I could hear was the buzzing filling my eardrums. My mouth ran dry, my vision blurred, and my heart beat so fast I truly believed I was having a heart attack.

It never occurred to me that everyone else continued with their lives. Xavier was the robotics team leader, Finley played basketball after school, and Sadie probably had a new leader to follow.

"Miss Broderick?" Mrs. Zwirek placed her hand on mine, but I snatched it away. "You'll have new courses as well, which is great. What art classes are you interested in taking? Abstract art, perhaps?"

I splatter black paint on the canvas, some on the left side, some on the right, and some on the dying grass. I toss the pallet on the ground and stomp closer. With a large glob of acrylic, I add all of it on the paper and smear my hands up and down. My eyes sting as the skies open up, and sheets of rain pour on my body.

When Aunt Vicky called Mom back, the phone rang once. "I'll do it," she said. "I don't quite understand what's happening with Rhiannon, but I'll help her in any way I can."

I peeked into our kitchen, so Mom couldn't see me. She sniffled, her eyes red and puffy, just like her nose. Her bottom lip quivered as she held her mouth.

"She needs change, Vicky," Mom whispered, twirling the cord beneath her fingertips. "She's not talking, barely eating, won't leave the house..."

The paintbrush switches to a deep blue. I dab it in the paint and streaks of color appear in random places. The dark blue changes to cobalt and ultramarine and cyan and turquoise. In between each blue, the harshness of the rain increases.

I laid on my floor, laughing so hard it hurt. But it was a good hurt. It was a hurt that said everything was truly going to be okay. When I opened my eyes, he was lying next to me with a smile that made my heart melt.

The sheets of rain cause my eyes to flutter. I probably should call it a day and run inside, but I can't explain it. The inspiration pours out of me, and if I stop, it might not come back. When I'm in the zone, everything around me becomes numb, my eyes focused, and my fingertips steady, like in Tori's art class and the potter's wheel. I switch from blue to yellow. The second the paint hits the canvas, it blends with the rain and the acrylic due to the precipitation, the dark with the light.

Austin sat on the bench, waiting for me to speak. I told him my story, why I was the way I was. His eyes didn't widen, and he didn't laugh, but rather he just sat there and listened.

With one last streak, I draw a messy heart in the bottom right corner. It may be cliché, drawing a heart like a little five-year-old, yet this one seems appropriate. I step back and stare at the canvas, abstract painting full of vibrant colors mixed in with subtle noir and navies. The colors drip as the rain pours from the sky. The more I watch it, the more I love it.

I pant over my knees and laugh. After I lift my body and face the sky, sheets of rain monsoon over me as I shut my eyes. My tongue sticks out and attempts to catch the water in my mouth. For a few minutes, I just stand there and let the rainfall shower over me.

Then, I grab my new painting, dash into the house, and grab one Polaroid camera. I photograph a picture of my magnificent artwork. As I write my signature and title on the back, my mind whirls, falling in love with not only the painting, but with the ideas. *Maybe I can create abstract monoprints, maybe I'll copy one photograph repeatedly in different angles, or I'll take a photograph and print it on the outside of a plasticine collage.*

While I stuff my picture into my shoe, my eyes tear up, falling with the futuristic imagination. I grab the house keys, and without thinking, I run to the backyard, despite the rain, and slide down the deep, deep trench.

Chapter 22
Austin

"You okay, Austin?" Allison asks, and hands me a slice of pizza. When Rhiannon wasn't there this morning, I lingered through the halls in a hope she was only avoiding me. But as I scan the lunchroom, she's nowhere to be found. Brielle sits at the same table as always with her book, cookies, and now headset. She must feel my stare because she looks in my direction, frowning.

Did Rhiannon tell her what happened?

"Austin?"

I fake a smile and nod. Allison's always been sweet and kind, and I don't think I've seen her mad. If my parents or I caused her to be discouraged, she didn't show it. Maybe I should do something for her, like a small gesture.

"Do..." She glances up with her permasmile. "Do you think I could cook tonight? Well, *attempt* cooking." I chuckle.

The Night at Times Square

She blinks with wide eyes. I think she might be surprised, like Persephone becoming captured into the underworld by Hades. She swallows and says, "Sure. I'll pick out the ingredients and—"

"Can I do that?"

She nervously laughs, and a worried crease forms in her brow. "Am I getting fired?"

"No! No, no, no! This's a way of saying thank you, you know, for all you..." My cheeks fluster. "I mean, I want to learn your ways."

"My ways?" Her smirking face raises her eyebrows.

I lean on the check-out desk and reciprocate her smile. "Someday, *years* from now, I'm gonna live on my own. I should at least know the difference between a spoon and a spatula."

"Well, then," she says, digs into her jeans pocket, and hands me a long sheet of paper, "as requested by your father."

After I pay, I head toward the normal spot, despite Rhiannon's absence, and see if Brielle knows what's going on with her. "Chang!" I turn to see Troy, standing and waving his arms frantically. I grin and move through the crowd toward him.

"Now that you're friends with Troy, you won't want to hang out with me."

I stop in my tracks and lower my gaze, my vision blurs. What if Rhiannon's right? Was I just hanging with her to bide my time? Would I invite her to sit with us? I shake my head and sit in the usual chair with the usual people, plus Finley. He and Greg are quoting *The Office,* the two of them laughing with word-for-word lines from the show. Troy joins in, but I can't crack a smile.

Someone cackles extremely loud. Jessyka serves a new group of popular friends, a wannabe serving their queen. In my opinion, the further she is, the better. Troy peers at her and punches me lightly in the arm. "Bros before hoes, amirite?"

"Yeah, I prefer your mom, anyway," I say, slapping the air repeatedly. He grabs my head, puts me under his armpit, and shakes my hair.

While we have a battle of 'yo mama' jokes, someone taps my shoulder: Brielle. As soon as Greg and Troy notice her, they silence, glare, and whisper, probably about her. Sure, when she was younger, it was easy for those two to make fun of her. But now, she carries an air of confidence. Why do they even bother?

Finley's eyes move from her to them, and back at her. "I'm sorry? I don't believe we have met," and he sticks out his hand. "Finley."

She blinks multiple times and faces me. "Can I talk to you?" She looks at the guys. "In private?"

Nodding, I follow her to the giant fireplace. There's a few students gathered here, but most of them either study, play with their phones, or read a novel. We sit down on the same couch. The roaring fireplace crackles, the heat warming my face.

No one speaks for a moment, so I ask, "What's up?"

"It's been two days, and she missed Halloween at school," she says, eyes narrowing. Brielle must know something's up. Why else would she interrogate me? "She told me you were going to Ms. Benner's house on Saturday, so you were the last person to see her." As I peer

The Night at Times Square

back at Brielle, a worried crease forms. "What happened?"

"I...I don't know." My palms sweating gives the lie away, but she nods and stares at the fire. My mind has been spinning all day, wondering where Rhiannon is. I get more worried with each passing minute. However, if Brielle is antsy, someone needs to calm her. "I'm sure she's...sick. Yeah, that's got to be it."

"I don't believe that." She turns to me, like she wanted to say how she didn't believe *me*. Brielle and Rhiannon have a stronger bond than I thought.

"Look," I say, a plea in my face. "I tried to call her, but—"

"You know her number?"

"Her house number, ye-yeah."

She scoffs. "Figures."

"What's that supposed to mean?" My fist tightens. "You don't even know me."

"That's right, I don't. But whose fault is that?" I lower my head because it's my fault. Throughout high school, I've ignored her, not even giving her the time of day. My hand pushes my hair back in silence. "If you want me to be a hundred percent honest, you aren't as great as she thinks you are."

Rhiannon talks about me? I can't help my smile.

"She might be a little fragile, but—"

"She's stronger than you think." For the first time, her mouth flies open. The fireplace grows hotter, and perspiration falls from Brielle. We're silent and watch the wood crackle.

In seventh grade, we were semi-close. Midway through eighth, I started hanging with Troy more and more and Brielle less and less until we didn't even say hi in the hallways. We didn't have a huge blow-out or anything. Without Rhiannon here, there's no reason for us to hang out. But Brielle and I could be actual friends again.

Standing up, I hold my hand for her to take. She glances behind me, and as I turn around, I see Troy and Greg staring at us while Finley chows down on the chicken alfredo.

"Want to come sit with me today?" She doesn't give an answer. I smile and nod toward a new seat. "Like you said, Rhiannon's absent and all, so..."

Brielle stares at my palm, and eventually, she accepts it.

Once I finish purchasing the ingredients, I open the door, slide off my shoes, and am greeted by Allison. She lights up and points to the drawer. I jog to the opposite side of the kitchen to grab an old apron. Actually, it's not really an *old* apron. When I was nine, we went to Falmouth, Massachusetts, for vacation, so Mom bought this as a souvenir.

Allison ties the apron around my waist and claps her hand. "Ready to work?" We begin with the eggs. She hits one gently on the side of the bowl and swoops it over the center, tossing the eggshells away. Easy, right?

Wrong.

Because when it's my turn to tap an egg, I hit it a little too hard, causing the egg to splatter onto the tile. My apron has a huge yellow stain in the middle. She hands me another egg, and this time, I softly tap it. Only some eggshells fall in the mixture.

Finally, it's finished, but I'm not thrilled with my handiwork. Although Allison does a splendid job at everyone else's omelets, mine is burned on the bottom and soggy on top. Before I eat, I walk to the bathroom, close the door, and run water from the sink.

I dial my cell phone, but Rhiannon doesn't answer.

After I walk through the kitchen, I hear a *slam!* from Allison leaving. I notice she left her purse on the counter, tucked behind the drying rack. Maybe she forgot it?

As I put her purse on the center island, I sit at the dining room table and play with my food. Pieces of my omelet are pushed across the dish, spreading out the eggs to make it seem like I actually ate something. When Mom places her omelet on her plate, she stops, turns around, and sits across from me.

Dad walks into the kitchen on his cellphone. While holding the phone in between his head and his shoulder, he scoops his omelet. But before he carries his food to his office, he stops and glances at me and Mom. She stops eating and stares into his eyes. When he glances at me, I nod toward us, secretly pleading, *Please, Dad? Please?*

"I have to call you back," he says, and with an angry associate continuing to yell, he hangs up and sits next to Mom.

My stomach growls. While I eat, my mind wanders to Rhiannon. How I confided my fears of escaping my culture, how I hate those stereotypical Asian nicknames like Jackie Chan, and how I'm disappointed by China's spot on Martin Luther King Drive.

Mom and Dad converse when I blurt out, "I think we should fix our spot."

They stop talking. She lays her fork down on her placemats. "What spot?"

"Where we used to go every Sunday."

He wipes his mouth and glances at Mom. "When was the last time we went there?" She shrugs and picks up her fork, but there's no more food to eat. "Son," he says and faces me. "Maybe—"

"We should change that." My voice commands to be heard, causing them to stop talking. I lower my gaze with a deep sigh. "I want our spot to be perfect, memorable...or even somewhat clean would be nice."

Dad chuckles. They stare at each other, and I don't know how, but they're able to have a silent, secret conversation about my request. As they turn to face me, Mom reaches across the table, grabs my hand, and squeezes it.

"Five minutes." Mom slides out her chair while Dad wolfs down his remaining food. She turns in his direction. "Do you want to drive? Or should I?"

"I'll drive," I say, and the two of them glance at me. "I want to."

"Okay." He reaches inside his pocket and tosses keys at me. "But yours smells. You're taking mine." My mouth drops. Dad's letting me take the Tesla?

In less than four minutes, the three of us slam the car doors and drive. I barely hear the engine move, no matter how quickly the car accelerates. When we reach the spot on Martin Luther King Drive, Mom and Dad's eyes

The Night at Times Square

widen. China's spot is a pit, fallen branches, tons of weeds, and high grasses that need to be mowed among the dead ones. Even trash is here from drunken teenagers. Dad opens his mouth to say something, but I do it first.

"The last time we were here was ten years ago," I whisper. "I loved...love it here. Every Sunday, we would bring our picnic basket, a blanket, and three beverages, one for each of us. We would spend hours here..." My voice trails into the distance.

Our last evening was when Dad and Mom got their perfect jobs. But since both of them needed more time, they halted our Sundays outings from their schedule and out of their lives. Although I said it was fine, I cried that night.

"Let's try something simple, like picking up branches?" I suggest.

Mom wraps her hair into a short ponytail, and Dad rolls up his sleeves. Even if it's forty degrees outside, I remove my sweatshirt. While we pick up some sticks, it's quiet on this busy street. Both of them sigh every three seconds. I thought it would be fun, but apparently not.

And then, I have an idea.

"Do you remember the games we used to play?"

My parents stop and stare at me. Dad grins. "You mean the games we used to trick you?" she says.

I snap. "Exactly!"

Then, we run to three separate empty trash barrels. She flings her shoes off her feet. "Who's gonna call it?" he asks.

"Me!" she says, raising her hand. Laughing, I give her a single nod. This game, Trashketball, is simple. On the count of three, we dash from one piece of trash and throw it in the barrel. Players can strategically steal some trash as well, and knowing Mom and Dad, they are still fierce competitors.

"One, two—" and Dad's off, picking up three pieces of garbage before she says, *Go*.

"That's cheating!" But she grins, running to his barrel and stealing two pieces. I laugh, running, hopping, and attempting to be the basketball star I wanted to be when I was eight years old. Rather than place the trash in my barrel, I shoot them from ten feet away, missing all of them.

At one point, Mom grabs Dad by the waist and pulls him back. I stop and stare at the two of them. Each of us has our own life, Mom with her surgeon work, Dad as a lawyer, and me with school and swimming. We barely spoke three words to each other until today. I lean against a tree and watch the two of them play. I've not seen them this happy in a long time.

Drip, drip, drip.

Precipitation falls on my nose sporadically, and I lean my neck back and stick out my tongue. When I lean forward, Dad and Mom do the same, wrapping in each other's arms, and simply kissing. Although I'm usually grossed out by adult PDA, I don't mind.

The light drizzle changes to sheets of rain. We sprint to Dad's car, me in the front and my parents in the back. When I glance at our new spot, my mind whirls with the possibilities. *Maybe we'll join our church again, we'll set up a group to stop littering, or we'll just come here, once a week, for the rest of our lives.*

The Night at Times Square

"We should do this on Sundays," Mom says and lays her head on Dad's shoulder.

My tears form, but I don't let my parents see that. "Sounds perfect."

Once we reach home, Mom and Dad head upstairs to pack for their business trips. Every time I glance at their bedroom, they're making out until they shut the door.

While they pack their belongings, I put on my AirPods, crank the volume up, and switch the heavy metal to instrumental pop music. At first, I dance to the rhythm and the beat, and after the song, I decide to do something drastic: clean.

I wash all the dishes without using the dishwasher, sweep throughout the tile and hardwood floors, and even vacuum the soft rugs in the living room. As I roll the vacuum's cord, Dad and Mom carry their suitcase holding hands. They stop abruptly with mouths open.

"I just thought..." I shrug, and Mom walks over and kisses me on the cheek.

"We'll be back tomorrow," she says and returns to holding Dad's hand. "Same spot on Sunday?"

I hug Mom and hover around Dad. When was the last time I hugged him? Then, I embrace him, close my eyes, and wait for the reciprocal. He does, and a slight wetness is felt on my shoulder.

With one last look at the newly clean home, my parents leave.

I plop on the couch and sigh. Cleaning was exhausting, and I'm about to turn on the television when my ears perk up. *Ding dong!* Did Dad forget something again? I run to the kitchen to find his keys right away, except it's not there.

Ding dong!

"Hold on, Dad!" I check the dining room, living room, and the kitchen, but nothing. Is it in his bedroom?

Ding dong!

"Coming!" After one final glance at the bowl where we put our keys, nothing is there. "Dad, I couldn't find your—" I swing open the door, expecting my father. My mouth hangs.

Rhiannon?

She's drenched from head to toe. Her hair sticks to her face, and the bottoms of her pants and shoes are black with dirt. As I stare at her fingers, they are covered with soot and mud and...paint? When I look up, she's staring at my lips, panting.

I immediately apologize. "I'm so sorry—" Rhiannon wraps her hands on my shoulders, steps closer on her tiptoes, and kisses me.

Chapter 23
Rhiannon

The first thing I noticed is how soft his lips are. I draw myself closer to him, lifting my body and making soaked handprints on his stomach and chest. With each second, the kiss grows more intense, like we can't keep our hands off each other. My hand touches his cheek, and he lets out a peaceful moan.

When I stop to breathe, I pant, and so does Austin. His cheek is smeared by my dirty hand. I gently brush off the mud. He lies his forehead down on mine, our heart beating in sync. "I've wanted to do that for so long," he whispers.

"Ye-ye-yeah." My teeth chatter, my legs quivering. "Me-me-me too." I'm not sure if it's from him, or if it's 'cause I just ran in the pouring rain in forty-degree weather, but that kiss was *so* worth it.

"Come in," Austin says, and I follow as my hands shake. With each step, my sneakers leave a footprint until I slide out of them. I drop my keys in the bowl. He touches my arm and spins me around, and I think we're going to make out again. Tucking my hair behind my ear, he scans me from head to toe. "Do you want to take a shower?"

I breathe in to say, "No, I have to tell you something," but a nice, hot, steamy shower does sound so inviting. Because I cannot find the words to say that, I nod. He holds my hand. I don't pull away, instead, my fingers wrap beneath his. Now it's his turn to blush.

Right before I step into the bathroom, he stops and says, "Wait right here." He disappears into a different room and then comes back with boxers, sweatpants, and a sweatshirt. Then, he hands me a tee, the one he constantly wears that says, "I'm into Fitness, Fit'ness Taco in My Mouth." I bite my bottom lip.

Somehow, the movement of my teeth stops. I whisper, "Thank you."

Once he leaves, I rip off my clothes, adjust the knobs, and hop in. Austin's shower is at a perfect temperature and water pressure. I stand there for a good ten minutes before I turn it off. His sweatpants and sweatshirt swim against my body, but it's warm and comforting and smells just like him.

Barefoot, I trudge through the hallway and into the kitchen. A loud tea kettle whistles, and he immediately cuts off the stove. "Would you like some?"

I nod. He pours it in with a little bit of milk and a lot of sugar. He places the mug on the kitchen counter and slides it over. After I blow the steam away, I sip and close my eyes. "Feel better?"

"Much," I reply and walk to the living room. When I sit on the three-cushioned couch, Austin rests on the

The Night at Times Square

opposite end with Gatorade and a sealed Oreos package.

"Sorry. My parents left a few minutes ago, and Allison's gone, and I just fill the fridge day by day. I didn't expect..." He laughs and stares into my eyes. "Anyway, I'm glad you're here."

We sip our tea in silence, but it's not awkward. I reach for a cookie and bite it. As I munch on the double-stuffed Oreo, I stare at his hair, and the frizz hints of chlorine. My eyes wander. The living room is covered with photographs of him and his boogie board, Hawken's swim team, and Austin on Christmas Day with a tooth missing.

"I especially like your picture," I say and point to the gap-toothed grin.

Chuckling, he places his drink on the coffee table and lays his arm on the couch. Back and forth, his eyes follow mine.

"I just..." I swallow and stare at his lips. "I had to see you."

"Really?" His mouth curls. "You know, going around the street takes the same amount of time as the shortcut, right?"

He might expect a chuckle from me, a fellow sarcastic comment to play in this game. But I want him to know that I'm serious, and when I finally move from his lips to his eyes, he blushes again.

"Rhiannon," he whispers. "What happened?"

My heart pounds as I sit up. I hold up one finger, hop off the couch, and jog to the entrance. Once I find my sneakers, I pick one up and hand it to him. He stares at the sneaker and inspects the shoe from toe cap to heel.

When he turns it over to the sole, a Polaroid picture falls on his lap. His eyes brighten.

"Is that—"

I nod and start to ramble. "When I tried to photograph, I just couldn't. I took a new path, though. Abstract pieces. I've painted a little in the past, so I wasn't completely new to it." He stares at a picture of my painting. "It's not much, and I'm certainly no Picasso, but—"

"It's beautiful," he says and glances at my lips. Then he returns to staring at the painting, his opposite hand presses the bottom of the Polaroid. As he flips the photograph, it has my signature on it, and underneath is the title, *Passion*. He glances up, his eyes watering.

"Is...is this why you came here?"

For the first time today, it's my turn to blush. Why is this so difficult? I rehearsed what I was going to say on the way over, but with one glance into his eyes, my mind goes blank. He puts the photograph down, scoots over on the couch, and places my hair behind my ear.

"I guess we both are inspired," he whispers this so softly I'm afraid I'll miss it. Austin strokes my arm with one hand and wraps me with the other.

We tell each other everything, what it was like growing up, who used to be our best friends and now are acquaintances, and where we'd like to travel to. I tell him about how I miss the water, about how I used to be an excellent swimmer, and about how I'm terrified of suffocating and drowning. He tells me about his superstition with Mickey Mouse, about his fascination with Greek mythology, and about how he'd wake up every

The Night at Times Square

morning eager for English class.

Tens, hundreds, even thousands of jokes are shared between us. My abs hurt from laughing so much. One by one, we empty the container of Oreos and share a Gatorade until it's all gone. When I look at the clock, it's been five hours.

At two in the morning, I rest my head on his shoulder and close my eyes. I never thought I could be happy again, like my internal button was broken, and I was forever stuck in misery. After Austin kisses my forehead, I stare at him.

"I thought you were never a night owl," he teases.

"I guess I shouldn't use the word *never*."

My eyes move from his lips to his phone, lying on the coffee table. When I raise, I can sense him watching me. I grab his phone, and for a split second, I'm in awe. My phone had been smaller and had a slight crack in the corner. His is flawless with a background of a gold medal around Michael Phelps's neck.

"One, two, two, four," Austin says, and I turn around. "My password."

Twelve twenty-four: Christmas Eve.

I open the YouTube app and search for a particular song. When "Count Me In" plays, I hold his hand and lead him onto the floor. On my tiptoes, I put both hands around his neck. He lays his on the small of my back. We sway back and forth, and quietly, I sing. He leans closer and joins in.

As the song ends, he says, "You have a great voice."

Our lips are inches away, his eyes drawn to the same place. If I've learned anything about him, it's that he'll let me make the first move, a thing I love. Xavier never did that. Slowly, I kiss him, and his tongue intertwines with mine. We sit on the couch, our fingers never letting go. He brings his hand behind my back, and I play with his hair while lifting my leg over his body. I straddle him as he touches my cheek. When we release our kiss, he asks, "Can I kiss your neck?"

I nod. He kisses my temple, neck, and collarbone. After I remove the sweatshirt I'm wearing, he stops kissing and touches the tee. "I like this shirt," I whisper.

"Good." Austin smiles. "It's yours."

Shaking my head, I kiss his neck. "I want to wear it whenever I sleep here." I slide back to his mouth for a long peck before I open my eyes.

He grins. "Deal."

And then, we intensified by a thousand. He kisses my cheek, neck, my collarbone. He drags his hand to the skin of my back, his touch soft and warm. As he brings his hand to the front, he cups in a circulation motion on my breast. I've never experienced anything like this before. My eyes shut, my toes curling. The second I gasp, he shoots up.

"Too fast?"

The Austin I've heard about is nothing like this man. The old Austin might've been the take-charge type, the one who was in control, the one who might make me feel weak and fragile. This Austin, though, is considerate, kind, and fucking sexy.

I glance at him and slide next to him. "Not at all," and my hand slides to his knee, his thigh, and his waist. While I kiss his neck, I untie his sweatpants and bring my hand down. His eyes flutter, unable to do anything. He sinks into the cushion. We kiss with a tiny nibble on his lips, and as I'm about to remove my shirt, his hand stops me.

"Rhiannon," he says, panting. "We don't have to if you don't want to." When I was with Xavier, we had a specific date to lose my virginity. I want to live in the moment, live free, live *alive*. I grab his hand and place it on my heart: steady and relaxed. I kiss him one last time, hop off his lap, and stretch out my hand.

"I really, really do."

Chapter 24
Austin

It's now 5:43 a.m., but I've been up since five staring at Rhiannon. Her lungs inhale, holding her breath in for longer than the average person. When she exhales, she releases everything at once. She's covered by her locks falling from the loose ponytail in the middle of the night. I tuck her hair behind her ear with her lips curled up. Every once in a while, she snores.

And it is so friggin' cute.

Most of the girls I've slept with, I wake up with a hangover ready to leave, or I snuck out while the lady-of-the-night slept. But this is different. The tiny details are so unique to me.

The way she snuggles me in her sleep.

The way she buries her face in my nook.

The way she inhales before saying anything important.

Rhiannon flips over, her lips still parted. She breathes

The Night at Times Square

heavily. While I sniff the air coming from her mouth, her breath smells like tea from last night, no gross morning breath. To be honest, I could just sit here for hours watching her sleep.

BEEP! BEEP! BEE—

I slam my hand against my alarm, cursing myself for not remembering today's early practice. Her eyes open, and she loudly groans, stretching so wide I quickly lean back. Otherwise, I'd be another punching bag for her.

"Good morning, *Alvin*," she teases, and I tickle her ribs. She scoots up so we are eye to eye, a smirk arising on her face. She kisses my cheek and then hides under the covers. I do the same with the biggest, *stupidest* grin, and as I'm about to say something, she brings one finger to her lips.

"What are you doing?" I whisper.

She shushes me again. "I'm trying to fool Chronos, so he actually freezes the space-time continuum." The fact that she made a reference to Chronos in Greek mythology puts me in awe. I kiss her on the forehead and remain silent for a good thirty seconds until we hear a loud *TICK* of the clock. She shoots out of the covers and sighs. "Not today, apparently."

Rhiannon leans on her side, and I mimic her actions, continuing to stroke her arm. She spaces out, something she does when she's coming up with a plan. "Let's skip school today," she says.

"What happened to, 'Only people who didn't believe in the importance of education skipped school'?"

"Well, I was wrong. Besides, what's one more day of not being in school?" She wiggles her eyebrows and giggles. I cannot get sick of that sound, the melodious laughter coming from her mouth. I wonder if this is something new or something returning.

I lower my body and kiss her nose. "Well, in that case, get some extra sleep."

As I'm about to leap out of bed, she pounces on top of my body. "Only if you sleep with me." I nod and attempt to fall back asleep, but my mind is wide awake.

Once I peek at Rhiannon's face, her eyes twitch at a rapid pace. It must be REM sleep. Carefully, I lay the covers off me and lift her. She rests on her side with her permasmile widening. I slide out of bed, put the sheets back over her, and tiptoe toward the door, gently closing it.

When I walk into the kitchen, Allison gathers her purse from the previous night and stops at the side counter. "Two mugs?" She turns around.

"She's in bed." I try to sound nonchalant, but my face tells otherwise.

"Is she *just* another girl?" She raises her eyes as I sit at the island. I bite an apple out of the fruit bowl.

"Rhiannon's...different."

The way she crinkles her nose whenever she calls me out on my shit.

The way she bites her lip when she's at a loss for words.

The way she makes me feel.

After she taps my hand, she leaves, closing the door behind her. I jump down from the kitchen's island, open the drawer, and pull out the Cape Cod apron.

The whole process takes about a half hour to

The Night at Times Square

scrambling the eggs, sizzling the bacon, and toasting the wheat bread. I cook two kinds of meat: pig bacon and turkey bacon. I unwrap my smock while I hear the pitter-patter of feet.

"You're making breakfast?" I spin around. Rhiannon wears my favorite T-shirt that she swims in, bare feet and bare legs, and no bra. When I glance at her eyes, she stares at me with a genuine smile. She pulls up a chair, and her eyes skim the mountains of food. She lights up when she sees the two different bacon.

One hand with my food and the other with Rhiannon's, I carry the plates to the island. I untie my apron and lay it down on the counter. However, once I turn around, I find Rhiannon eating my bacon. I don't mind, though.

"So," I say, "what do you wanna do today?"

She chews and swallows, grinning. "I have an idea."

Two hours later of slowly getting ready, we hop into my car. I tap the top of the Mickey Mouse bobble head. We stop at her house to grab some items, and as I'm about to step out of the car, she shakes her head. "Wait here," and before I protest, she's up the stairs, engages her key, and enters the house. For about ten minutes, I play with my phone until I hear the jingle of keys.

I glance up, and my mouth hangs. Rhiannon looks absolutely beautiful. She wears jeans, a light jacket, and a simple white tee. Her hair is down, dancing in the wind. I am trying to find the words to express how I am in awe, how gorgeous she is, how one look at her makes me melt, inside and out. She tucks her hair behind her ear while blushing. Forcing a laugh, she asks, "What?"

Say something...anything...ANYTHING!

I close my mouth, shake my head, and face forward, like a moronic idiot.

Rhiannon jumps into the car while I stare at her. When she glances up, she beams red and passes me her camera and a water bottle. I hand her my phone while she plugs in my GPS. "Take a right onto the main road," says the robotic voice.

I peer at her. "What are we going, Fleetwood?"

"You'll see, Alvin," and she holds my hand.

Twenty minutes of driving, I've never been to this part of town. Streets upon streets upon streets, the narrow road is filled with small ranches and abandoned apartment buildings. As we drive closer to the inner city, these houses grow even smaller. But as I glance to my right, Rhiannon bounces in her chair, so excited that I'm filled with anticipation, too. Pointing, she screams, "There!"

I slam on my breaks. There's twenty people of different ages crossing the street in front of Jeff. Some wear bright pink caps, while others sport knitted ones that say, "Triple Dog Dare You." Once I glance up, a huge inflatable boy wears a pink bunny suit and doesn't look too pleased. I laugh.

"*A Christmas Story*," I say. "Really?"

She hits me gently. "Yes! Ever since I was ten, I've always wanted to come here. It's like living in New York City and never going to the Statue of Liberty. That part of Manhattan has been inches away, but I've never visited." My scan shifts to the iconic house. "Have you been here before?"

"I actually haven't."

She snaps her fingers. "Exactly!"

"Okay, we'll go in on *one* condition."

"You name it."

"Next time you're back home, you see the Statue of Liberty."

Her lips curl, and she sticks out her hand for me to receive it, her way of saying "deal." As I kiss Rhiannon on the forehead, I pull into the Free Parking lot, but every spot, even handicap ones, are occupied. Apparently, *A Christmas Story* Museum is well known because people from all over North America stop here. Their license plates prove it, like Toronto, Montana, and New York.

Backing out, I shift into gear, move five miles per hour, and search for a place to park. We turn onto a different side street. Houses with broken windows stand, and pit bulls bark ferociously at us. Rhiannon's hand touches my knee. "Maybe we should look again?"

"Good idea."

There's one spot at the end of *A Christmas Story* Museum street that some people may think isn't large enough. But me and Jeff? We can do it. Inches away, I creep behind the Mercedes in front of us. Rhiannon shields her eyes with her hand and holds her breath until we break.

After I open her door, she squeezes my hand and dashes. We reach the house as she lets go and pulls out her camera. She photographs the giant inflatable Ralphie, a butterfly shivering, and the inside of a window. During her snapping away, I lean against a telephone pole. I stare at her jeans, her white tee, and her denim jacket, all of which are a little too big. When she crouches down to photograph the scattered leaves, my eyes draw to her—

"Stop looking at my butt," she says, but she's still facing forward. *How does she know?* As she turns around, we hop in line until we're at the front entrance.

"Tickets, please." The voucher woman sounds like a robot, just like my GPS. It must be the look on our faces that causes her to sigh. "Go to the gift shop. You can buy tickets there." We scurry down the mini staircase. Rhiannon links her arm with mine, crossing the street and into the gift shop.

The building inside is massive. Hundreds of leg lamps align the wall and floor, mug lamps and shot glasses and even custom ones, like *The Nightmare Before Christmas*'s Sally and Jack's. A pink Christmas tree towers over everything in the store, and the television plays the iconic scene where the boy's tongue gets stuck to a pole.

"Wow" is all I can say. "Just, wow."

I turn my head to say something to Rhiannon when I realize she's trying on different hats. Once I reach her, she hands me a knitted hat that reads, "Triple Dog Dare You," while she tries on a replica of pilot hats. It's supposed to be from the movie, but she loves its appearance in *Up*.

"Adventure is out there."

She turns. "How'd you know?"

"You told me once, I think two weeks ago?"

Grinning, she steps forward. "Something like that." Then she turns in the full-length mirror's reflection. "Well?" She adjusts the hat for a perfect fit. "What do you think?" I step forward and lace my fingers with hers. After I add my hat, we look at each other.

"I'd say we're a good-looking couple."

The Night at Times Square

"I'd say so, too."

As we purchase the ticket, hats, and a copy of *A Christmas Story* for Hank, we sport our souvenirs and linger around the replica cars. There are a bunch of the old 1940s motor vehicles in mint condition. I bend to look beneath the hood when I see a flash. I immediately blush and turn around.

"I search for undiscovered beauty," she says, "or hotness. Either or."

In the third building, the door opens, and about twenty people file out to take pictures with their phones. Above the porch stands a dark-complexion man, around thirty, who talks to each individual person. His gap-toothed smile brightens anyone's day, and he wears a solid red polo, a backwards black cap, and has a brace on one leg. I squint and adjust my glasses, my eyes widening.

"Fleetwood," I squeak and beckon her with a huge smile. I point to the man as he comes down the stairs. "See his necklace? It's the same necklace as The Flash. I haven't seen that necklace anywhere! Not a real one at least."

"Wow," she says, nudging me. "First, you make references to Greek mythology, and now this? You are *such* a nerd. An adorable, sweet nerd, but nevertheless, a nerd."

I try not to laugh and whisper, "Don't tell anyone," and she crosses her heart.

"Ladies and gentlemen," the man announces. His booming voice doesn't need a microphone. "The twelve o'clock tour starts in three minutes," and motions us to follow him. He's like the leader of a marching band, and one by one, we stride. As we reach the lady at the ticket booth, she smiles and holds out her hand without a word.

We step into the house and shuffle into the living room. The background plays the opening soundtrack song of *A Christmas Story*. Unlike the original film, this living room and entryway are much smaller. There's an out-of-use fireplace, a godly Christmas tree, a giant box that reads "Fra-gil-e", and three cushioned chairs. Behind me, a staircase in a zigzag formation climbs to the second floor. The kitchen is on the first.

The door closes, and the air gains ten degrees. I take off my hat and stuff it into my pocket, but Rhiannon doesn't remove hers. While the man hobbles to the front, I can see his necklace's solid gold and not a toy. He checks his watch to wait for noon, and I take this as an opportunity to impress her. "Fun fact, The Flash can process information so quickly he can predict the future and every outcome."

She blinks and then asks, "Can't Dr. Strange do that?"

"Well, yes, but—"

"And doesn't Superman travel faster than a speeding bullet?"

"Um—"

"It sounds like he got the short end of the stick."

"No, it doesn't," both me and our tour guide say, and Rhiannon and I turn around.

"Did you know after being poisoned by Poison Ivy's thorns, The Flash ran to stop the toxin from metabolizing his bloodstream?" Even *I* didn't know that, never mind Rhiannon. He nods and adds, "Yep, he circled the Earth six times."

The Night at Times Square

At exactly noon, our tour guide claps his hands and rubs them together. "Welcome to *A Christmas Story* Museum tour with yours truly, Ernie!" He applauds, but no one joins in. With a shake of both hands, he says, "Yay," in a sheepish voice.

Everyone laughs.

"Where're you from?" People yell out different states, like Florida, California, New York, and Massachusetts.

When everyone is silent, I scream, "Ohio!" and a few spectators chuckle. Ernie raises his eyebrows.

"Is this a daily thing for you, or..." The crowd laughs, including Rhiannon and me. Then, he tells us the "boring" part, which I find fascinating. Only about fifteen percent of the movie was actually shot here because the producers paid the owner $20,000 to use it *without* scoping out the interior. Most of the movie was shot in Canada, but that year's winter was unseasonably warm, so they had to create artificial snow. Melinda Dillon, the actress who played Ralphie's mom, was actually pregnant. That's why she always wore heavy clothing!

"Okay, now I'll give you about fifteen minutes to explore."

Everyone scatters, half head up the stairs while the others stay on this floor. As we run into the kitchen, Rhiannon turns on her camera. She photographs the oven's inside, the bird's-eye view of the kitchen table, and of me underneath the sink.

Then, we skip up the stairs and enter the spare room: a cluttered cabinet, an iron board filled with magazines, and an outdated flowered wallpaper. My smile stretches as I glance at her. She holds up her camera. "Try it."

Carefully, I cling to the strap and bring my eyes to the preview screen. It looks foggy until I adjust the lens. I scan around the two twin beds when I notice an old movie poster for *The Wizard of Oz*. After three tries, I take the perfect picture, or a halfway decent one. I spin around to see Rhiannon's grin spreading. She motions me to keep going, which is *exactly* what I do.

I photograph Ralphie's bathroom.

I snap a picture of an old Raggedy Ann doll.

I zoom into the faded, maroon wallpaper with white boats and lighthouses.

After I finish, I turn around, expecting to see her behind me, yet she's not here. Although I try not to seem panicked, my heart pounds against my chest, and instantaneously, sweat forms on the top of my head and falls in my eyes. I search in every room upstairs. When I run down the stairs to the awning, I stop.

Rhiannon stares at the Christmas tree, her eyes dashing from the tinsel to the bright lights and funky ornaments. While I trudge down the staircase, Ernie sits down in the rocking chair and says, "You can touch the tree if you want."

"Really?" she asks, but continues to gaze into the lights. Once I reach Rhiannon, I watch her, analyzing every ornament, every tinsel, every green, fake branch. There's even an open box of the BB gun underneath the tree. I walk up to her and wrap my arms around her, and she leans back.

"He had a Christmas tree just like this one," she whispers, and I patiently wait. "We agreed to only buy one gift for each other. In the previous years, we spent so much money with all the stupid, *useless* presents." She swallows. I can only feel her tearing up, so I squeeze her hand to reassure she could continue.

With a deep inhale, she says, "It was Christmas Eve. Although everyone loves Christmas Day, Christmas Eve was always my favorite, even more than my birthday." I smile, thinking *Mine, too.* She chuckles, but it's not her usual one. "He handed me a gift, a small box with an overly large bow. When I opened it, I gasped. A necklace with a velvet pink bow wrapped in a shimmering chain and a silver heart at the center labeled 'Love.'"

She turns around with her arms now on my shoulders. We sway to the music of *A Christmas Story* playing in the background.

"I hated that necklace."

Rhiannon forces a chuckle and digs her face into my chest. I don't dare say anything. Instead, I wait, stroking the small of her back when she looks up.

"But it didn't matter. From Christmas to January first, I wore that necklace every single day until..." We stop swaying, and she lifts up my chin, making me feel so small. "I'm telling you this because *if* you want to be with me, there are things in my past I need to share."

She waits for me and bites her lips. Rhiannon is a brilliant, intelligent, mature woman, and I'm in no way, shape, or form worthy of her. I've done some terrible things in the past, and the fact she wants me *despite* everything I've done, means everything.

"Rhiannon, I want to know."

Then she tiptoes up to my face and kisses me, but it's not any kiss, a passionate kiss, a kiss that occurred last night multiple times. I play with her hair, my tongue moving in and out of her mouth. She gasps as I move down her neck until I hear a loud crunching.

We stop making out and lethargically, turn toward the chip sound: Ernie, eating a bag of Doritos. I forgot he was sitting inches away from us. "My apologies," he says, and he chuckles. "I would've gotten up and left, but my right leg"—he points to the brace—"has been killing me today."

Rhiannon unwraps her body from mine, leans on the adjacent wall, and smiles. "What happened? If you don't mind, that is."

"Not at all."

As Ernie tells us his injury story—breakdancing, of all things!—I wrap my arms around her and kiss the top of her head.

When we reach the car, the two of us hop in, and before she can say anything, I ask, "Rhiannon?" I glance at her, a wide smile appearing on her face. "I want to show you something. But you have to close your eyes."

"Are you going to kidnap me?"

"Yep!" I smirk. "It's so much easier for me if you close your eyes. Too much time to tie you up. Cops may get suspicious."

"As long as I know what's going on."

After I put on my new hat, we drive to the opposite side of the city and pull into a tiny parking lot. I hop out of Jeff and open her door. She flies out. I hold on to her arms so that if she trips, I can save her.

"Such a gentle, polite kidnapper. Four stars."

"Why not five?"

"Well, you are stealing me, possibly for my unpinning doom, so..."

When we cross the street, she grabs my arm tighter with one arm and a water bottle in the other. She might be afraid because there are hundreds of cars zooming, but I assure her she's safe with me.

It's a tiny uphill trek on the sidewalk, and looking down, I notice Rhiannon takes three steps for my one. I slow down. In the middle of our path, I spin her toward the sea. "Okay, so I saw you checking out the picture at the museum, but I figured you'd want to see what it looks like in person."

She opens her eyes with her mouth agape: Hope Memorial Bridge. On this cloudless day, a ship travels out to sea, and multiple cranes rest in the bay. She places the water bottle down next to her and leans over the side. For one second, I panic and am afraid she might fall off. The air smells like seaweed and low tide.

This was a bad idea.

"You know what?" I force a laugh. "Never mind. I mean, it was stupid. Have you smelled it up here?" I hold my nose. "And besides, I was just joking. Who cares, right? I thought you would like it because of the picture and—"

Rhiannon turns around and presses my lips with her fingers. "It's better than the photograph, really." She drags my hand over to the edge of the railing and leans on my arm. I close my eyes and listen to the waves crashing on the river's shores. We stay like this until her stomach growls.

"How about I get you something to eat? You liked

Aladdin's the last time, yeah? It's right down the street and—"

"Pistachio baklava?"

I nod, and she's about to follow when I say, "You stay here. I'll be back in ten minutes." She doesn't protest.

I jog down from the bridge to one block and ring the shop's door. This store's extremely busy, and all my guys are working the cashiers because there's a long line of people. "New guy!" Frank nods in my direction. "Help him out."

The new guy wipes his hands on his new apron and clears his throat. He wears diamond studs in his ears, gelled hair, and greasy fingers, despite sporting cooking gloves. Frank laughs once he realizes I was staring at the new guy's hands.

"He just got hired," he says. "He used to work at a car shop. The grime will fade...*eventually*."

"I take it you've been here before?" the new guy asks.

Although he helps a different customer, Frank snorts and says, "You'll get to know him, don't worry. Austin gets so much food from here we could survive with *just* him."

New guy chuckles. "Well, then, welcome back. I assume you want an amazing sandwich, right?"

"Actually, my—" I stop. Is Rhiannon my girlfriend? Are we exclusive? Do we have to have that conversation? "I mean, *we* would like two pistachio baklava and two whatever you recommend." My face gets so hot I remove my hat and place it in my pocket.

The way she stares into my eyes, into my soul.

The way she kisses ever so softly.

The Night at Times Square

The way I'm falling for her.

The new guy grabs two pistachios and two chocolates and wraps them up. "Austin," says Frank. "This isn't *the* girl, is it?" He wiggles his eyebrows and fumbles with the music player.

"It is." I smile.

He continues ringing up a different customer. "Well, where is she?"

"She's waiting by the bridge," and I point to the right. The new guy rings up my order as the Fleetwood Mac song comes on: "You Can Go Your Own Way." I beam. Maybe the universe is aligned, or perhaps it's just a coincidence that a Fleetwood Mac song happens to be playing when I'm talking about her. Once I see Frank, his wink tells me it wasn't the universe or a rare coincidence at all.

"Hilarious," I say, and as I look up, the new guy's finger hovers over the cash register.

"What's...what's so funny?" He peers up.

"Oh! The girl"—I blush—"is named after Fleetwood Mac."

He chuckles, but then the smile fades. He drops his hand and walks out the door. Frank blinks a few times, rolls his eyes, and rings up my order. He mumbles while I look at the silhouette getting smaller as the new guy jogs up the street. I glance at Frank. "Something wrong with him?"

"It's your whole generation," he says. "Other than you, of course. He just leaves without an explanation." *If I had a dollar every time Frank used the term* your generation, *I'd be a rich man.* "Anyway, he'll be back. He probably left for a smoke. He's been three hours here this morning without one. Just gotta remember to ask me, you know?"

I nod and grab the bag. Grabbing my hat from my pocket to the counter, I slide my money back into my wallet.

"Hey, Mark? Will you come to the front desk? Xavier went out for a smoke."

Now it's my turn to drop my bag.

"Xavier? From-from-from Brooklyn?"

The blood drains from my head, and I'm holding on to the counter. A ringing sound overtakes the others. I close my eyes, attempting to breathe. Even though it might be just a coincidence that some guy has the same name as Rhiannon's ex, I don't think it is. The way she described him, the shortness of height, the love of working on his car, his mom being a jeweler.

Just like Rhiannon, I can't breathe.

At some point, Frank came across the counter. He pats my arm with his shaky hand. *How long was I out for?* "Are you okay, kid?" Everything comes to focus, the ringing stops. Frank's face is full of fear.

"Is Xavier from Brooklyn?"

Please say no, please say no, please say no.

Frank's brow frowns. "How'd you know?"

I have three choices: fight, flight, or freeze, just like I've done in the past. But this time, I choose to run toward her, for Rhiannon. I dash toward the door, ignoring my new hat, ignoring the voices calling my name, and sprinting as fast as I can before it's too late.

Chapter 25
Rhiannon

I'm fascinated by the sea.

Waves crash on the shore, a ship blows its horn, and the multiple seagulls caw overhead. Cuyahoga River seems still, but as I gaze at its beautiful cyan color, the tide moves in, and the wind picks up, causing the water to become rough and wavy. The canal walls are strong and steep. The red buoy sways more and more, with a goldfinch landing on the tallest point. She clings to the cellular antenna, reminding me of a bobblehead.

Chuckling, my eyes wander from sea to land. Hundreds of cars speed past without honking their horns, but unlike before, it seems serene. I lean on the tall pole and watch a woman with a baby stroller. She nods her head toward me. While they pass, I glance at the baby girl, smiling and waving. The wind howls, and the little girl tucks her blanket closer to her body.

As I turn to watch the river, I could stand here for hours and listen to the shore. I close my eyes and hear the waves: *crash...crash...crash.* I open my water bottle and take a few sips. Maybe I'll stay here forever, a new life, new experiences, and a possibly new boy—

"Adventure is out there, right?" he asks and clears his throat.

I hear the sound of a clamorous beat. Pound!...Pound!...Pound!...The hammering of his step, the hoarseness of his voice, the constant clearing of his throat. Maybe it's not him. It can't be him. It just can't.

"Rumor has it, Xavier didn't pick Ohio State or NYU. He attends Cleveland State," Finley had told me. How many people are there in Cleveland? Three hundred thousand? Four? After a few moments, nothing else was said. Did I imagine it?

"You used to love that movie." I drop my water, splattering it onto the concrete sidewalk. The bottle rolls down the sidewalk and falls into the sea. My ears perk up, goosebumps form along my arms and on the back of my neck, shivering as if I was in negative thirty degrees in the Arctic. I don't need to turn around right away.

I know that voice.

Is it really him? Is it just another flashback? Or a blackout? The pounding of his feet stops. "I want to talk to you."

With a deep inhale, I turn around with eyes wide open. He looks exactly the same, same dirty-blond hair, same blue eyes, hasn't lost or gained any weight. When I follow my stare to his polo, a logo from Aladdin's appears. And, of course, he plasters on his smile.

That *fucking* smile.

Once he reaches six feet away, I shake my head and

say, "Not another step." I'm impressed that I don't squeak. But as I move backward, I slightly slide, clinging to the pole. He quickly walks forward to make sure I'm all right. "I said, 'stop!'"

Halting, Xavier raises both hands. My knees quake while I try to seem as calm as possible. When he releases his hands from the upright position, we're silent, almost *too* silent. My heart quickens, and I breathe, like I did during the gym incident, like I did when I saw Finley, and like I did right before I told Austin everything that happened.

However, I refuse to let Xavier know this. I cross my arms and say, "Well? Say whatever you want to say."

"You look good."

"Thanks?" The coldness of my tone causes him to drop emotion from his face. Why is he here? What is he playing at? And what gives him the audacity to believe I'd want to ever see him again?

"How..." His eyes gaze into mine, but I won't cower and won't back down. He glances away. "How've you been?" I've imagined every outcome of what would happen if we saw each other again. I've even pictured what would happen if we were the last people on Earth because of a zombie apocalypse. In that scenario, it's a fight to the death.

That's why I keep up with my boxing.

Yet, he seems genuine, almost kind, but I'm not that girl he used to know. This girl has walls built around her for protection, and recently, I tore those down for Austin, but I'm not doing it for Xavier.

"Fine" is all I say. I stare into his eyes, but I end up

losing this contest, my eyes falling to the sidewalk.

"Look, Rhiannon," he says. He steps forward and puts his hands in his pockets. Instantly, I think, *Does he have a knife?* My boxing pays off, and I crouch with my arms ready to punch.

He steps back and throws his hands in the air, one of them in a fist. "I fucked up, okay? I know I did."

My mouth opens a little, and my arm falls. I may've thought of every scenario, but not this one. There're new ideas about what I could have done, about how Dad stepped aside and let Xavier talk to me, about how we could've coexisted, and about how I might've stayed in school. But at the time, I wasn't strong enough for any of those options, so what I *did* do was the best decision I could have made.

I remain quiet with the river crashing on the canal's walls. He scans me and waits for my "I forgive you" speech. I cross my arms once again. He must conclude that it's not happening.

"Listen," Xavier says. He walks toward me so we're three feet away and places something in my hands. "I tried to go to Cleveland State. It was a fresh start for me, a new state, new scenery, hell, new people who didn't know who I was. But, I couldn't forget the past, so I took off the first semester, had picked up a job with my uncle and later Frank, and—" He stops, and his cheeks blush. "I decided to see a therapist."

I can't help it but laugh. "You? A therapist? I thought therapists were overpaid listeners who used the phrase, 'and how does that make you feel,' too often?"

He sheepishly smiles and shrugs. "People change."

He glances up. "You've changed."

"Having a near-death experience will do that to you," the words fly out of my mouth, and the smile which he carries drops.

"Yeah...I...I know."

Xavier had held me by the throat, and I was about to pass out, fluttering between the current and the inevitable phases of life. I wish our relationship wasn't important, because it had been my *entire* world. I experienced the flashbacks, the ones you get when you might die: being partners in science class, our first kiss at Vinegar Hill House, the silly games we would play with my parents and his, and the night at Times Square.

Then he walks to me and holds my hand. My locks blow from the sea's breeze. Although his hand hovers to touch my hair, he brings it down.

"Rhiannon," he whispers, and I hold my breath. "I'm so, so sor—"

"Hey!" Austin sprints to me, and even though I've pulled my hand away from Xavier, I still have the items within my fist. Austin weakly smiles as he stares into my eyes and steps in front of me. "Are you okay?"

This man is a protector, unafraid of whoever is between the two of us. My heart melts, and if I wasn't so stunned that he was showing me his brave side, I'd definitely make out with him, leaving Xavier in the dust. Austin caresses my cheek, and I close my eyes and lean forward.

"I just wanna talk, that's all," Xavier says. I open my eyes, expecting Austin to be staring back at me. However, he's facing Xavier. At first, I'm proud of him because he finally got rid of his fear of confrontation. But he takes a step, leaps forward, and punches Xavier's stomach.

Then I notice an item within my grasp: the infamous necklace. I glance up, and at this point, Xavier cowers under Austin. Inch by inch, Austin throws punches, but Xavier crunches so he takes the punches on his hands. They're inches away from falling off the bridge.

I snap out of it. "Look out!"

Although Xavier stops his tracks, Austin jumps and swings wide, but he slips on the water residue. The edge of the bridge is shallow, and because of his height, he wobbles, flips over the ledge, and falls into the river with a loud *Smash!* A random person screams.

"Austin!"

I scramble, lean over the bridge, followed by Xavier, and search for Austin's air bubbles. Nothing appears. I step up onto the ledge and hover above the deep, dark water. Clinging toward the pole, I sway back and forth, my breath catching itself. The sea becomes farther away than it actually is.

Xavier swung his arms like a mad man, knocking my camera off the ledge and onto the floor, smashing it.

Another flashback. Another fear-stricken moment. *Another blackout?* Shaking my head, I peer down at the murky sea. The water's waves might as well be shards of glass that will cut into my flesh. My throat tightens, and I touch my neck, searching for the bump Xavier gave me. But it's invisible. I bring my hand off my collarbone and into a fist.

Trauma has to wait.

With a large breath, I drop the necklace and dive into

the lake with the side view of bare trees and tar and rocks. I can imagine Xavier yelling, "What are you doing!" As soon as my body becomes submerged, the icy-cold water hits me, pins and needles stabbing my bones. The river's current is stronger than I thought, tossing and turning by the undertow. I swim out of the current, but I'm rusty.

He pushed me out of the way, and I slammed against the mantle.

Not now, not now, not now.

Closing my eyes, I swim upward and gasp the millisecond I hit the surface. My teeth chatter, and my legs go numb. I attempt to steady myself, but the waves crash into me. *Come on, Broderick! You have to find Austin!* Three breaths later, I'm somewhat stable.

While I search the rocky sea, no air pockets arise. I dive. It's so hard to see in the murky river, swimming deeper and deeper and deeper. My eyes sting as I hope to find Austin. I hold my nose to gain what little time he might have left.

Xavier pulled me by holding my necklace until it broke. I stumbled and fell onto the brick mantle, face-first. My chin throbbed and blood oozed onto the floor.

Not now, not now, not now.

I force myself to forget those flashbacks, forget to hear Finley screaming, and forget the past as I inhale and search for anything that might be Austin. The seaweed clumps together, and I dig through the algae in search of a sign. My eyes water, but I can't cry, can't give up my hope, and can't think about what might happen if he—

"There!" When I glance over, Xavier points toward the water. "Three o'clock! Near the seaweed!" Before saying, "Thank you," I deeply hold my breath and dive with eyes wide open. Fish scatter away as I approach. How deep is the lake here? Twenty feet? Thirty? The deeper I submerge, the more I force myself not to breathe. I can't think of anything except rescuing Austin, saving Austin.

Xavier turned around, picked me up, and held me by my throat. He lifted me off the rug and slammed my back against the fireplace. He clenched my neck, and I tried to wiggle out of his grasp, but he wouldn't let go.

My eyes widen as navy-blue spots appear.

Not now...not now...not—

I see Austin lying on the sand, hovering above the rocks and gravel and shells. His glasses lie beneath the sea, but I couldn't care about those. Once I reach him, I turn my feet onto the lake's bottom and shoot upward and I try to drag him through the current and my ears pop and my eyes flutter but I have to keep going—

I tried to inhale, kept trying, trying, trying; nothing escaped.

Keep going—

I hit his arm, his fist, and at one point, his face, but my punches were weak.

Keep going—

As my arm fell to my side, I struggled to stay conscious. I couldn't breathe, couldn't breathe, couldn't—

Then, a bright yellow light grows bigger and bigger and I switch my arms and push through the river as we break the surface. I gasp, but Austin's heartbeat is shallow.

"Help!" I yell and scream and I push him along, and glancing up, Xavier dives off the sea's shore. Each second that passes, Austin's breathing becomes fainter. I'm still swimming, swimming, swimming until I reach Xavier and we each grab an arm and my muscles go limp and my throat and my lungs are all so tired. But I keep going.

As we climb onto the shore, Xavier and I drag Austin to the semi-level surface. The seagulls caw and fly away into the distance. When I look at him, his blue lips are parted, his skin frozen to the touch. His face draws pale, almost like a ghost. I've never seen that white before. After I kneel next to him, I press two fingers against his collarbone and neck.

Xavier's eyes grow, a hand clasping over his mouth. "Call nine-one-one," I say, but he doesn't move.

"Is he—"

"Xavier!" I snap. "Call nine-one-one! Now!" While he dials, I compress Autin for thirty seconds with two rescue breaths: still nothing. I breathe into his lungs, fighting tears through stinging eyes. The only person more panicked than me is Xavier. He cries and kneels next to me, attempting to tell the dispatcher what is happening.

Every second Austin and I spent together flashes before me: when we collided in the beginning of the school year, when we had our first real conversation in Cleveland Museum, when I held his hand at Aladdin's, when we argued about my potential, when I realized I still had passion and needed to let him know, when I kissed him in the rain, when we had our first night together. The more I compress, the more I realize I love him. I think I always have.

Please, don't die.

With two more rescue breaths, Austin's lungs inflate.

He coughs, and water comes out of his mouth. I turn his head so he doesn't choke on his phlegm. He doesn't talk or even blink, rather he remains motionless. I hold two fingers up to his neck pressure point.

If I wasn't scared he wouldn't survive, I'd leap onto his body and cry tears of joy.

Xavier taps me on the shoulder. I jump because, for a moment, I forgot about him. His black-and-yellow sneakers lay neatly next to his folded polo. He hands me his phone. "Hello?"

"Is he breathing?" the dispatcher asks.

"Yes." Barely.

"Conscious?"

"I don't think so."

"Okay, stay on the phone with me until the ambulance arrives. What is your name?"

Xavier pulls his shirt over his head, but he still shakes. I don't know if he shivers from the coldness of the water or Austin's unconscious body.

Tears fall from my face, and I bury my mouth beneath my hand. My throat closes up, my lungs hurting. "Is he going to be okay?"

"We're going to try."

As she says this, an ambulance siren blares, growing louder and louder. When I glance up, cars pull over to let the ambulance rush through. Fifteen people, from ages of twenty to sixty, are filming the event. Were they here the entire time?

The vehicle parks at the river's edge. Two EMTs rush down the hill with a gurney. "Move!" one of them yells. The crowd parts, some leaving while others capture the

The Night at Times Square

EMTs on their phones. Once they reach Austin, they slide him onto the gurney along with an oxygen mask, prop it up, and run through the path. I stare at them while they leave, closing the ambulance's door and speeding off into the distance. Right after, the last of the spectators disappears.

"Ma'am? Ma'am?" a voice coming from my hand repeats herself.

I swallow. "Yes?"

"Have the EMTs taken him?" I nod and close my eyes. "Ma'am?"

"I'm nodding."

The voice exhales from the other line and ends the call. There're a million questions I need answered, one including where the ambulance is taking him. But as Xavier places his hand on my shoulder, I think he already has that information.

If not, we are driving to every hospital until we find Austin.

Chapter 26
Austin

Beep...beep...beep...

Before I open my eyes, I hear a machine. I wince when I gently touch my ribs. My nose cast pushes on my cartilage, and I have a constant pound in my head. I might as well have been hit by an eighteen-wheeler. My mouth is stuck in the back of my throat while my tongue swells. Knives stab my back and left shoulder, and my right eye just hurts...*everything* hurts.

Am I dead?

Other senses activate, like the smell of latex, the cleanliness of a pillow, the stiff mattress, the sound of *drip, drip, drip*. There's another voice, too. As my eyes open, I see Mom, Dad, and even Troy lying on each other's shoulders with their eyes closed. But Rhiannon sits in a chair next to me, her head lowered toward my right hand.

"After the ambulance took you away, I asked Xavier if he knew where the EMTs went," she whispers. When I peer down, she strokes my hand. Does she know I'm awake? I can feel her tears falling and landing on my palm. "He knew...Of course he knew."

She scoffs, laughs a little, and wipes her eyes with her free hand. I smile at that sound, and although I want to reassure her I'm okay, my lungs hurt. "But first, he was gonna drive me somewhere else." The last time I went to this same hospital was when my mom was in a car accident. She was in a coma, and the nurses told me to talk to her. That must be what Rhiannon's doing.

She kisses my hand. It tingles, like a spark of electricity. "After you were in the ambulance, I demanded Xavier drive me to Hawken. He dropped me off, and I searched for Troy. Luckily, he had your parent's numbers. They each took the next flight home."

I remain motionless, wanting to hold her, but it's like I'm paralyzed and can't move or talk. Am I paralyzed? Did I hit the water at an awkward angle? Or is it PTSD, and I can't talk for now?

"Once the doctor said you were going to survive, your dad drove your car here. Wanna know how he got to your car in the first place? An Uber." Her soft giggle turns me to mush. Her shoulders pulse as she leans closer to my hands. "I know you're gonna be okay, Alvin...I just know it."

With all the strength I have, my fingers curl up beneath her palm. She shoots up. She smiles and covers her mouth and continues to sob, but it's no longer from sorrow. I try to sit up, and as soon as she realizes I can move, she leaps onto my torso. I wince from the pain. When she looks up at me, pulling away from me because she must realize the agony I'm in, I don't care. I wrap my arms around her.

Now I cry, weeping, sobbing, letting myself go as she does. As I glance up, Troy, Mom, and Dad bawl, too. Rhiannon releases me, followed by Dad sprinting and embracing my body. I collapse on him.

After five minutes of just holding each other, we release. Mom walks up to me and places her fingers on my cheek. She whispers, "She's the one." I chuckle and glance at her. At this point, my throat hurts so much from all the crying that I can only mouth the words, "I know."

Mom tells me about how Rhiannon dove into the river. She swam in search of my body, even though the water was freezing, and she even did CPR.

My eyes fill with tears again. "You swam?"

"Yes."

I grin. "How was it?"

"Pretty fucking cold." The smirk on her face grows. "Haven't you lived in Cleveland all your life?"

Everyone laughs, and as I glance at Troy, I nod; he knows what to do. "Mrs. and Mr. Chang?" He rubs his hands together. "I'd like a nice hot chocolate. Wanna get some with me?" My parents look at each other, stare at Rhiannon, and leave. As they exit, Troy winks, and for once, I don't blush.

"So," I ask, "how long was I out for?"

"Almost a day."

My eyes get bigger. "Almost a day?"

She nods, not being able to glance my way. "I was worried." Her eyes water again, and I wipe away those tears from her face. "Really worried," she whispers. I lift her chin and kiss her—a long, soft, *amazing* kiss.

Before this school year, I didn't know what I wanted out of life. I was a cheater, barely practicing swimming over the summer, and drinking far too often. I was the cliché of clichés: the popular guy, unable to keep a woman for more than one night.

But then I met her.

"Rhiannon," I say, and she gazes into my eyes.

Say something.

Say something.

Say something.

With a deep breath, I shut my eyes. *Now or never, Chang.* "I love you." My eyes remain closed, my heart rate monitor has a rapid *Beepbeepbeep*, and my chest and my throat want to throw up.

What if she doesn't say it back?

All the blood comes rushing to my head, my face getting hot. Then, it's her turn to lift my head, to kiss me, and although I don't open my eyes, I feel her breath, hear her slight giggle, and smell her peppermint scent.

Chapter 27
Rhiannon

Tori drives us from Cleveland to the Brooklyn Bridge for December break. Unfortunately, in this bumper-to-bumper traffic, the four-hundred-mile trip takes us nine hours so far. We still have twenty minutes once we cross the arch.

I hold up my aunt's phone so I can FaceTime Brielle. *Ring...Ring...Ring.* On the third buzz, she's beaming with her Christmas tree in the background. Her cat curls under the branches, purring so loud it's audible. "Miss me already?" she asks.

Laughing, I bring two fingers to measure one centimeter. "Just a little."

"I'm so pissed my parents wouldn't let me visit your family! Who *cares* if it's my last Christmas before college?"

"Your parents...and possibly you." She chuckles. "Don't worry, we get two weeks off in March."

Brielle opens her mouth when her mom calls her name. She rolls her eyes. "I gotta go. Text me when you get there, okay?"

"Of course."

After we disconnect, Tori and I listen to Cher on her CD player. I rummage through twenty CDs when I spot a unique band that I've never heard of: Hill Billy Idol. "How 'bout this one?" I ask and hold it up.

After glancing at the album, Tori smirks. "You're not gonna like it."

"How would you know?"

As she switches her lane, she shrugs and keeps her eyes on the road. I slide the CD into the player and press Play. Immediately, I wince and cover my ears. Hill Billy Idol is full of bluegrass music, banjos and all. With only ten seconds of airtime, I hit Stop. "You're right," I say, put the album back in its case, and play *Spring Awakening* soundtrack again.

Once I put my feet on the dashboard, I roll down the window, stick my head out, and breathe. The breeze smells like salty air and shrimp, but I think the shrimp is my imagination. Sure, the beeps sing their orchestral song, but still, I missed this place.

"Well," Tori says, "now I know why I never drove here. I'm going to pee my pants if we don't make it soon."

I close my eyes and reach my hand out the window, waving my arm like it's swimming. "You can always pee in a cup."

"That's gross, Rhie." She rolls her eyes, but the twitch of a smile comes on. "Really gross." After we cross the bridge, her truck speeds up, dodging tiny SUVs left and right. The New Yorkers honk their horns and swear out their window.

Sounds like home.

As we slow down, she babbles about Manhattan and how excited she is to do the touristy events. "What about the Statue of Liberty? Empire State Building? Oh! The Wax Museum!" She bounces in her seat. "You are *so* gonna get sick of me."

I laugh. "Actually, I've only been to the Statue of Liberty."

Tori side-eyes and raises her eyebrows.

This time, I'll do all the sightseeing. For the first seventeen years of my life, I thought wearing a fanny pack, asking for directions, and taking a Kodak disposable camera would be disgusting. I live in Brooklyn, for crepe's—

HONK!

Tori slams on the brakes. My seatbelt lock engages, and my feet fly, kicking the air. She swerves into the fast lane. As soon as she moves into the proper lane, she breathes and pulls over to the side of the road. With her hazards on, she turns around.

"You okay?"

I turn around. Austin—I mean, Alvin—squishes against our luggage, his knees against his chest, and his glasses crooked on his face. He rubs his crust-covered eyes and yawns. Since the only vehicle Tori has is a truck, he hopped in behind us. We stuffed our duffle bags, suitcases, and a few blankets in an effort to make him as comfy as possible. It worked great, until now.

He pushes the luggage so he has maximum leg room and wipes the dirt coming from the truck's floor. "Yep," he says, "just risking my life over here. No big deal." Tori's eyes grow, and her mouth drops. But I pat her knee.

"He's fine." I spin around. "You've been through worse."

Alvin leans forward and tickles my ribs. I giggle and bounce my feet against the dashboard. "Children?" Tori raises one eyebrow. Alvin and I stop and face forward. But I can feel the weight shift to the direction of my seat and receive a kiss on my cheek.

For the rest of the ride, I reach for him behind me and squeeze his hand. When Alvin returned from the hospital, he told everyone his real name, and surprisingly—or not surprisingly—no one made fun of him. It's like having a new/old name is the equivalent of the next chapter in his life, and I'm lucky to witness it.

"You're gonna take the next left," I tell Tori.

"The Chipmunk Song" plays on the radio. I sway back and forth with the beat, humming the iconic melody. When I glance in the rearview mirror, Alvin smirks, sways along with me, and mouths the lyrics, word for word. I reach for his hand and kiss it.

As we turn left, my knee bounces, and I attempt to watch the buildings. I visited my parents for a day at Thanksgiving, but I didn't come home. What does the house, my old home, look like? I can't picture it because for nine months, I stared at the pavement whenever I stepped outside, which wasn't too often.

But as Tori slows down, my face brightens. Through my parent's window, I can see the Christmas tree's lights glow, the fireplace is lit, and the candy canes, gift boxes, and tinsel are everywhere. Outside, there's a blow-up Santa Claus, Rudolph, and Hermie the elf. Closing my eyes, I can picture the old memories, caroling at nearby houses, matching pajamas sets, and watching *A Christmas Story* two times, once Christmas Eve, and once Christmas day. I'm able to lean back in my seat, slightly tearing up at this gorgeous, *wonderful* house.

We hop out of the vehicle. I open the side door after I text Brielle that we arrived safely. Aunt Tori hands me three duffle bags and shoves the blankets to the side, clearing a path for Alvin.

After he slides out of the truck, he wraps his arms around me, and I instantly feel safe and warm. Gosh, his embrace is so wonderful. I glance up and say, "Be honest, was it really that bad?"

He chuckles. "Not at all. I fell asleep three times."

"Oh, we know. You were snoring."

"Really?" His cheeks turn pink.

I nod. "It was pretty adorable."

His eyes lower to my lips, and right when I close my eyes and lean forward, someone asks, "What did Baby corn say to Mama corn?" As Dad barges through the door, Alvin and I separate a good ten feet away from each other. "Where's Pop corn!"

Dad gives Tori a hug and stops short, scanning me from head to toe. Not much has changed, still weigh the same, still wear sweatpants and sweatshirts, and still have a makeup-free face. Yet, his eyes brighten, and he glances at Alvin and back at me.

"Finally?" Dad asks, and I'm thinking, *Finally what?* But then it dawns on me: *Finally, I'm happy.*

"Finally," I say.

Dad picks me up, squeezes my body, and gently puts

me down. He walks ten feet to Alvin. They're the same height, but Dad has a dad bod, a.k.a. a little too many cookies, no arm muscles, and wears shorts with high socks, despite the current freezing temperature. He sticks out his hand, and hesitantly, Alvin grabs it.

Dad brings his hand back at ricochet speed, and because it's so unexpected, Alvin stumbles forward. "You hurt her," Dad says with a stern face, leaning closer, "and I'll make it look like an accident."

My mouth drops.

"I'm kidding!" He slaps Alvin on the back. "He knows I'm kidding, right?" and he knocks Alvin's shoulder, his way of saying, "I'm not joking." I roll my eyes while I hug Mom.

When Alvin reaches for an outstretched hand, she gently smiles, embracing him.

"I'm surprised your parents let you come."

"They didn't at first," Alvin says and looks at me. "But someone can be very persuasive." Not only did he beg, I did too. Tao and Yan caved, but on one condition; we treated December twenty-third and the twenty-four like they were Christmas Eve and Day. That's why we're so late.

Austin picks up my duffle bag, his, and Tori's. He struggles with the uneven weight. But Dad just smirks and watches my boyfriend wobble up the stairs.

"Tori gets the guest room," Dad says, "and you two get Rhiannon's." Alvin stumbles, turns around, and stares at me. "Rhie, you're not a little kid anymore. I know that now."

I smile and lean on Alvin's shoulder. As I gaze into

his eyes, I think, *That's incredibly sweet,* until—

"But no sex under my roof."

"Dad!"

My cheeks redden, so do Alvin's and Mom's. "Kirk..." and she gives the *ultimate* Mom look of the century. He doesn't budge, though.

We climb the stairs and enter my bedroom. It remains untouched, the pink walls, flowered comforter, and pictures of Xavier, Sadie, and I strategically on a cork board. Ten stuffed animals like Charmander, Eevee, and Vulpix smile down on us, and boy-band posters fill the walls.

So many boy-band posters.

After I place Maybelline at the bed's head, I turn around to see Alvin's grin spreading. "I never expected...*this*." On top of the DVD player, there are three DVDs, and two are identical. He picks both copies of *Legally Blonde 2*. "Two? I'm surprised to see *one*, but two?"

I dig my head in my hands. "I'm so ashamed."

I hear him putting the DVDs down, walk over to me, and lift my chin. My hands wrap around his shoulder, and I sway to the lack of music on my tiptoes. He joins me, kissing my forehead. "We could add some ambient music with your *outstanding* boombox."

"Unless you want to listen to One Direction, all my records are back at Tori's."

We sway, walk to my bed, and jump onto the comforter at the same time. As soon as we turn toward each other, we kiss. I wrap my leg over his body, and he strokes one thigh beneath my sweatpants.

*Gurgle...*When we release our kiss, I tilt my head and

smile. "Truth number one, I am *starving*. Truth number two, I'd prefer shrimp over a pizza at the moment."

Austin continues stroking my arm. "And what's truth number three?"

"I don't know if I've mentioned it, but I love you," and we kiss. "Have I mentioned that?"

"Once or twice." He smiles. "But you haven't said it since we exited the car." He mouths those three little words, and I do the same.

Then, I hop off my bed and give him an arm. "Let's go explore!"

"In the kitchen?"

"No! We don't have shrimp, but—" I point to the outside world.

He laughs and says, "Rhiannon, it's nine o'clock at night."

"That's the beauty of Brooklyn; you can eat almost anywhere until two in the morning."

Eyes open wide, he asks, "Really?"

"Really, really."

We run down the stairs and put on our jackets. I grab Alvin's hand and yell, "We'll be back by midnight!" and slam the door. The temperature drops even lower, and I add my gloves to the ensemble. We hold hands and swing our arms, singing loudly different classic Disney songs. My cheeks hurt from all the smiling I've done recently.

"How about this restaurant?" I ask and point to Otis.

He stops walking and wraps his arms around me. "Doesn't matter to me," and we kiss.

"Seriously, though. If I don't eat soon, I'm going to be extremely *hang*ry."

Alvin kisses me again and unwraps his arms, but still our palms are clasped. "Let's do it."

After looking both ways, we jaywalk, hopping over sewer grates and onto the sidewalk. When we're about to enter the restaurant, Alvin freezes and sticks his hand against my chest. I peer up and draw a shade of white.

Xavier texts on his phone with one hand and the leftover bag in the other. Maybe he'll just leave. Austin and I side-step behind the pole, escaping from this potential awkward moment. Then, I stop. The last time we saw each other, we never had any closure.

With a deep inhale, I scream, "Adventure is out there!" Xavier halts, backtracks, and spins. Squeezing Alvin's hand, I smile, wave, and drag him by my side. We hold hands, although he holds mine tight.

"What...What are you doing there?" he asks with a nervous chuckle.

"The holidays, of course." I glance at him. "This is my boyfriend, Alvin." Xavier immediately holds his arm out, hovering where Alvin's arm should be. Both boys stare in my direction. I nudge him, and he grabs Xavier's. They shake hands, a little longer than comfortable.

When they're released, Xavier clears his throat and says, "So...You going to Otis?"

I nod. "Is it crowded inside?"

"Very." He chuckles. "But you know Tony. He'll make room for you, either at the bar or near the bathrooms."

I glance at Alvin. "How romantic."

"It would be *ultimately* romantic if he would give us a seat *inside* the bathroom," he says.

"Oo! Men's or women's?"

"Women's of course. I have standards." We kiss, stare into each other's eyes, and laugh. I'm about to slobber him with more kisses, but someone coughs.

"Anyway," Xavier says, gazes down the concrete sidewalk, and kicks some snow. The three of us awkwardly watch our feet: Alvin with his Air Jordans, me with my white Vans, and Xavier with his faded black-and-yellow sneakers. "It was unseasonably warm today, but now it's chilly."

He's trying to keep me there longer by asking questions he already knows the answer to, but it's the thought that counts.

"Do you think it's cold back at your aunt's?"

"It's always cold in Cleveland," Alvin and I say, which makes us laugh. I nuzzle into his sweatshirt. As I glance at Xavier, he smiles, a genuine smile. He breathes in, wanting to continue this conversation. He never wanted to stop, though.

I interrupt. "It was good to see you, really."

"You too." With his free hand, he picks up my palm and kisses it. "Goodbye, Rhiannon." As he leaves, he hums a little lick by Fleetwood. I laugh and lean into Alvin's chest, thumping like a rabbit.

Once Xavier rounds a corner, I ask, "Wanna go in?"

"Yes." Alvin kisses me, and as we start, he says, "But only if we get a table *in* the bathroom."

"I'll try my best."

We enter the restaurant. I lean against the doorway. Alvin taps against the hostess's booth with his mouth open: the roaring fireplace, the hanging plants, the above light fixtures, fairy lights. He wraps his arms around me and kisses my head.

"I can't think of any reason why someone wouldn't stay here."

When I flew home for Thanksgiving, my family didn't cook turkey or stuffing, rather, we saw the Macy's Thanksgiving Day Parade, had dinner at Vinegar Hill House, and visited the Statue of Liberty. As I boarded the plane that same night, I missed my parents, but I saw my future at Richmond Heights.

On my tiptoes, I kiss him for a long, long time. "I can think of *one* reason to go to Cleveland."

"Oh really?" He grins. "And what is that?" I smile and am about to answer when the hostess power-walks to her desk.

"Broderick, I haven't seen you in months! The chef set up a table just for you," she says and beckons us to follow our place.

Alvin leans into me. "It may not be the inside ladies' room, but it's the next thing," and kisses me on the top of my head. I giggle, watch as he follows the hostess, and gaze toward the ceiling.

Yep, all I needed was change.

Acknowledgments

When I was in between my beta readers and my line editor for *One Term Left*, I was visiting my aunt Denise in the outskirts of Cleveland, Ohio. The suburb paints a beautiful picture as well as her entire house, sculptures, drawings, and mono prints. I knew I wanted to have a character named Rhiannon (one of my students had that name, and I love it), and, like my aunt's sculptures, I molded a person, her past, her present, and her future. We went to all the places pictured in the book, such as Aladdin's, Cleveland Art Museum, and *A Christmas Story* museum. I even spent the day at Hawken School.

I would like to thank my beta reader and formatter, Caitlin Angelo, my line editor Rachel Garber, and my cover artist Lianna Moisescu. If it wasn't for all of them, *The Night at Times Square* wouldn't exist.

About the Author

C.M. Francis was born and raised on the outskirts of Boston, Massachusetts. She earned her bachelor's degree in film and animation as well as a master's degree in elementary education. When she's not working, she's always daydreaming about her characters, story ideas, and creating different plot lines. Other times, she gathers her thoughts on long walks on her favorite trails or exploring new places. For more of her writing, check out her previous novels, *The Day I Died* and *One Term Left*.

Find her online:

https://www.cmfrancis.net/

https://www.facebook.com/TheDayIDied1107/

https://www.instagram.com/cmfrancis1107/

Made in the USA
Middletown, DE
16 October 2024